Regent's Study Guides
General Editor: Paul S. Fiddes

Praying as Believing

*The Lord's Prayer and
the Christian Doctrine of God*

Regent's Study Guides

Praying as Believing

*The Lord's Prayer and
the Christian Doctrine of God*

Timothy Bradshaw

Regent's Park College, Oxford
with
Smyth & Helwys Publishing, Inc.
Macon, Georgia

ISBN   (UK) 0-9518104-56   (US) 1-57312-198-3

Praying as Believing
The Lord's Prayer and the Christian Doctrine of God

Timothy Bradshaw

copyright © 1998

Published by Regent's Park College, Oxford OX1 2LB, UK
in association with Smyth & Helwys, Publishing, Inc.
6316 Peake Road
Macon, Georgia 31210-3960, USA

The paper used in this publication meets the minimum
requirements of American National Standard for Information
Sciences—Permanence of Paper for Printed Library Materials,
ANSI, Z39.48–1984.

Library of Congress Cataloging-in-Publication Data
Bradshaw, Timothy.
    Praying as Believing:
    the Lord's Prayer and the Christian doctrine of God/
    Timothy Bradshaw.
    p.   cm.—(Regent's study guides: 6)
    Includes bibliographical references and index.
    ISBN 1-57312-198-3 (alk. paper)
    1. Lord's prayer—Theology. 2. Theology, Doctrinal.
    3. God. I. Title. II. Series.
    BV230.B684   1998
    226.9'606—dc21   98-17455
                                                CIP

Contents

General Editor's Preface

What are theologians of the present day saying about God? Pastoral leaders who take courses in theology to prepare for their ministry are bound to be faced with the thoughts, for example, of the great Swiss theologian Karl Barth, or the German theologian Wolfhart Pannenberg, or the British theologian John Macquarrie, or the American school of Process Theology. Moreover, these modern Christian thinkers seem to be in continual argument with 'great names' from the past—Spinoza, Nietzsche, Kant, Schleiermacher, Marx. How shall we assess what they have to say about the nature and acts of God? Why should it matter in the least bit to members of our local congregations anyway?

In this book, Timothy Bradshaw sets out to answer these questions in a way that is completely relevant to the life of all Christian people. He surveys some major developments in modern theology by bringing them up against the test of worship. How does modern thinking about God stand up to the challenge of prayer, and especially the challenge of the master-prayer of Christians, the Lord's Prayer? 'Theology' means literally 'talking about God'; how well then does our theology help us to 'talk to God' in our prayers? Conversely, what might the great prayer of Jesus tell us about the very being of God? Answering these questions also brings a great deal of illumination to the nature of prayer itself.

What follows, then, is not the usual kind of study of the Lord's Prayer. Timothy Bradshaw certainly explains what the petitions mean, but he wants us to press beyond them to find what they tell us about the God to whom they are addressed. In the light of this, he invites his readers to explore with him the meaning and worth of modern Christian thinking about God. This study is a remarkable attempt in our day to discover the truth of the ancient Christian saying, *lex orandi lex credendi*: 'the rule of prayer is the rule of belief'. To this task the author brings many years of experience in preparing candidates for the ordained Christian ministry both in Baptist churches and in the Church of England, as well as his ongoing pastoral experience as an Anglican minister in a local congregation.

This is an opportune time for such a venture. On the British scene, the ecumenical forum Churches Together in England has set up a 'Millennium Coordinating Group' to plan ways in which Christian churches of all denominations can seize the opportunity of celebrating the year 2000 to bring the truth of the gospel to our society. One project is to focus on the Lord's Prayer, to 'promote the use of the Prayer and to teach the meaning behind it'. Regent's Park College offers this Study Guide as one contribution to the material being produced. Churches Together in England, of course, has no responsibility for this book, which rests solely with the college; but the college hopes that the Guide will be particularly useful for ministers and other Christian leaders who are prepared to take the time and effort to test their theology by their praying. This is not a 'popular study', but it is an accessible one and should provide a resource for the writing of material at other levels.

The 'Millennium Group' of Churches Together in England noted that there is no longer a universally agreed version of the Lord's Prayer. While it is certainly not possible to impose the use of any one translation, it was felt helpful to recommend a common text of the prayer that could be focused upon in the various writings and study groups that were sharing in the project. The version chosen was that of the English Language Liturgical Consultation, already used in many service books, and it is this that is also used in the present study. It is reproduced, with permission, below.

Our Father in heaven,
hallowed be your name,
your kingdom come,
your will be done in earth as in heaven.
Give us today our daily bread.
Forgive us our sins
as we forgive those who sin against us.
Save us from the time of trial
and deliver us from evil.
For the kingdom, the power, and the glory are yours
now and for ever. Amen.

Acknowledgements

Quotations from Scripture are from The New Revised Standard Version, Copyright © 1989, Division of Christian Education of the National Council of the Churches of Christ in the United States of America. Used by kind permission of the Oxford University Press Inc., New York.

The text of the Lord's Prayer was originally prepared by the International Consultation on English Texts and revised © 1990 by the English Language Liturgical Consultation.

Quotations from the poem 'The Wreck of the Deutschland' by Gerard Manley Hopkins are © 1967 by The Society of Jesus, and also used by kind permission of the publishers, the Oxford University Press, Oxford.

1

Introduction
Christian prayer and the Christian doctrine of God

1. A two-way process

Doctrines about God, and the ordinary Christian experience of prayer and worship, have often been held strangely asunder by thinkers in the church. This book aims to bring them together so as to gain mutual illumination and interaction, for the sake of theological and pastoral insight. Any view of God which fails to engage with the ordinary experience of prayer and worship may be interesting, but can hardly be considered Christian.

Prayer and theology are inseparable. Theology without any obvious commitment to engage with the God who is the subject of the study becomes arid and often negative, isolated and complaining that few take notice of its efforts. Just as philosophy which becomes detached from the world inhabited by ordinary people gains a reputation for eccentricity and uselessness, so it is with theology which loses touch with the roots and experience of our common faith and worship. Prayer and worship in their turn lose by neglecting serious reflection on the God who is worshipped. All worshippers presuppose some theology, some ideas about God and the world. The only question is the quality of this presupposed, sometimes preconceptual, theology. The picture of God we have will affect our prayer life. The process is two-way.

The Reformation saw the church undertake a criticism of doctrine and practice in the area of our *relationship* with God through Jesus and the Spirit. It is becoming apparent that this generation is witnessing a scrutiny of a doctrine that was not reassessed at the Reformation, or even since then; that is, the doctrine of the very being, nature, and the acts of God that is usually simply called 'the doctrine of God'. The Reformers took over their doctrine of God from their medieval forbears uncritically. The second half of the twentieth century has witnessed much thorough questioning of this traditional way of understanding God in relation to the world, which was inherited from medieval times and from the age of the Church Fathers.

The immediate dynamo for getting such an examination of the received tradition going has been the problem of evil and mass suffering, and the question thrust upon the mind of European Christianity since 1945 is how to do 'theology since the holocaust'. The problem of

suffering on a massive scale has made Christian thinkers especially ask
about the relationship of God to this world he created. Such questioning
has produced much rich fruit, particularly in insisting that the doctrine of
God should not be divorced from the focal figure of Christian faith: Jesus
and his life, death, and resurrection. The death of Jesus in particular has
become a sharply focused lens through which God has been perceived.[1]

A further stream of thought feeding similar theological reassessment
has been the work of the existentialist thinkers, critical of talk of an objective God somewhere 'out there'.[2] Yet another influence has been the
school of thought called 'process theology', which has taken a rather different track of reconstruction by linking God more closely into the
processes of the world than the tradition of 'classical theism' had ever
done.

There seems to be a need to take stock of such advances in the light
not only of Christianity's explanation of itself to the outside world and its
inner theological coherence, but also of spirituality, worship, and prayer.
It might be regarded as strange, for example, that worship is not one of
the formative factors of theology named by the theologian John Macquarrie[3] in his influential textbook on the principles of Christian theology. A
modern category, not included by Macquarrie, which today is claiming a
place among the formative factors is 'praxis', that is, the impact of the
Christian community on society and its economics, as popularized by liberation theology. But worship should be of equal significance as a factor
helping to shape theological statements, along with the established categories of revelation, experience, scripture, tradition, and reason.

Whereas the category of 'praxis' is now well accepted as one theological norm among others, worship is less so recognized. A book ahead
of its time in this regard was *Jubilate* by Daniel Hardy and David Ford.[4]
In that book the authors identified the twin explosions of critical theological thought and the Pentecostal movement. Now, ten years later, the latter has become a massive force in the world church, especially in Latin
America where millions are turning from the established Roman Catholic
Church to Pentecostalism. Even the Catholic liberation theologians and
their communitarian 'base communities' seem unable to check the enthusiasm for this movement, although their focus on 'praxis' was meant to
appeal specifically to the poor and powerless. 'The church has opted for
the poor, but the poor have opted for the Pentecostals', one Vatican offi-
cial is alleged to have said. David Martin, the sociologist, puts the same

point slightly differently by saying that 'the church has opted for the poor, but the poor have their own options'.[5]

The factor of 'praxis' ought not to have been ignored, but neither should the worship factor, unless academic theology is simply building itself a ghetto, disconnected from the spiritual realities of the church in the world. The poverty-stricken of Latin America are, it seems, first finding new life and hope in the spiritual renewal of Pentecostalist worship, and then finding their praxis flowing from there. In this we may discern a return to the traditional pattern of grace fuelling works, and an inversion of the agenda of liberation theology, which tends to blur that distinction. Paradoxically, worship and praxis are deeply intertwined in the experience of the poor.

Western Europe has no less its movements of the Spirit and exuberant worship, but it also exhibits a kind of theological reversal of the Pentecostal movement. Some Christian thinkers are rejecting the notion of a God who is real and addressable, while they wish to keep the term 'God' and maintain liturgical practices which, in their view, perform a useful socio-psychological function. This movement goes well beyond the liberal Christian agenda with its attempt to reinterpret doctrine in terms of modern categories, into an atheism which retains Christian theological language.[6] The emotional tone of this is cold, stoical, and individualist. 'God' is reduced to the aspirations of the human heart, especially the heart of a certain type of late twentieth century Western individual.

2. Theology and experience: some significant witnesses

Our understanding of God and worship must, then, take into account not only supernaturalist movements such as Pentecostalism, but reductivist movements which make inverse claims about God and prayer. It must take into account the whole history of theological contribution to this question. Notwithstanding the charges of aridity and detachment from the roots of actual faith which have been levelled at them, theologians have in fact sought to think their way into God in a manner which acknowledges him to be much more than a merely rational matrix of reality.

Indeed it can be argued that the theologians who have made an impact have been those to tap into the experience of personal need for God at particular times in history. No doubt this could be claimed for Luther's radical reading of the cross of Christ, which shapes his whole picture of God. Long before Luther, the same could be said for Augustine and his personal struggles over sexuality, the will, and the blessing of grace. In the Middle Ages, Anselm's theology had a sharp sense of human sin as a kind of contempt for the divine honour. Abelard was struck by the love of the human Jesus; in this he anticipated Francis of Assisi who was to see, and imitate, Jesus as a figure of vulnerable goodness in need of no moral or metaphysical rationalization. Personal experience was inseparable from the theological endeavour of all these thinkers.

This is also true, in the post-Enlightenment era, of Friedrich Schleiermacher.[7] Often considered to be the initiator of modern theology, Schleiermacher was a sincere believer who wished to commend the Christian faith to 'the cultured despisers of religion', by pointing to a common human sense for the infinite. He believed that the human sense of dependence was brought to its highest pitch in a 'feeling of absolute dependence', that is, a sense of the indwelling presence of the divine, which conditions us completely and sustains the universe. He developed his theology by using this sense of 'utter dependence' as the key for interpreting the classical doctrines of the Christian faith. This spiritual experience he found to be present with a unique power in Jesus of Nazareth, whose own total sense of 'God-consciousness' has the effect of transforming the consciousness of the human race.

The doctrine of God, for Schleiermacher, thus takes second place to the experience of God; the doctrine is an attempt to register the reality of the experience, as a hospital monitor reads the pulsing heart beat of the patient. Doctrine is a kind of index of reality itself, which is God as experienced by us. Schleiermacher was therefore concerned to relate the faith of the community to academic theology in the strongest possible way. There is a sense in which Schleiermacher, 'the father of modern theology', is also following the more traditional pathway of 'faith seeking understanding'; faith and experience take the prior part, certainly faith seeking elucidation in contemporary terms. The notion of God developed by Schleiermacher was, however, one of a divine grounding of all reality, a view of God as immanent in the world. Prayer and worship become primarily a matter of adjusting to the sustaining divine energy of the universe in an attitude of trustful surrender, of 'self-abandonment to the divine providence'.[8]

If Schleiermacher encouraged the educated bourgeoisie to 'get in touch with their feelings' and relate these to the divine, his most fierce critic, Karl Barth, held that this route was deeply mistaken; it was confusing our *feelings* about God with *God*.[9] Barth wished to reclaim a revelatory understanding of God and so to reinstall God into his seat of judgement and grace, rescuing him from the company of the chattering classes and their moralizing or aesthetic priorities. God is the God of Jesus Christ in the sense that God's being is in Christ to save us from our sins. Worship is thus directed to the transcendent God on this basis of salvation and grace.

David Tracy[10] has suggested that Barth's break with Schleiermacher's way of thinking is less great than Barth supposed, because Barth was also appealing to an *experience* of God, although a different one from that tapped by Schleiermacher. Barth felt constrained to stress the feeling of 'absolute dependence' in a way which focused on deeply rooted human sin and evil, that is as a sense of need for redemption from the grip of sin and radical evil which Augustine had earlier insisted upon. Barth articulates the deep distortion of the human will, its capacity for brutality and its need for grace from outside its own resources, a theology for 1917 when Christian Europe was tearing itself savagely to shreds. For the point here is that experience and theology, even such a weighty theology as the Word Incarnate, coincide again even in Barth.

3. Jesus, theology, and prayer

Both Schleiermacher and Barth bring together the person of Jesus and the fact of God. We must somehow read the two together; again and again that is the insistent Christian testimony and *experience*. This experience is a spiritual reality which cannot be escaped, however inconvenient intellectually this may be. Somehow we know that God defines himself through Jesus. The church knows God to be this God, 'full of grace of truth' (John 1:14). Christians have not generally felt that this link is sufficiently described in terms of Jesus as a kind of divine visual aid to understanding. A divine act occurred in the life and ministry of Jesus that lit up and changed the human predicament, and which involved the passion of God, a fact which theologians in the second half of this century have been exploring with great determination. The order of *being*, and not just the order of *knowing*, is somehow transformed by the life, death, and resurrection of Jesus.

If Jesus gives us the clearest window into God, a claim which schools of thought stemming from both Schleiermacher and Barth affirm, then we are on safe ground if we develop our doctrine of God *and* our grasp of prayer from the understanding held by Jesus. The simple suggestion made here is that the 'Lord's Prayer' which Jesus gave to his disciples offers us a way into the theology of Jesus, as well as providing the classic prayer for the church; indeed the theology and the prayer coincide. This should provide a starting point and a method which will satisfy both conservative and liberal Christians. The Lord's Prayer serves as the classical place to examine both prayer itself and the Christian view of God and the world, since even highly sceptical critical scholarship is likely to admit that the prayer must, in essence, go back to the historical Jesus. If any words or ideas of Jesus at all have been deliberately handed down by the disciples, then surely his prayer would be among them.[11]

This prayer in all its simplicity opens up to us the living understanding of God held and experienced by Jesus of Nazareth. The prayer life of any person, if genuine, must open the heart of that person's understanding of who God is and what kind of relationship God has to his people and to the world. The Jewish scholar, Geza Vermes, tells us that this prayer stands very much in the Jewish tradition:

> It is hardly surprising that the understanding of God as the heavenly Father typical of the preaching of Jesus, dovetails into the development of Jewish religious thought precisely where it is expected. . . . the idea of the divine Father moves on the collective level from the Creator/ Begetter of the Jewish people (within mankind) towards the loving and affectionate Protector of the individual member of the family.[12]

Vermes agrees with James Barr that the thesis popularized by Joachim Jeremias,[13] that 'Abba' was the child's form of address—'Daddy'— in Aramaic, cannot be sustained. 'Abba, Father' is not a childish form of address. But the basic idea of close personal trust enshrined in Jeremias's interpretation remains in Vermes's view:

> What lies at the heart of his [Jesus'] intuition and gives individuality and freshness to his vision is the conviction that the eternal, distant, dominating and tremendous Creator is also and primarily a near and approachable God.[14]

Jesus might be said to focus all the depths of the Hebrew wisdom and understanding of God.

Vermes makes clear that this is no naive, immature view of God; the world is a tough context, evil and suffering occur, and Jesus does not offer a sentimental fatherly image, which was perhaps one danger of Jeremias's

'Daddy' interpretation. The nature of the suffering of the innocent one who prayed this prayer cannot be forgotten.

4. *The shape of the Lord's Prayer*

In praying 'Our Father in heaven', Jesus thus prays to the Hebrew God, the creator, the king of the universe, transcendent and glorious, wrapped in a robe of light, worthy of all praise. This God is nevertheless approachable, the covenant-giving Lord whose nature is to grant and build communion with his creation. This God cares for his world and his people. The Father is 'in heaven', in and of a different realm of being from that of creation. The imagery portrays height and depth, transcendence and immanence; 'on earth' is later contrasted with 'in heaven', and the two are complementary, registering the distinction between two realms of reality while not making the difference into a dualism of two incompatible entities. Moreover, the analogy of the heavenly Father contains the ideas not only of care, trust, and respect but also of personal communication, or at the very least, of 'approach'. The value of this analogical language of fatherhood is equally to rule out the contrary ideas of pantheism and deism from the vision of Jesus about God.

The first phrase of the prayer has oriented the self to God as the accessible yet transcendent one. The heart is lifted up from the confusion and despair of the world to the throne of the heavenly grace, to the ultimate reality and truth. This alone is a fact of Christian prayer worth rehearsing: it is God-centred first and foremost; it is worship of the absolutely worthy. The human mind fills with this reality of the Father. By orienting ourselves around the transcendent God, worldly things fall into perspective.[15] There is an infinite difference between ourselves as creatures and God; even a perfect sinless human being would not equate with God, and would still worship God as the one to be adored in wonder, love, and praise infinitely 'above' the created person[16] who likewise senses his own absolute dependence on the supreme reality. The deepest meaning of our experience of things rests in the creator.

While the relationship between creator and creation is theologically primary, that between the holy God and sinful humanity is, sadly, very closely related to it. Perhaps this sense can be picked up in the second phrase of the prayer, 'hallowed be your name'. The word translated 'hallowed' is *hagiastheto*, from the root *hagios*, meaning holy. The Septuagint Greek translation of Isaiah 6:3—the cry of the seraphs praising God in the Temple—'holy, holy, holy is the Lord God of hosts', uses precisely this term. There is the connotation of purity, absolute goodness, sheer dependence, and utter worth of the supreme object of worship. In the face of this holiness the Hebrew tradition often reflects the unworthiness of the worshipper; this was so in the case of Isaiah who felt a deep sense of his own uncleanness, which was symbolically purged with the burning coal from the altar.[17] God is absolute purity, living holiness, and goodness.[18]

Christians feel the tension between the Fatherhood or approachability of God and the utter holiness so far removed from sinful humanity; but they also feel that this is resolved by the very fact that the church prays, in the name and nature of Jesus, the prayer Jesus taught. Hence there is access to the heavenly throne through 'the great high priest who has passed into the heavens'.[19] This awe-struck awareness of the extent of divine holiness compels an acknowledgement of the wisdom of trinitarian theology. As Paul confessed, 'God has sent into our hearts the Spirit of his Son, crying "Abba, Father!" ' (Gal 4:6), so we discover that the triune God enables and helps us to pray. To be even more specific, the Christian consciousness of prayer to the holy Father includes the background of the sacrifice of Christ as that which underlies the communion of the sinful with the utterly holy.

This spiritual fact can be seen in the vision of Isaiah in the Temple, the burning coal symbolising the purification of the worshipper's lips and person. It is also apparent in the link between suffering and intercession that recurs through the biblical witness. For example, the suffering servant of God in the book of Isaiah[20] both sacrifices himself and intercedes, as does Jesus in Hebrews, who offers himself as the priestly sacrifice and lives at the level of the divine, 'at the right hand of God', making intercession for us. Sacrifice and prayer combine in the face of the holiness of God, and in the movement of the worshipper to God in and through the Spirit of the self-giving Son.

From a total orientation to God as God, independent of any other concerns, we move to the will of God in history and creation. 'Your kingdom come, your will be done. . . .' We move from attention to the being of God to the works and plan of God. Immediately we run into a paradox of grace and mercy: God asks us to pray that his will be done. This is extraordinary. This phrase concentrates a dense theology in itself; indeed it encloses in all its apparent simplicity wonderful complexity and mystery.

God is the God who works out his purposes by ways that include the importance of his people's willing and praying the divine will into action.

The implication is that divine activity, or rather some divine activity, is made conditional for its outworking upon faithful human prayer. This links up with the authentically Christian experience of the grace of God at work in the world, pointed to with such clarity by Donald Baillie in his classic *God Was in Christ*.[21] He describes, following Paul, Augustine, and the Reformed tradition in particular, the experience of a believer struggling with every ounce of effort, often with a sense of real isolation and weakness, for a good cause. But later that person sees that God was always there, leading the way and enabling, with 'prevenient grace'. Looking back, God was at work, and yet at the same time the human effort was total and genuine.

We can apply this experience of the paradox of 'fully divine, fully human' to God's choice to work through human effort and prayer, and especially through the prayer 'your will be done'. God chooses to limit himself, so as to achieve his purposes through the total co-operation of his faithful people. He chooses to be conditioned in his works in the world by the freedom he brings into being in his people. This happened to the highest degree in the life of Jesus: God was in Christ constantly, and Jesus was always fully open to divine grace. The two sets of intentions and goals coalesced without conflict (or without sin, to put it another way). We might add that if God wishes to bring humanity to the fullness of his love and goodness, he 'needs' to work from the inside of the human heart; his omnipotence would be defeated if human hearts and wills were merely forced externally, since this would not achieve moral and spiritual victory. Once again then the fact of prayer points us to an important feature of the Christian doctrine of God, the way that his power is 'magnified' when it works through human obedience and co-operation.

This means that God intends the closest trustful communion of life with his church, which, as has been indicated, must shape herself into the pattern of Jesus and his sacrificial way. 'On earth as in heaven' surely reinforces this mutuality and entrusting of the self to the other; the communion between God and his people, patterned on the perfect trust between the Father and the Son, entails God's trusting or committing his purposes to his praying and acting faithful. It also entails the counter movement by the church of responsive, sacrificial life conditioned to the divine purposes, or the kingdom of God. Being patterned and conditioned by the kingdom surely rules out any notion of modern Western consumerist prayer, any 'prosperity gospel'. It is the truest delight of the disciple to live out the way of Jesus, his truth and life, a way of costly self-giving rather than of worldly acquisition through the supposed agency of God.

The hope of the coming kingdom also has a future reference, an eschatological orientation whereby the present world, the current scheme of things, is relativized by the coming triumph of God and the vindication of his people. This, as Wolfhart Pannenberg has argued, follows from the resurrection of Jesus, which was this vindication in advance,[22] the total revelation of God, and the declaration of his victory in history. This event is true for God as it is for us. It is from this position of victory gained, heralded by the resurrection of Jesus, that the world can be utterly sure of the final outcome. God is not struggling, in some sense, against evil as if the battle might go against him; Christ is risen, the battle is won. If the cross of Jesus reveals the genuine involvement of God in the suffering of the world,[23] the resurrection reveals the security of his victory. This double-sidedness comes through in the Lord's Prayer in calling on God to do his will, while at the same time being sure that ultimately he will bring in the kingdom.

5. *The will of the living God*

In grappling with this double aspect of God's will, Thomas Oden has drawn on a distinction, found in the process theologians, between the divine 'primordial' and 'consequent' wills; so we might well differentiate between the unchangeable, overarching purposes of God and, within this, the contingencies and adjustments in and through which God works.[24] But we must also notice that the assured coming in of the kingdom reinforces the distinction between God and his world, however deeply he is involved in and with it. God has a covenant relationship with the world, but he also has an existence outside created time. Here we reach a storm centre of debate with the process theologians, for whom God and the world comprise one entity, as the life to the body; the life is free to use the body and yet cannot exist without it.[25] Much could be said to challenge this concept, but here we are simply concerned to pick out the implications of Christian prayer for the doctrine of God; it has to be said that this kind of panentheist ('everything in God') or process view cannot easily fit in with the fact of prayer.

When the church prays, she worships the perfectly good and holy God and not a God who is somehow developing into true perfection. The church prays to this God as Father, the most real and alive 'being' there is, the source of all life and goodness; for process thinkers, the 'primordial' pole of God's being means an abstract idea or principle which becomes actual in created 'consequent' enactments of the ideal. The church does not experience worshipping an abstraction or ideal so much as the supremely real and alive. Moreover, given the process view of a God with a dual polarity, prayer itself would be part of the enactment of the divine ideal through the 'consequent' pole of divine being: it would be as if God's consequent nature were worshipping God's abstract and primordial nature through human agency! Christian worship demands a more transcendent vitality to adore and to which sacrifice of self is made. Process thought provides a God who is deeply integrated into the world, but one who is not sufficiently 'other' from the created process in order to satisfy as an object of total devotion and worship.

Process thought, however, rightly warns against a theology of a distant deist God, uninterested in the details of life, remote and inaccessible. The Lord's Prayer points us to God's fatherly care of creation, and calls on us to pray for this provision rather than take it for granted as if it were simply a mechanical system. 'Give us today our daily bread.' It is right to ask for our needs and the needs of others, although not for excess or luxury which may not be compatible with prayer 'in the name of Jesus', and sharing in his character.

What of the problem of unanswered prayer, of suffering and oppression experienced by those who pray and are disappointed, by the mother whose child dies of cancer despite prayer of the most heartfelt kind? Here we reach a point where neither philosophy nor theology can give a neat answer; there is no system whereby prayer automatically leads to worldly blessing, that is happiness in the sense defined by Western consumerism. But faith in the midst of the blinding storm, holding fast to God even by hurling anger at God at times, by weeping with God, this is the essence of the Christian approach to such suffering. The plea 'your kingdom come' may also be charged with such faith and hope in trial and agony.

If the fundamental aim of God goes beyond a hedonistic kingdom of worldly enjoyment to the creation and re-creation of Christlike, holy people, things take on a new perspective, as they do if at the climax of all life there is to be a 'wiping away of every tear' by the 'Lamb in the midst of the throne'. At the end of all the arguments and wringing of hands, the Christian response to suffering is to trust in the transcendently holy Father revealed in his good faith by Good Friday and Easter; only this can face both the scale and depth of suffering, such as under the demonic application of technology by the Nazis against millions of people. Our trust is that the judge of all the earth will do right, and that things are quite different when seen from the perspective of heaven rather than 'on earth'.

Strangely enough, the process view can be linked with the so-called 'pre-millennialist' view of history, in that both envisage a form of happiness, for those who follow the way of the divine calling, which is far too this-worldly. The earthly reign of a thousand years by the elect over the rest of the world, as envisaged by 'pre-millenialists', seems to lack the vision of Jesus, for whom self-sacrifice is true glory. So also the goal of enhanced 'enjoyment' advocated by process thought cannot equate with the truly Christian vision of holiness as ultimate blessing.

The final phase of the prayer, 'forgive us our sins . . .', recalls the purity and goodness of the God who is untainted by sin and who can therefore forgive in his love and mercy. Again, this basic experience of praying must imply that God is *perfect* in *vital* goodness, so neither developing in goodness nor existing unchangingly as an abstract principle. God is enacted holiness, *living* goodness, the source of forgiveness and re-creation. This reinforces the fact that God aims at producing holy people in covenant with himself and his kingdom; his apparent carelessness in allowing us to suffer, or worse our nearest and dearest to suffer, has to be seen in this light. Jesus in Gethsemane models this truth. The kingdom of God is built through costly sacrifice and faithful prayer, and we are part of that kingdom. We are led back to our Father, who is however the heavenly Father, not simply a worldly 'sugar daddy', and to our trust in him. But there is also a clear note of struggle on the part of God as well as his people in bringing in the kingdom and turning back the kingdom of pride, sinfulness, and hardness of heart.

This summary of the significance of the Lord's Prayer should serve to set out the issues to be taken forward in the following chapters, which will follow the structure of this pattern prayer, beginning as it does by addressing the one called the 'Father'.

Notes to Chapter 1

[1]Perhaps the most famous theologian linked to this movement is Jürgen Moltmann and his book *The Crucified God. The Cross of Jesus as the Foundation and Criticism of Christian Theology*, trans. R. Wilson and J. Bowden (SCM Press, London, 1974).

[2]Notably Rudolph Bultmann, for example, in his collection of essays *Existence and Faith*, trans. and ed. Schubert M. Ogden (Hodder and Stoughton, London, 1961), pp. 213-25.

[3]John Macquarrie, *Principles of Christian Theology*, rev. ed. (SCM Press, London, 1977), pp. 4-17.

[4]Daniel W. Hardy and David F. Ford, *Jubilate: Theology in Praise* (Darton, Longman, and Todd, London, 1984).

[5]David Martin, *Tongues of Fire* (Blackwell, Oxford, 1990), p. 227.

[6]Examples are: Don Cupitt, *Taking Leave of God* (SCM Press, London, 1980); essays in (ed.) Colin Crowder, *God and Reality. Essays on Christian Non-Realism* (Mowbray, London, 1997).

[7]Friedrich Schleiermacher, *On Religion. Speeches to the Cultured Despisers of Religion*, trans. J. Oman (Kegan Paul, London, 1893); *The Christian Faith*, 2d ed., trans. H. R. Mackintosh (T & T Clark, Edinburgh, 1928).

[8]The original title of a Roman Catholic work of spirituality by Jean Pierre de Caussade, English translation under the title *The Sacrament and the Present Moment*, trans. K. Muggeridge (Collins/Fount, London, 1996).

[9]This criticism is expressed by Karl Barth in his essay 'Evangelical Theology in the Nineteenth Century' in Barth, *The Humanity of God*, trans. C. Deans (Collins, London, 1961), pp. 24-28.

[10]David Tracy, *Blessed Rage for Order* (Kegan Paul, San Francisco, 1988), p. 27.

[11]Geza Vermes, in his recent book *The Religion of Jesus the Jew* (SCM Press, London, 1993), p. 164, provides a useful summary of the continuum of modern scholarly opinion on the matter, saying that 'the majority view is that the original Lord's Prayer can actually be traced to Jesus, though no agreement has yet been reached concerning the language in which it was formulated'.

[12]Ibid., p. 179.

[13]Joachim Jeremias, *The Prayers of Jesus*, trans. J. Bowden, C. Burchard, and J. Reumann (SCM Press, London, 1967), pp. 58ff.

[14]Vermes, *The Religion of Jesus the Jew*, p. 180.

[15]The chorus written by Helen H. Lemmell and much sung by evangelical youth groups in the 1970s:

> Turn your eyes upon Jesus,
> Look full in his wonderful face,
> and the things of earth will grow strangely dim,
> In the light of his glory and grace.

illustrates the need for divine orientation and yet fails to satisfy a fully Christian view because surely the things of earth fall strangely *into perspective* in the light of his glory and grace. (Chorus from the hymn 'O Soul are you weary and troubled?' Copyright ©1922/1950, Singspiration Inc.)

[16]Friedrich von Hügel discusses this interestingly in his *Essays and Addresses*, First Series (Dent and Dutton, London and New York, 1921), p. 43.

[17]Here we bracket off the problem for Christology that Jesus in the Gospels is never portrayed as repenting from sin, and the teaching in the Epistles is that he is uniquely sinless.

[18]Thomas C. Oden, in his *The Living God* (Harper & Row, San Francisco, 1987), has a fine exposition of divine holiness, especially pp. 96-104.

[19]Hebrews 4:14. This whole epistle concerns the fact of Christian worship of, and access to, the supremely holy God, in and through the mediation of Christ.

[20]E.g., Isaiah 53:12, 'for he bore the sin of many and interceded for the transgressors.'

[21]Donald Baillie, *God Was in Christ* (Faber & Faber, London, 1948), especially ch. 5.

[22]Wolfhart Pannenberg *Jesus—God and Man*, trans. L. Wilkins and D. Priebe (SCM Press, London, 1968) ch. 3, or more simply put in his *Apostles Creed*, trans. M. Kohl (SCM Press, London, 1972), p. 96.

[23]Most strikingly argued by Paul S. Fiddes in *The Creative Suffering of God* (Oxford University Press, Oxford, 1988), pp. 25-31.

[24]Oden, *The Living God*, pp. 92-96.

[25]See, e.g., Charles Hartshorne, *Man's Vision of God* (Archon Books, Connecticut, 1964), pp. 180-88. This subtle concept can also be found in the philosophy of Hegel. See, for example, G. W. F. Hegel, *Phenomenology of Spirit* [1807], trans. A. V. Miller (Oxford University Press, Oxford, 1977), pp. 1-138; cf. the exposition of this aspect of Hegel in Edward Caird, *Hegel* (1883, repr. AMS Press, New York, 1972).

2

'Our Father in heaven'

1. Jesus and the Father

The Gospels witness to Jesus as teaching, 'Pray then like this: our Father', and the church has taken this as foundational. Christian prayer is addressed to God, the God known by Jesus the Jew as Father. Jesus did not deny any of his Old Testament tradition,[1] and he can be said to distil the Hebrew experience of God in his own teaching and spirituality.

He is portrayed as consciously communing with his Father in prayer privately and also not rejecting public worship in the Temple or synagogues. He claimed to depend upon God for his ministry, which in turn brought the kingdom of God into the midst of events. He trusted and obeyed his Father in the face of temptation and terrible trial, particularly as mediated through the story of Gethsemane. He is said by Luke to have set his face like a flint to go to Jerusalem where he believed his ministry would reach its crisis, trusting in God that right would come from this climax.

In this process of trust and faith, Jesus is not depicted as simply a religious genius who invented a new mode of spiritual life. Rather he defines himself as standing in a tradition of faith arising from divine revelation. There can be little question that Jesus did have a 'feeling of absolute dependence' on the God of Israel, as Schleiermacher put it,[2] but that feeling or orientation was shaped by the self-disclosure of God as found in the Hebrew Scriptures.[3] His use of the term 'Father' as a primary way of addressing God might be regarded as a summation of the wisdom of the Hebrew tradition of God and his relationship with his people.

Jesus had faith in a sovereign creator who sustains all things, sending the rain on the just and the unjust (Matt 6:45), so that no conclusions can be drawn about people from their prosperity or otherwise. This God cares in detail about people, according to Matthew's impression of Jesus, which has him asking, 'Are not two sparrows sold for a penny? And yet not one of them will fall to the ground without your Father's will' (Matt 10:29). This is no detached and remote creator, but one at work in and with his created order. Jesus expects people to pray, not only communally in public worship but specifically 'in secret' where no one else can observe piety, where it is a matter of personal relationship with the heavenly Father (Matt 6:1-8).

This tells us something about the nature of God, and at the same time the nature of prayer, in the theology of Jesus. The God of Jesus is one who reigns yet also is one who cares with total commitment and detail. This God cares for particularities, not only general laws and principles. The Hebrew God is a realist for whom individual lives matter. The message of the book of Job has been absorbed into Jesus' theology of God and man. We cannot tell why suffering happens to someone, and we certainly should not presume to impose our own grid of judgement, but we do know that God cares passionately; such is the implication of what we read in the Gospels. God is not a timeless truth or ideal floating in the heavens, to which we try to make our lives correspond here below. The flesh and blood realities of what actually happens in history concern the heavenly Father deeply.

The Hebrew God has to be regarded as 'monarchical', that is, one God who reigns supremely. This God named himself to his people, according to the tradition of Moses in Exodus 3:14, as Yahweh. This in itself seems important. The Hebrew people did not regard themselves as having discovered or uncovered the divine principle in the universe, the unchanging truth or moral ideal. Rather they found themselves dealt with and addressed by a God who sought relationship and commitment. Martin Buber, the Jewish scholar, translated the name Yahweh as 'I am present',[4] rather than the more common 'I am who I am'. He thought his translation warranted by the Hebrew and by the context of Moses and the people needing reassurance, resulting in God promising to be present with his chosen, to remain present and to help them.

> Again and again, when God says in the narrative: 'Then will the Egyptians recognize that I am YHVH', or 'you will recognize that I am YHVH' . . . The Egyptians shall come to know that I (unlike their gods) am the really present One in the midst of the human world, the standing and acting One; you will know that I am He who is present with you, going with you and directing your cause.[5]

Earlier in the biblical narrative Abraham represents the wandering tribes of Israel, and Abraham uses the word 'Elohim' for God. For Buber:

> In the religion of Israel the term Elohim, as expressed in our own range of concepts, means the totality of divine forces or the divine substance, regarded as a single person. Abraham's god, however, is a wanderer like himself. He has no fixed spot, no 'house'; he wanders hither and thither; he takes his folk and leads them wherever he will; he moves on with them from one place to another.[6]

This underlines the sense of presence, and by extension omnipresence, of God; 'where can I flee from your presence?' asks the Psalmist (Ps 139:7), of the God for whom 'even the darkness is as light to you' (v. 12).

God transcends the boundaries of space and time, while caring intimately for the history which happens within space and time. This surely is very close to a provisional understanding of what Jesus meant by 'our Father in heaven', 'heaven' indicating the 'beyondness' of God and fatherhood his care. Jesus begins the prayer with this theology of God, inculcating a corresponding attitude of wonder and trustful obedience; the majestic Lord of the universe, the object of total adoration and worship. This cosmic ruler knows us intimately, 'You know when I sit down and when I rise up'. 'Our Father in heaven' crystallizes this tradition of adoring wonder and secure trust.

The Psalms convey the passion of the adoring soul towards God, and this intensity of the divine worth is concentrated into the prayer of Jesus the Jew.

> Bless the Lord O my soul.
> O LORD my God you are very great.
> You are clothed with honour and majesty,
> wrapped in light as with a garment.
> You stretch out the heavens like a tent,
> you set the beams of your chambers on the waters,
> you make the clouds your chariot . . .
> you make the winds your messengers,
> fire and flame your ministers. (Ps 104:1-4)

The outpouring of praise includes a whole implicit doctrine of God and his absolute worth. It is to this God that the Lord's Prayer directs our attention in the first place.

Christian prayer therefore can never be a matter of undertaking certain religious duties by rote. It is a matter of communion with the heavenly Father, not simply keeping to a code of ritual practice imposed on the worshipping community. Prayer taught by Jesus excludes 'heaping up empty phrases' either repeating what has already been said or using words which cease to have meaning, in other words, impersonal religiosity. The very address of 'Father' defined as the one who knows and cares, not as an autocratic ruler concerned only to exact obedience, makes Christian prayer 'personal' rather than mechanical, albeit personal in a way that includes the sheer majesty of God and the utter inequality of the two parties in the relationship of prayer. There is an emphasis on the need for private prayer: 'When you pray, go into your room and shut the door and pray to your Father who is in secret' (Matt 6:6); this way of praying must have become the norm for the earliest Christian community known by the Gospel writer. Its doctrine of God as Father and practice of prayer to this Father 'who sees in secret', depend upon each other.

Matthew's Gospel has a passage pointing to the 'Wisdom tradition' as part of Jesus' self-understanding and spirituality, another aspect of the Hebrew inheritance finding its focus in his prayer life. Matthew 11 has Jesus comparing the reaction of his critics to those of John the Baptist. The Baptist lived an ascetic lifestyle, 'neither eating nor drinking', evoking the suspicion that he 'had a demon' (Matt 11:18). But Jesus did not espouse the lifestyle of an ascetic:

> The Son of Man came, eating and drinking, and they say, 'Look at him! A glutton and a drinker, a friend of tax-collectors and sinners!' Yet God's wisdom is proved right by its results. (Matt 11:19)

Jesus ends by appealing to the fruits of his ministry; if they are good, then he will be justified by these results, and we notice that in making this defence he seems to identify himself with the divine Wisdom. He may well be referring to the classic wisdom passage in Proverbs 8:22-36 in which Wisdom is personified as a playful princess at the side of the creator as he creates in the beginning. The poem speaks of a delight and joy in creating:

> When he marked out the foundations of the earth,
> then I was beside him like a master worker [or, 'like a little child'];
> and I was daily his delight, rejoicing before him always,
> rejoicing [or 'playing'] in his inhabited world
> and delighting in the human race.

Perhaps the 'eating and drinking' of Jesus in Matthew alludes to such rejoicing in creation. The element of play we find in the wisdom poem does occur immediately prior to this Gospel saying, when Jesus compares the critical spirit of his generation to children in the playground who call to their playmates, 'We piped to you and you did not dance, we wailed and you did not mourn'. Jesus, in the words of a modern hymn, is the 'Lord of the dance'[7] of creation, identified with the delight and play that was at the beginning of all things and is somehow woven into the making of the cosmos, somehow reflective of the nature of God.

This motif of the divine Wisdom, appropriated by Jesus in his self-definition as his ministry developed, is strengthened by Jesus' sayings in Matthew 11:25-30. The parallel passage in Luke 10 begins:

> At that same hour Jesus rejoiced in the Holy Spirit, and said, 'I thank you, Father, Lord of heaven and earth, because you have hidden these things from the wise and the intelligent and have revealed them to infants'.[8]

Luke captures a delight and joy in the Father by Jesus at the revelation of the true wisdom. This reflects the poem of Proverbs 8 in its emphasis on the creation as involving the mediating of Wisdom in joy, wonder, and delight. Perhaps this poem proved something of a stepping stone in Jesus' self-interpretation, as well as the understanding of the earliest Christian community. The wisdom of God, according to Paul,[9] is manifest not in a system of utility or philosophy, but in the person of Jesus. Christian prayer includes the note of joyful freedom, something the Pentecostal movement in particular has recovered.

Divine wisdom is to be marvelled at and praised. The note of rejoicing and praising is very important and part of the meaning crystallized in the term 'Father' in the teaching of Jesus. This goes beyond a rational natural law harmoniously holding things together. The Father reveals all things to the Son who mediates wisdom, true wisdom and not the cold logic of the world, to those who are weary and heavy-laden (Matt 11: 27-30). True wisdom is communion with the Father, and the Gospel writers depict Jesus as conscious of being that Wisdom, of God which 'goes between' the Father and the children of humanity. Jesus introduces them to the Father, as well as teaching them to pray to the Father in a distinctive manner of communion.

Jesus' ministry of healing may also be put in the light of the wisdom of creation. In healing the sick Jesus brings creation to what it is meant to be, putting right what should not be broken, so restoring delight and joy to oppressed humanity. Through this ministry the kingdom of God is made present, the creation is restored, and the joy of wisdom renewed. Jesus keeps death and disintegration at bay in several incidents in the Gospels, and his exorcisms are described in terms of conquest of the power of darkness, liberating creation from its frustration and self-destruction. The activity of Jesus brings release and freedom, and opens up the creative options for humanity, restoring God's destiny for his created order. Obviously the nature miracles of Jesus in the Gospels convey the message of divine Lordship over the forces of nature, the stilling of the storm, for example, but at the same time these episodes also contain the message of restoring creation to its true peace and joy, with its hostile aspects subdued.

In such activity the Gospels depict Jesus as bringing in the hope of restoring creation to what it should be, to its destiny under the creator, the heavenly Father who cares about the fall of a sparrow. It is a mistake to divorce salvation from creation, and the ministry of Jesus cannot be interpreted as so doing. The theological significance of what has been dubbed the 'Nazareth Manifesto' may have been too much restricted to events in history in recent interpretation. Jesus in the synagogue cites Isaiah in identifying his ministry:[10]

> The Spirit of the Lord is upon me
> because he has anointed me to bring good news to the poor.
> He has sent me to proclaim release to the captives
> and recovery of sight to the blind,
> to let the oppressed go free,
> to proclaim the year of the Lord's favour.

Such acts not only bring human *history* to fulfilment, but also *creation*. Jesus seems to have cited such eschatological prophecy in interpreting himself to genuine enquirers,[11] giving the impression that his self-consciousness must have developed along the lines of fulfilling such prophecy and hence being involved in the destiny of creation. Jesus reveals the purpose and character of God in his ministry, and in so doing he gathers up the teaching and experience of the Hebrew tradition in his theology and person. Love and holiness cannot remain concepts, but must be alive and must finally involve community. Praying to the Father is no retreat into immaturity or irresponsible escapism from the tough realities of life; Abba is not 'Daddy' to the adult disciple. Worship of the Father commits the disciple to sharing in the divine mission and ministry in the world.

2. *Prayer to the Father through Jesus*

The Fatherhood of God in the teaching and ministry of Jesus thus crystallizes or distils the insights of the Hebrew tradition, so that 'Father' becomes the normative address for the worshipper, summing up all the Hebrew doctrine of the creator, sustainer, and carer. But once we have said this, we come to a point of decision that was first reached by the early church and which remains today. That fork in the road divides those who are content to regard Jesus as a fine prophet pointing us to God—standing in the shoes of Jeremiah, Amos, and Isaiah—from those who cannot escape the claim of much of the New Testament that Jesus himself is one in being with God.

In other words, the Christian moves on from saying only that Jesus *teaches* us to pray to the Father, and adds to that undeniable truth the fact that Jesus enacts and *gives a way* to God, into which we need to be inducted. Jesus did preach and teach and model a spiritual life, spiritual in the very Hebraic sense of fulfilling creation and not denying it in favour of an abstract realm of existence divorced from this world. Jesus was indeed God's visual aid, but the faithful have found this understanding necessary but not fully sufficient. More has to be said, if justice is to be done to both the experience of faith and to the testimony of the prophets and the apostles.

This watershed has often, in the history of scholarship, been associated with the difference between the Gospels and the Epistles, with John's Gospel being included with the latter for its intensity of interpretative theology. The Jewish scholar Geza Vermes is happy with the picture of Jesus in the Synoptic Gospels (Matthew, Mark, Luke) as a charismatic Jewish prophet. But the church made its major error, he thinks, by deifying this prophet, thus parting company with the Hebrew tradition of the one majestic God in covenant with creation.[12] He thinks that the resurrection of Jesus was possible, but that this would not have deified him any more than Elijah in having been taken into heaven.

This is actually a more positive view of Jesus, in some ways, than that of the nineteenth-century liberal theologians, for whom Jesus was a teacher of righteousness who preached 'the fatherhood of God and the brotherhood of Man', and who taught that the 'kingdom of God is within us'. Jesus was thought to have brought this message to us, but it then became overlaid with Greek ideas and myths to produce a dogmatic 'super-history' of the trinitarian life of God beyond our history. Paul is held largely responsible for this error of starting to worship Jesus the man who above all wished to focus our attention on the Father. Unlike the otherwise similar view of Vermes, however, this line of interpretation does not accept the resurrection of Jesus as a possibility, unless we take it as a metaphorical idea.

Such an interpretation insists on the character of God revealed by the life of Jesus as loving and just. God is open to the faith of anyone who turns to him, as the Father of the world in the sense of the creator and sustainer. Prayer by anyone who is weary and heavy-laden, at the end of their tether and unable to cope, will be heard by the loving and just God of all creation. An extended, opened form of liberal Judaism, shorn of its particularity of race and blood ties, emerges. Such a view seems eminently reasonable, pointing to the Father as Jesus taught about him; Jesus himself is therefore a unique revealer of the divine, a window into God.

Why did the Christian experience take the other fork, the path which did define Jesus beyond this liberal Jewish vision? Somehow Jesus seemed more than a historical figure, a charismatic rabbi, or prophet. The figure of Jesus impressed itself on the lives of believers in a way which brought newness of life, forgiveness, and the Spirit. The picture of Jesus emerges as not only a great teacher about God and how to relate to this God of Israel, but as an enactor of the divine purpose. His final act seems to have been one of total self-giving in line with the plan of the Father, in the pain of this enigmatic horror of Calvary. This was a life-act of obedience to the Father, whom Jesus believed cared about him and related to him as his beloved Son, in whom he was well pleased.

This life-act of faith turned out to be transformatory for those who believed. Something new opened up, and a release of spiritual communion with the Father was given. The resurrection of Jesus was not held to be simply a resuscitated corpse, a 'conjuring trick with bones',[13] but a renewing of created life, a fulfilling of destiny. Jesus was found to be not only the revealer of the shape of reality but also the moral and spiritual saviour. The nature of this salvation involved the sense of immediate closeness to God the Father in a way which compelled the belief that somehow Jesus was of God's very being. The disciples came to believe that the identity of Jesus was divine, and that sharing his life meant sharing in the life of God, transforming human existence radically.

The Epistle to the Hebrews interprets Jesus as mediating between the Father and humanity; Jesus is the great high priest who has passed into the heavens, victoriously giving up his life so as to pioneer a new and living way, a relationship with God which fulfils all that went before. Jesus is seated at the right hand of the Father, the place of final vindication and glory, and makes intercession for us from this position of security and peace. This is not an intercession with any doubt as to the result, since the almighty Father has the Son at his right hand, in the reigning role.

This idea of intercession has its roots in the Last Supper, when Jesus is portrayed citing Isaiah 53, the song of the suffering servant; the words about the servant, that 'he poured out his soul to death' (Isa 53:12) seem to be echoed by the words of Jesus, that 'this is my blood poured out for many'. Probably, then, it was following the lead of Jesus himself that early Christians identified Jesus as this suffering servant of God who 'was numbered with the transgressors; yet he bore the sin of many, and *made intercession* for the transgressors' (Isa 53:12). Jesus is the great suffering intercessor. There is also the note of praise and triumph here; he has been through the pain and injustice to be vindicated and to share that joyful communion of acceptance with those who trust him. Disciples share in the life of Jesus, rather than merely copying his example: such is the distinctively Christian decision about Jesus.

Christian prayer to the Father thus entails sharing in the life of Jesus who brings us into the closest possible communion with the Father. 'God has sent the spirit of his Son into our hearts, crying "Abba, Father" ', says Paul (Gal 4:6). The witness of the New Testament is that such prayer to the Father takes place within a special relationship forged through the triumphant moral and spiritual victory of Jesus who remains effective as the mediator of this 'new and living way' (Heb 10:19). Prayer and worship offered by those surrendered to this new way is eschatological, as the Letter to the Hebrews claims; such prayer fulfils the ancient prophecy of Jeremiah that the time would come when a new covenant would bring a closer, more intimate relationship with God into being, a relationship which the church associates with the name 'Father' (Heb 10:16). A new confidence arises in the hearts of the disciples because of the security of the victory of Christ in God and in human history.

Anthony Hanson's effort to state this is worth quoting:

The risen Jesus, we claim, became the medium whereby the fruits of the incarnation are made available to men. . . . We do not worship the body of Christ, and Paul never suggested that we should. In the body of Christ we can worship God manifested in human nature. This, I believe, is what Karl Rahner means when he writes that 'Jesus the man . . . is now and for all eternity the permanent openness of our finite being to the living God of infinite, eternal life'.[14]

The mediating place of Jesus is no mere scholastic nicety for theologians and church officials; it is the experience of countless disciples down the centuries that God has become real to them since turning to Christ whole-heartedly. Further, it is also the experience of very many Christians that this closeness to God, associated with surrender to the way and person of Christ, brings with it a sense of God within their human lives as the Holy Spirit. The Christian view of prayer is trinitarian and dynamic.

This experience of worship, climaxing with the joyful acknowledge-ment of 'Abba, Father', accords with the picture of prayer in the Synoptic Gospels, as taught by Jesus to the disciples. He introduces them to the regularity of calling God 'Father'; the lofty one, high and lifted up is the one who knows and cares. Sharing in the life-act of Jesus' dying and ris-ing to newness of relationship with the Father, physically enacted in baptism and the holy communion, deepens the link with God as Father.

This means that prayer passes through the lens of Jesus' enacted life, or orientation. Worship entails an act of the will and heart, and Jesus lived out such a life of worship and self-offering to the Father in perfect love. The movement of the perfect self-offering of Jesus orientates our wor-ship. The Letter to the Hebrews sets out this understanding of worship through Jesus quite plainly:

> Therefore, my friends, since we have confidence to enter the sanctuary by the blood of Jesus, by the new and living way that he opened for us through the curtain (that is, through his flesh), and since we have a great priest over the house of God, let us approach with a true heart in full assurance of faith, with our hearts sprinkled clean from an evil conscience and our bodies washed with pure water. (Heb 10:19-22)

This language speaks of access in prayer to the Holy of Holies, to the cen-tre of pure divine presence hitherto prohibited to the people. Now through Jesus' sacrifice, his flesh, a way exists for communion with the holiest, and not in fear and trembling but in confidence. The very same idea can be seen in the book of Revelation in the Seer's phrase, 'the lamb in the midst of the throne' (Rev 7:17); interestingly this final New Testament text seems to indicate worship being addressed both to 'him who sits upon the throne' and 'to the lamb', before whom the 'elders fell down and worshipped' (Rev 5:13-14). Hanson here aptly says that 'we must applaud the wisdom of Pannenberg when he maintains that Jesus Christ could only be known to be both God and man at and after his resurrection.'[15]

It is significant that the first trinitarian formulae in Christian history seem to be baptismal forms, the words interpreting the water-baptism of those entering the faith. This formally inducts the believer into the dynamic trinitarian movement of God sending the Spirit of his Son into our hearts, evoking worship of the Father. As Stuart Hall explains in his study of the early church:[16] after baptism and anointing, the candidate was allowed to pray with the faithful for the first time, which until then had not been allowed; this signalled that there was a new way of praying, in the Spirit, open only to the baptized, those sacramentally sealed into the body of Christ.

3. Image and relationship

From the fact that a radical access to God is given to those who share in the life of Jesus, we must conclude that God is *his God*, the God of Israel who can and does enter into this kind of relationship with his created order. God is to be worshipped and prayed to in a way which goes beyond external obeisance or submission. This is shown in the delight in creation enjoyed by the Father, and in the desire for confident and rejoicing relationship with those who enter into the movement of praise and trust established by Jesus, the beloved son.

Jesus is 'the image of the invisible God' (Col 1:15), in whom all creation holds together. Hebrews speaks similarly of the Son 'through whom he created the worlds. He is the reflection of God's glory and the exact imprint of God's very being, and he sustains all things by his powerful word' (Heb 1:3). The first believers consistently concluded that as the word and wisdom of God, Jesus was the very image of God. Jesus also becomes the head of the humanity, the 'second Adam' whose act of obedience at Calvary reversed the Adamic act of disobedience at the tree in the garden, the sinful state of old humanity. He becomes representative man for restored humanity, taking responsibility for humanity in every way, 'born of woman, born under the law to redeem those under the law' (Gal 4:14). He is the pioneer and perfecter of our faith, tempted as we are, yet without sin, according to Hebrews, fulfilling the true destiny of created humanity.

In these ways the witness of the Old Testament is brought forward into the New. Genesis speaks of God creating men and women in his 'own image and likeness' (Gen 1:26), as distinct from making them 'after their own kind', the equivalent phrase for the other orders of creation. The 'kind' of humanity is invested with divine characteristics, the central aspect of which must be the quality of loving God and our neighbour. Given the nature of the worship opened up by Jesus for humanity, the phenomenon of this fellowship of prayer discloses much about God. It discloses that God desires and indeed bestows *koinonia*, fellowship, with his created partners who are invested with something of their maker. It discloses too that God opens himself up to his created partners in inviting prayer as co-operation in fulfilling his purposes.

Worship of God in the Hebraic tradition of Jesus, is an absolute and life-shaping priority. It is the first of the commandments, and in Jesus' summary of the law, total love and worship of God forms the ground of all else in human life. This is more than a demand or an imperative, although it is both. It is a natural fact that we adore our heavenly Father, for it is our orientation and destiny. There is but one object of absolute love and worship, on whom we should be 'absolutely dependent', as Schleiermacher rightly says, and joyfully so rather than simply dutifully. Worship of God, absolute love of God, cannot be reduced to any other category of human response. This worship is that of sons and daughters, 'not slaves', according to the New Testament.

Christian worship, in theology and experience, defines human beings most truly: they are made in the image of God for communion with God. C. S. Lewis helpfully distinguished, in present human experience, between 'likeness' to God and 'nearness' of approach to God:[17] humanity is 'like God' in many ways, but it somehow fails to actualize this quality or potential in the right way in its conduct. Disciples who pray 'our Father' reinforce their truest identity as those created to know and love God as sons and daughters. The question of who we really are gains its deepest answer as we pray this prayer.

Further, an implication of Jesus' pointing us to God as Father seems to be that creation is not a necessity but stems from the free and generous act of God, portrayed in majestic terms in the grand opening anthem of Genesis. Worship is due to this God, and to nothing else, since everything else is created, and to worship the creature is idolatry. The world is not God, but stems from God who is the source and ground of everything, delighting in the creation which in turn praises its maker for the overflowing generosity of existence.

The fact of this worship eliminates the notion that God somehow worships himself, or actualizes himself, through the medium of the created order. The created order has not been brought into being with the ulterior motive of divine self-discovery or self-affirmation. The history of human consciousness is not itself a form of divine life in finite mode, as the philosopher Hegel maintained. Such an emanation of God into a finite form of God would place qualifications against the sheer grace of creation, and would import into that act a version of what Hegel called 'the cunning of reason', whereby the absolute spirit acts for itself while appearing to bestow freedom on the finite will.[18] The Hebraic and Christian doctrine of creation entails the pure delight and generosity of bringing the non-divine realm into being. It also points us to a 'respect' for what is created, as Daniel Hardy and David Ford have emphasized.[19] When we pray, we know we pray to God, to one who loves us; we know we are created beings privileged to respond genuinely to our maker.

The orientation of Christian prayer totally inverts the cynicism prevalent in our late twentieth century, delighting instead to *acknowledge* this Lord of the universe. While modern philosophers invoke a 'hermeneutics of suspicion', this has no place in worship, which is predicated on the utter trustworthiness of the heavenly Father, often in the face of terrible circumstances. Divine Fatherhood and the kingdom, twin pillars of Jesus' teaching about the divine nature and character, hold together in this attitude of worshipful trust, honour, and gratitude for existence itself. The attitude of worship may be *childlike* in this totality of trust in divine goodness at the very depths of all things, but it is not *childish*.

Pessimism as a way of life and thinking is resisted in the Christian mindset, because of a natural confidence in the heavenly Father. The sermons of many South African Christian ministers in the years leading up to the settlement of 1994 illustrate this confidence in the Lordship of the God of Jesus Christ, often proclaimed in the teeth of bitter oppression.[20] The character of this God, and the orientation of the church to our Father in heaven, forms the granite of the universe. Prayer implicitly resists pessimism, not so much by any false optimism or shallow heartiness, but primarily by the disciplined, regular, and glad acknowledgement of the heavenly Father.

The sheer fact that God is the 'heavenly' Father, with an existence transcending our own, erodes pessimism that is either theological or psychological. Ultimately, God is God and is *this God*. Whatever mess and confusion we see the human race making of itself, the world process is not God: we are pointed beyond it. God and the world are intimately related, but God and the world are distinct entities. This is challenged in a good deal of contemporary theology, and will recur in our discussion, but even before we embark on any further enquiry, it appears evident that the worship of God must be by one reality towards Another that is its source. Delight in God, just as God's own joy in creation, involves a difference in being, although of course it also requires a relationality. A strong single-entity model of God and the world renders primary features of worship—love, delight, and rejoicing—difficult to sustain, leading on the face of it to a form of monistic self-gratification rather than *mutual* joy, respect, and trust.

If God and the universe are fundamentally a single integrated entity, if the world is 'God's body',[21] then praise of God is self-praise, washing back from God's body into his emotional or mental aspect, giving him a pleasure that emanates from him in the first place. As with all theological proposals, there is some truth in this model, but it will need to show how it preserves sufficient distinction between praiser and praised if it is to be a Christian theological construct. The fact of worship here can be seen to serve as something of a litmus test for theology, in that any theological construct which fails to give sufficient *space* for the creature to worship its maker needs to be revised accordingly. If there is not a sufficient *distinction* between God and his created humanity, there cannot be sufficient *relationship*. Worship, signalled by the address 'our father in heaven', arises from total respect and honour felt towards God, overflowing into praise evoked by the object of pure worth. There needs to be sufficient independent existence on the part of the worshipper to bestow honour to the worshipped, for the lover to love the beloved. On the other hand, there needs to be sufficient commonality for a relationship to be possible. The suggestion made in Genesis that we are made in the image of God underlines this fact, in that we are given sufficient commonality whereby a relationship can take place between God and his people.

This commonality exists prior to any mention of the distortion of sin. This shared reality is prior in time to evil. The 'image of God' and 'covenant relationship' with God are two interlocking biblical concepts. However great the disparity between the one who is high and lifted up, wrapped in a robe of light, and his creatures, yet in the case of human beings there is the possibility of relationship, which is due to the divine generosity and woven in at creation. In terms of the 'labels' and 'logos' fashionable in Western culture as markers of identity, and so of purpose and goal, Christians bear the label of adult children of 'our' (not simply 'my') heavenly Father. This label needs to be internalized so as to become the way we think of ourselves in the world. This identity carries with it true freedom and true responsibility. Our personhood comes from God and lives in relationship with this God.

4. The trinitarian Father

God has projected, or invested, something of his character into humanity so that there can be these relationships. This suggests that in God himself there is some form of relationality that corresponds to relations between God and humanity, and to relations between human beings themselves. The divine love creates us in a kind of analogy to himself, in such a way that this analogy is partial, so preserving the great difference between creator and created order. Any analogy compares one thing with another, and the very need for such a comparison shows that there is a clear difference between the two items. For example, a pebble is not an acorn but may look like one, so that we can use the analogy that 'this pebble is like an acorn.' By contrast, to say that one pebble looks like another pebble is not really an analogy, since two different kinds of things are not involved.

God is not humanity, but there is an analogy that has been constituted by God. This analogy seems to consist of the capacity to relate in a way we call 'personal'. The analogy does not equate a human person with God, and it is a limited analogy. This can be simply shown in terms of the second Genesis story of creation, the Adam and Eve narrative, in which to 'become like God' is the great temptation to be resisted. To be as God, to be unlimited in freedom, the temptation felt by Jesus in his temptations in the wilderness, is to overleap the proper boundary of the divine and the human. We are to keep to our proper order of being, not to claim equality with God in terms of power, authority, and knowledge. The very context of the Genesis narratives in which the idea of 'image' is set ensures an interpretation of the image and likeness of God in humanity which fully allows for disproportion.

Jesus perfects the image of God *in* humanity, since he is the very Word of God *to* humanity, and this places limits on any analogy between the divine and the human. It also fits into the double aspect of the image doctrine, the vertical and the horizontal. God has reached into the human situation out of his loving character, and has established his kingdom in the person of Jesus and his disciples who continue the 'Jesus mode' of life and worship. Creation bears the stamp of divine care and generosity, and the restoration of creation also is the act of God invested with the

character of God. Christian worship is to be caught up into this movement
of God's saving action, from God the Son to God the Father.

Christian worship of the Father, with the Spirit of his Son in our
hearts, is not only a matter of experience, but concerns the being
('ontology') of God; this has led the church to develop another analogy,
that God is triune. The unity of God cannot be a purely mathematical
unity, but must rather be like the unity of the human mind or person with
a richness and life that extends beyond itself. God is the God who desires
to reach out, to 'overflow'.[22] This desire is not best regarded as contrary
to his nature, perhaps as some trick played on humanity to set up a world
full of woe but with sufficient goodness in it to make fruitless effort
worthwhile. God is not that sort of being; he is sincere, transparently honest, and genuine in his love. We know this through Jesus. The Gospel
assumes that the being of God matches the disclosure of God in Jesus,
and is not masked by it. Behind a loving Jesus is not an unloving God,
although this version of faith is held surprisingly often, as many pastors
have discovered in disciples who have kept their fears hidden.

The triunity of God has been perceived by Christians in the light of
the person and work of Jesus, with all his theological inheritance of the
Hebrew God, and the impact of the Holy Spirit in life and worship. The
richness of divine life overflowing must exist *in and as* God, as well as
towards his creation. In Christian understanding, the Fatherhood of God
has taken on this trinitarian sense in addition to the meaning of a benign
ruler of the universe that is apparent in the Hebraic tradition. The
Christian mind has come to hold that the *action* of God in Christ and in
the Spirit reflects the *life* of God in himself.

We must recognize the limits of theology when it tries to map the
very being of God as if by some architectural plan. But the analogy of
threefoldness in a single being is exactly aware of these limits, wishing as
an analogy to affirm something, yet remaining a figure of speech. The
main point to be grasped is that Jesus is real for God the Father, as is the
Father for Jesus, and that this reality each for each will not prove temporary. God defines himself in this way, since this is how he is. God is
Christlike, and Jesus lived out God's life in history. The church shares in
the life of Christ and so relates to God as Father. The New Testament
speaks of this dynamic knowledge of God in and through God, and the
church has experienced this and patterned its worship accordingly for
centuries, in public and in private.

To abstract from this dynamic movement of worship and speak of God apart from our worship of him as triune becomes more abstruse and difficult, moving from the concrete experience to more speculative theology. But as Karl Barth affirms,[23] the pattern of this dynamic overflow of creating and saving love is no accident, but arises from the divine being and so reflects it. Barth speaks of the structure of Father, Son, and Spirit as paralleling that of revealer, revelation, and the state of revealedness; so the trinitarian *action* of God can be carried back from experienced salvation into the *being* of the Godhead.[24] The 'economic' trinity (God at work in the world) corresponds to the 'immanent' trinity (God in his inner life and being).

In this way the fatherhood of the caring God of the Hebrew tradition coincides with the triune Father who is the source of all being, including the divine being. Christian spirituality believes that this Father is the self-same God of Hebrew belief, not a kind of 'third' part of that God. But the term 'Father' in the context of trinitarian discourse takes on a different function, since it means the originator of the Son and Spirit, who as the one God created the universe. When we use worship as the test of our doctrine of God, we find that adoration is directed towards the trinitarian Father by the Son, and that loving pleasure is directed towards the Son by the Father.

This structure of relationship is symbolized in the Gospels, as in Jesus' baptism in the Jordan where the Spirit descends on Jesus as he hears the voice from heaven saying, 'You are my Son, the Beloved; with you I am well pleased' (Mark 1:9-11). John's Gospel develops this motif greatly in terms of the Father-Son bond existing before history and flowing out into the world in love. 'As the Father sent me, so I send you', says Jesus to his disciples (John 20:21), patterning their ministry on his own dynamic trinitarian identity. The pattern and life of mission is rooted in the sending of the Son by the Father, as is the responsive pattern of worship that is prayer to the Father through the Son in the power of the Spirit.

Christian theology has moved 'upwards' from the dynamic trinitarian God of experience, and from the concrete historic revelation of the life and destiny of Jesus, in order to seek definitions of the trinitarian *being* of God. Two kinds of analogy are commonly used, one psychological and the other social, each trying to speak on the basis of the dynamic of the lived trinitarian revelation. The 'psychological' analogy detects a rich pluriformity in the human mind and extends it to God; for example,

Augustine pondered the threefoldness of being, knowing, and willing within the same mind.[25] The Eastern tradition circles around a 'social' analogy, based on experience of relationships; the Father is the source of the divine being, eternally bringing forth the Son and Spirit to produce a continual existence of love and mutuality. God gives God, and the disciple is caught up in the life of this astonishing generosity which knows no limits.

A notable difference between the two traditions of analogy is that in Western theology, based on Augustine's thought, divine essence is taken as the common uniting factor, whereas for the tradition of the East (exemplified in the 'Cappadocian Fathers') the Father is the primary person from whom the Son and Spirit come. But for both approaches, God's love is real in himself, even without creation to love; and for love to be real rather than just an idea awaiting fulfilment, it must be alive. God gives God; the Father gives the Son. This divine life reaches out to us: the deepest word that can be said of Christian worship and prayer is that God has sent the Spirit of his Son into our hearts, so that we cry 'Abba, Father'.

5. The language of God as 'Father': the challenge of Christian feminism

'Mutuality' has become a significant concept for the issue of theological language. It has played a part in feminist criticism of male terms in the doctrine of the Trinity, especially the term 'father', which has attracted the charge that it reinforces male domination of society. If the trinitarian terminology is a kind of cipher for mutuality at the very heart of God, then should the church replace the traditional terms with others more acceptable to those who are offended by male language?

Moltmann argues that feminist criticism has had three waves. The first was to reject the trinitarian theology altogether and to seek a different religion, God 'beyond the Father', using neutral terms such as 'depth of being' to escape the history of theology.[26] The second wave of criticism wished to insert the feminine dimension into the trinity by adding new images to balance the traditional male ones. In particular, the Holy Spirit can be shown to have had such connotations as far back as the patristic era. Already we have seen that the divine wisdom is personified in Proverbs 8 as a playful princess at the dawn of creation, and the Syrian Church could describe the Spirit as 'mother' because of the comforting nature of the Spirit and because by the Spirit we are reborn.[27]

Third, feminist criticism sought to find in the traditional figures a feminine aspect,[28] reconstructing the trinitarian persons by importing into them two sets of gender qualities, and so bringing into being the notion of a male *and female* 'Father'. Moltmann wonders whether this does not reflect an overly individualistic notion of the human person, with each individual self-contained in sexual duality, not needing the other. This is an interesting cultural development with roots going back into a long-standing mystical perfectionist tradition. As John Passmore informs us,[29] mystical perfectibilists held that in the state of perfection there will be only one flesh, that the final secrets will not be unveiled 'until the two become one, and the male with the female is neither male nor female'. It is expected that a state of androgynous or hermaphrodite perfection can be reached, transcending the duality of male and female, reaching a point of unification and still joy.

But does such a revision as this last one offend the principle of mutuality that the doctrine of the Trinity seems to teach? Or, on the contrary, does the notion of hermaphrodite 'persons' of the Trinity protect the doctrine from the notion of sexual communion in God, in the same way that the exclusion of the female terminology did? It has been argued that the Old Testament tradition, which uses female imagery for God very rarely indeed, was sealing off its doctrine of God from surrounding pagan fertility religion by using only masculine language with which to address God. Elizabeth Achtemeier has sympathy with this view:

> It is not that the prophets were slaves to their patriarchal culture, as some feminists hold. And it is not that the prophets could not imagine God as female: they were surrounded by people who so imagine their deities. It is rather that the prophets, as well as the Deuteronomists and Priestly writers and Jesus and Paul, would not use such language, because they knew and had ample evidence from the religions surrounding them that female language for the deity results in a basic distortion of the nature of God and of his relation to his creation.[30]

Janet Martin Soskice argues that the title 'father' can be saved for feminist use. Following the analysis of Paul Ricoeur, she points out that 'Father' in the Old Testament is not used of God to denote a 'begetter' of the world or of Israel; rather, Israel is the people *adopted* by this God. Only with the New Testament does the metaphor of 'begetting' appear, in the Father's begetting of the *Son*. Moreover, this particular begetting powerfully embodies a motherly characteristic.[31] Soskice here simply seeks to advocate the retention of the address 'Father' but argues for an exclusive use with regard to God as the Father of Christ and of 'sisters and brothers in Christ'.

This debate reveals the different nuances of usage of the term 'father' and the vital importance of context. For instance, Moltmann is happy to use the trinitarian term 'father', but discards the address outside the trinitarian context. To call God 'father' in a purely theistic sense would be to fall into the patriarchal hostility to women. The trinitarian context, however, includes a motherly aspect in the father, as this father not only begets but 'gives birth to his son'.[32] Now, all this gives reason why the Lord's Prayer should remain normative for Christian worship; the phrase 'Our Father in heaven' clearly connects the fatherhood of God to Jesus, and given the church's trinitarian understanding of Christ's identity, feminist criticism has strengthened the use of the prayer by ensuring its purgation of literalist connotations of maleness in God. Such language is, in effect, a kind of theological and liturgical mathematics, a-sexual algebra that cannot now be altered without reimporting what it purified from the Old Testament era.

The trinitarian debate about fatherhood in the early centuries of the church's life involved the nuances of origination. The argument raged around the question as to whether the origination of the Son by the Father was analogous to the act of 'making' something or 'begetting' someone. The consensus emerged, after years of struggle and bitter debate, that the Father originates the Son 'eternally' and 'from his own being'. This means that the analogy 'Father' is not being used in this context to depict the mode of begetting life as human fathers beget, that is, sexually. In the early centuries, the way that the origination of the Son occurs was described in the imagery of a natural 'coming forth', for example, like light from the sun, so moving from the human fatherly analogy to one from the inanimate world. Thus the language of fatherhood in the trinitarian tradition develops in a way that affirms only *some aspects* of human fatherhood. The fatherhood of the triune God is not simply to be described by the analogy, partial and pale image though it be, of human fatherhood, but by the partial analogy of only an *aspect* of human fatherhood.

Karl Barth contends that the worshipping community best approaches the topic of language about God from the 'top down', that is, from the perfection of the divine fatherhood.[33] In this light we should interpret human fatherhood and see its imperfection in the light of the wonder of the divine fatherhood and sonship; likewise says Barth, ' "lordship" is not first and properly what we know as the exercise of power by man over man, but the *kuriotes* [lordship] of God exercised and revealed in Jesus Christ'.[34] Barth is concerned not to measure God by human standards, but conversely to elaborate the implications of revealed divine fatherhood. While not living in the late twentieth-century cultural context of feminist criticism, he might well have sympathized with women who are angry at male oppressiveness and therefore find masculine language for God difficult. He would point out that language of God is meant to point beyond the human to the divine, who is revealed in Jesus Christ.

Barth's response would be Christological rather than propositional, or fixed to defined terms. That is, he is always seeking to attend to the revealed Jesus Christ. Since, however, Jesus is revealed as praying to the Father, and teaches his disciples to do so, there is a strong reason to suppose that Barth would not approve of substituting the term 'mother' for father. Nevertheless, he points out that the terms 'father and son' are only analogical, referring to a 'higher and lower' in God, and that the earthly relationship of Jesus and his heavenly Father is transposed within the very being of God.[35] Barth seeks to understand God *through* Jesus and his story, which must be real for God as for us who are caught up into his story.

Of particular relevance here is that Barth claims to root his theology in the real knowledge of God through faith and worship, in an encounter which uses human language as its instrument to point to himself. Barth therefore seeks to pass theology through the prism of worship and to listen to the testimony of the prophets and apostles in so doing. While he does see the broken nature of our theological words, and the fallibility of tradition, he might nevertheless have argued that the revealed God of Jesus is the self-naming father, whose name is a given datum for worship first and foremost. Although a human word, it is the word taken up or adopted by God for the purposes of his self-revelation.

While suspecting that Barth would not be at ease with the notion that the term father is dispensable, since it is so closely linked to the very self-understanding of Jesus, the issue highlights a certain ambivalence in his theology: on the one hand propositions are secondary, but on the other God has ordained the Scriptures as normative in a way that other texts or words are not. God, Barth admits, can reveal himself through 'a flute concerto, a blossoming shrub, or [even] a dead dog',[36] but the church is not founded on such possible revelations. Likewise, we might say, we might well use feminine terms to address God, but the Lord's Prayer has a normative status, as have the trinitarian formulas attaching to worship as found in the New Testament.

A watershed of opinion seems to be reached in the church today as to whether the traditional language of prayer should be reconstructed and, if so, whether any norms remain by which such changes can be controlled. The conservative fears the importation of sexual generation into the divine being, for example, whereas the classical tradition has excised this possibility with its asexual but masculine language. Here the church might do well to be guided by its theologian, Karl Barth, in accepting that the language of the 'father and the son' is not dispensable according to some other terms we may prefer; rather, this is the language which the church has understood to derive from the revelatory story of Jesus, who seems to have been one of the historic forces on the side of women. Barth's logic seems to be that if such church language has been support-ing oppression of women, that is because the self-disclosure of God has been abused by sinful men. The interpretation of the Father needs to be rigorously Christological: God is Christlike.

If we pass the debate arising from the feminist protest through the lens of worship, we see that its ferocity and bitterness have at times con-tradicted the vision of one God and the unity of the Spirit claimed by the church. Christians risk splitting into more and less feminist modes of worship and liturgical language. The alternative of using a neutral phrase such as 'ground of being' to denote the object of worship may serve a use-ful purpose in theological discussion, but as a term with which to address God, it is too impersonal and more metaphysical than biblical. The language of theology does not fully overlap that of worship.

Eastern Orthodox theology strongly affirms that 'Father' is a name, the name which God has revealed as normative and that cannot be changed. This might, however, be qualified through careful theological exposition, so that someone praying to the Father might be made more aware of qualities often associated with the feminine. The trinitarian God transcends sexuality, but not relationship, and the phrase 'being as com-munion' has become well known as expressing this, following a leading work with this title by an Orthodox theologian.[37] Communion, however, is itself not an entity without persons who engage in communion or fellowship, and the Orthodox indeed stress that 'persons', and so the per-son of the Father, are the object of worship. Mutuality itself cannot be worshipped or communed with any more than can 'being'.

Each side in the debate can accuse the other of literalism. Feminist critics can argue that the traditional language is analogical and hence adjustable, not set in concrete. Conservatives can argue that objection to the classical language of Father and Son involves failure to get beyond a very literalistic use of the terms, that some terms are needed, and that to introduce female names is to lapse into less sophisticated faith and worship. Pastorally, churches existing in this cultural climate are hard pressed to know what to do. A constant Christological check on the usage of language of worship may be the only advice to offer, which will ensure the classical formulations are not used in ways which contradict the Gospel they purport to serve. Communion with the God of the historical Jesus involves sharing in the way he prayed to his God and imaged God; hence, it must be right for the church to protect this tradition while seeking to be sensitive to the claims of all people.

This debate highlights the significance of the Old Testament, and worship of the God of Israel, as the normative context for understanding Jesus and his prayer to the Father. But this might itself be questioned. Is Jesus after all to be interpreted against the background of the Hebrew theology of God, however broadly it is necessary to regard such a theological tradition? Or should the figure of Jesus be set against other backgrounds in order to understand his significance and spirituality? This issue was forced onto the early church's agenda as different theological systems were asserted by 'Gnostic' groups who claimed that the Old Testament God of creation was inferior to the New Testament God of redemption. In response, the Christian theologian Irenaeus affirmed the unity of the God of the Old and New Testaments, and the unity of creative and redemptive purposes of God in Christ, who was the recapitulation of created humanity, the second Adam. He therefore helped to link the Hebrew God to the God of Jesus and affirmed that creation came from the act of this one, monarchical God.

Against the background of a Gnostic cosmology, the interpretation of Jesus and of prayer would have been very different indeed. The work of early Christian teachers such as Irenaeus provided the framework for the classical doctrine of God's relation to the world, with its accompanying view of prayer. The doctrine of the Trinity might be said to have linked the New and Old Testaments organically, teaching that the Hebrew God is the God of Jesus Christ. This in turn prevented the development of a cosmology of different deities with Jesus standing within history in the tension between, and seeking a path of redemption from an evil world and its history.

The Hebraic tradition of God always saw the divine as an agent active in the world and passionately interested in the world in all senses of the word 'passionate'. It would be hard to conceive of the doctrine of the Trinity arising without that theological background that was funnelled into the term 'Father' on the lips of Jesus. The Jesus of history and the Christ of faith cannot finally be split apart, as the historical Jesus used the term 'Father' in such a way as to invest new meaning in it. It is the God of Abraham, Isaac, and Jacob, the 'I am who I am', who is focused in the address of 'Father' as used by Jesus. While God is universal, and beyond domestication by us, to say that God is a 'God of many names', each of equal significance and insignificance, would not only imperil the historical link with sharing the prayer of Jesus; simultaneously it would undermine the spiritual 'concreteness' of that prayer.

6. Is there a 'real' Father?: the challenge of 'non-realist' believing

For some, however, any notion of an objectively real God is a relic of the past and needs to be reinterpreted along other lines more accessible to secular people of the Western type. In the last century Schleiermacher had sought to commend the faith to the 'cultured despisers of religion' by focusing on the sense of dependence in the human heart. While showing the reasonableness of faith by way of this experiential path, Schleiermacher did not advocate the non-existence of God. Today some wish to commend the language of the faith to the cultured despisers of religion, while retreating from claiming that God is in any sense real or objective. Anthony Freeman's book *God in Us*[38] summarizes this move from a liberal position, such as that adopted by Schleiermacher, to what he calls a radical understanding of the word 'God'.

The traditional view of God is described by Freeman as 'supernaturalist', believing in a God who exists and who intervenes in the affairs of the world, revealing himself in the person of Jesus and forgiving our sins. The 'liberal' view, which Freeman himself first adopted after being unable to accept a supernatural deity, was more agnostic but still asserted the existence of the divine which affected life through the will and action of human beings. Instead of prayer being answered in an 'interventionist' fashion as for the supernaturalist, prayers 'increasingly take the form,

"Lord, help us to do things" '. Freeman comments that 'somehow it's easier to imagine God's affecting my actions than to imagine his acting directly on the physical world'.[39]

Freeman's former 'liberal' view seems to affirm *that* God is, but to resign any claim to talking about what or *who* God is. In fact, this seems to be a rather negative and narrow view of the liberal tradition, since in the normal kind of liberal theology the person of Jesus colours the character of God. But the main point for Freeman is that he goes on to conclude that God as this mysterious being beyond human existence has to be denied, as has even a divine existence beyond the category of 'being'; nevertheless, the *practice* of religion, for Freeman, ought to continue as a worthwhile enterprise for the human spirit. 'Now I have decided to change my use of the term God. Instead of referring it to a supernatural being, I shall apply it to the sum of all my values and ideals in life',[40] says Freeman, testifying that this denial of the objectively real God has brought a sense of liberation like a conversion experience, and has in effect lost nothing. The more academically rigorous version of this move into 'non-realist' theology is to be found in the many works of Don Cupitt,[41] and historically is the heritage of Ludwig Feuerbach.

Feuerbach explained religion as projection. Human beings have projected their best and highest aspirations onto an imaginary deity, and in so doing have devalued human potential and self-worth. Worth has been given to God; lack of worth is left for the human race.[42] Karl Marx developed this idea powerfully, teaching that worship of God drains the sense of esteem and value from humanity, causing it to doubt its own greatness and moral capacity. The qualities attributed to God—for example, love, wisdom, and justice—are human qualities evaporated and condensed into a being named God.

Declaring, 'Ever since we embraced just one God, he has always been in fact the sum of all our ideals',[43] Freeman re-states the view of Feuerbach which was first worked out some century and a half ago. For Feuerbach, we ought no longer to talk of God's being, intelligence, morality, and love; rather, we should reverse this statement and call these things divine. The secret of religion is therefore atheism, according to Feuerbach as to Freeman so much later, and this is not bad news for them but is positive as true humanism. The truths found in the myth of religion, they argue, are truths of the human condition. Marx drew on Feuerbach's criticism of religion strongly to argue that not only was religion false, but it served a pernicious purpose in drawing the sting of revolutionary fervour;

it was an opiate for the suffering poor and oppressed, and therefore not merely harmless.[44]

Such projection theory, as Daniel Hardy and David Ford point out,[45] cannot be disproved. It is a counter claim to that of the religious claim of the existence of God. Christian theology claims the contrary, that God has projected himself to us, ultimately in the person of Jesus, but in a sense also in the created order and especially in humanity, the image of God. Christians affirm that the highest human aspirations of love, beauty, truth, goodness, and justice flow from God, and in some way are woven into our existence. The Christian perspective thus argues a correspondence between the highest in human value and God who grounds this absolute value. This also gives a firm rationale for using analogy to speak of God, seeing the basis for this usage in creation. The sociologist Peter Berger acknowledges the force of Feuerbach's argument about the truth of religious projection, but suggests that this projection may well also have a genuine point of reference.[46] He uses the example of mathematical constructions that have been made, only to be confirmed by empirical scientific discovery later; that is, the mental constructs *actually did* mirror the way things are. Accordingly, the theological claim is that the initial projection was from the divine into the created order, and that this has been reflected in the human act of projection.

Marx took up Feuerbach's criticism of religion enthusiastically, interpreting the Reformation as a victory over *external* religious authorities that had chained mankind, and hailing Feuerbach as implementing the final victory over the authority of religion within the individual. This *internal* authority, in Marx's view, had also now been proved to be a fiction, and a fiction harming the prospects for a mature and fair development of the human race. What both Feuerbach and Marx would therefore have made of the proposal (by Freeman and others) that we should continue religious practice and forms of worship despite the denial of the truth asserted in such forms, is hard to guess. One of the main points of their criticism of religion was to free humanity from the subservient attitudes of harsh self-negation that were involved in religious observance. To continue with them could well seem to lack seriousness. On the other hand, perhaps continuation with religious practice, but reinterpreted so as to make clear that humanity is being celebrated and not anything else, might come close to the spirit of Feuerbach's work if not to his actual recommendations.

In fact, a very important question to be put to the 'radical' or 'non-realist' interpretation is that of worship. Can human moral orientation, as an interpretation of what we mean by God, be an object of worship? This question is sharpened when we perceive that these values are clearly no more separable from actual human beings than they would be from the deity who has been rejected. In other words, such worship entails worship of real humanity. This is a very interesting and clarifying question, not only about the nature of the non-realist position that is being advocated as an option for the church, but also about the nature of worship itself.

No doubt there is more than a grain of truth in the criticism that the history of Christianity has been stained with lack of respect for humanity in the name of God. The stigmatizing of sex in the Western Church as sinful rather than part of creation seems to exemplify this failure to celebrate humanity in its fulness, in the name of a God who is angry at sin that supposedly passes through the race through the sexual act. Much sin-laden spirituality has similarly failed to do justice to the created potential of mankind, exaggerating negative aspects of humanity while finding good only in God.

Dietrich Bonhoeffer's *Letters and Papers from Prison*[47] express denial of a God who oppresses and renders humanity immature and irresponsible, keeping it childish and unable to work seriously in the world. This line of theology contains some of Feuerbach's criticism of religion in the name of humanity in all its potential. Bonhoeffer's controversial phrase, 'man has come of age',[48] expresses something of this right concern to celebrate the real capacities of humanity, and to warn against negation of human beings as if glory could be given to God by diminishing his own creation. Bonhoeffer, however, does not recommend us to worship humanity, but to be mature human beings and to act *as if* God were not a given reality, *as if* we were on our own and wholly responsible for the development of society, and so to take this responsibility with utmost seriousness. Worship of humanity might instead be an *irresponsible* attitude to take, or to encourage by using religious forms as a means of affirming human worth. The paradox of Bonhoeffer's letters and papers is that they were written in a Nazi prison, and so seem to celebrate humanity 'come of age' in the midst of unspeakable state-organized criminality.

Bonhoeffer's reminder to us to behave with total seriousness and to take responsibility for life is salutary; no doubt religion has in many and various ways impeded this maturity of the human race. But he did not reject God; rather, he set humanity in the context of God who is real, but not the overpowering, even disabling, deity of much spirituality. Bonhoeffer speaks of trusting others who are worthy of trust, in the mists of the choking atmosphere of lies and betrayal in wartime Germany, but not of worshipping others. His is a mature and helpful message. But is 'non-realist' theology mature in identifying human value with God, using liturgical language that was designed to adore the creator? Is this somehow the inverse of the maturity called for by Bonhoeffer? Is it an over-estimation of humanity, a deification, which simply fails to fit the true facts of human history?

Worship cannot be self-worship; it needs to turn its face to the sun. While a realistic celebration of human potential is very necessary, adoration of the self or the race to which we belong breaks the limits within which we live, overreaches our own status in a Promethean fashion. This is the implication of the 'non-realist' programme, and it falls down badly at the point of worship and prayer, while persevering with ritual and liturgy. Perhaps it can be argued that this use of ritual has a dimension of social control: in a similar way Auguste Comte's 'Catholicism without Christianity' retained an ethical undergirding for behaviour. It can surely be accused of irresponsibility, the like of which Bonhoeffer would have disliked.

This discussion does not seek to win a debate on logical grounds against projection 'from below' by human beings, in favour of the traditional projection 'from above' by the creator. It is doubtful whether such a debate can be won by either side on rational argumentation. Nor is this observation an attempt to win an argument by bringing in the factor of a 'felt need', a factor Feuerbach precisely puts his finger on. But the 'worship factor' is being deployed here as a criterion of theology, and a neglected one. Can any purported contribution to Christian theology that wipes away the utterly central fact of worship and adoration be taken seriously? Indeed is not the implication of self-worship destined to prove damaging and dangerously over-optimistic, given the record of humanity in the late twentieth century? Serious attempts to address the grave problems of humanity need both optimism and realism, rather than flights of romantic fancy about the human spirit and its infinite worth. The fact, often overlooked, is that the Christian faith *does* attribute such worth to the human being, made in the image of God; an example of this is its opposition to euthanasia. But this is not to worship humanity.

The suggestion that the 'non-realist' approach to the question of God abolishes a core Christian reality is not only very grave for that approach, since it claims to be the future of the Christian way, but also helps us to clarify what we mean by worship. 'Non-realists' wish to speak of worth and value, but not in the Platonist sense of a real entity over and above the flesh and blood life of humanity. Value is being celebrated, but located firmly in the historical dimension. Worth is being thereby affirmed and praised. Now, it is true that poets have for centuries been using the language of adoration in their love poems; in the marriage service of the *Book of Common Prayer* the groom tells the bride: 'With this ring I thee wed, with my body I thee worship, and with all my worldly goods I thee endow'. Such is the language of total trust, self-giving, and honour, directed to another human being. Does this indicate that the non-realist may be less in error than has been suggested?

The language used by our poets in such texts sounds like religious adoration, and in some respects shares in its intensity of self-surrender before the glory of its object, the beloved; this is a self-giving that is not enforced by sheer power but is evoked from the free heart, or it would not be genuine love nor anything like Judeao Christian adoration of God. We need to note that such adoration and love is addressed to and evoked by particular people who are held in wonder. Praise addressed to abstract principles or values is not of the same order; and in fact, it tends to be an imitation of the concrete style of love poetry. The adoration of human love is always directed to an other, who is held to be peerless in beauty, goodness, and glory of some kind.

This is why it is *like* religious language, having the covenant structure of asymmetrical mutual love and praise from one to another. This concrete particularity is important, for the beloved is like no other, is unique and irreplaceable. Her qualities are hers alone. Such language therefore is not really used to praise abstract values so much as people who are endowed with such wondrous properties. This is an important point in differentiating love poetry from the non-realist use of worship language for celebrating human values. Such values certainly do not exist outside real life, and can be exemplified by humans, as is shown by the telling of the stories of Jesus by 'non-realist' believers. But all this remains at the moralist level of affirming values themselves, not the level of praise and adoration, which needs a personal object to receive glorification.

Further, the one who praises a non-realistic God, celebrating what is human, must himself be included in what is praised. This point is not only a criticism of 'non-realism'; it also stimulates those who believe in an objectively real God to ponder on the fact that their praise, too, is not detached from its object. The church does not worship from a detached stance, isolated from God and calling its praise across a chasm. Rather, the church shares in the life of God as she worships the Father according to the dynamic of prayer that Paul expresses, through the Son and in the Spirit.[49] The church therefore shares in the life that she is praising, and experiences salvation and acceptance.

Christian worship is joyful, focused beyond itself, precisely not moralistic. This reflects the nature of the relationship between worshipper and worshipped, one of glad reconciliation. The church worships as 'in Christ', secure in that filial status, and therefore celebrating this as an aspect of praising the Father. An element of being glad to be in the position of true worship comes to be part of worship itself. Such an awareness is not at the top of the mind of the 'realist' worshipper, not a fact to be focused upon, but rather has the character of a logically indirect although psychologically simultaneous celebration. As the worshipper focuses on the Father, so the sense of privilege and thanks often increases, with the implication, or reflection, of the worth of humanity conferred by God.

In the projection towards God in worship, the church finds herself conscious of being indwelt by the Holy Spirit and sharing the divine recreative life. The faithful become aware of the presence of the Spirit fostering worship. The believer in a 'real' God therefore shares with the 'non-realist' a sense of gladness in the human condition, but attributes this also to God. A eucharistic structure might be seen in this aspect of worship, expressed in the double movement in the prayer of thanksgiving in the Eucharist; God bestows his grace upon his people in Christ, and his people respond with thanks (*eucharistia*) 'in Christ', with their sacrifice of praise.

There is a receiving from the Father and a responsive offering of our souls and bodies to be a living sacrifice as the Holy Communion is taken: the receiving entails a giving back. This implies that in Christ believers offer themselves to the Father in perfect confidence, the confidence born of the resurrection of Jesus by the Father. Worship focuses on the glory of the Lord, but not simply from a self-negation or abasement; worship is offered from a position of glad relationship as a son or daughter. This contrasts starkly with efforts to attain a dimension in life, perhaps through transcendental meditation, focusing on the inner abyss.[50]

The 'non-realist' understanding of God can thus prompt us to explore the true dimension of joy in worship. But it is important to say that the interpretation of worship as a celebration of human value, cutting away any sort of objective reality of the God who bestows and renews humanity, seems unreal and possibly dangerous. Even to talk of the 'deification' of humanity, while denying any limits to humanity under a creator God, looks like going beyond an assertion of the maturity of a humanity that can cope with ordering the world, towards something far too over-confident.

While the debate between those who think 'projection' is happening from above (from God) and those who think it is happening from below (from human beings) cannot be settled by mere logical argument, the theological debate within the community of faith does have to take into account the factor of worship. Can worship be experienced as real if it is simply being directed to the human race which has evolved a good value system? If it is only the latter, then it becomes a form of words that is either misleading or only for the very sophisticated moralist. One can sympathize with the elation felt by the 'non-realist' at being converted from a realist position, if this is felt as a shaking free from the bonds of an oppressive deity; but equally one must acknowledge that there is an elation in heartfelt praise given to the God of Jesus Christ.

A well-known version of the projection theory is that of Freud, who focused upon the place of the father figure in his account of how the Christian faith arose in the human heart. Religious ideas, according to Freud, are illusions, fulfilments of the primitive and powerful wishes of mankind. The strength of these illusions lies in the power of the wishes. Humans project into existence a means of coping with their fears, desire for justice, and for an antidote to death. The need for protection turns out to equate with the human longing for a father, a figure of awe and yet of care. The Freudian criticism particularly attacks any personal notion of God, as a projection of this powerful father.[51]

In particular, Freud relates the Christian view of God to his famous theory of the Oedipus complex of repressed guilt in the human heart. In the ancient Greek myth, Oedipus, in order to gain Jocasta, killed her husband King Laius. Laius, however, unbeknown to Oedipus, turned out to be his own father and Jocasta his mother. This story illustrated, for Freud, his theory of the young male's desire for his mother and his resentment of his father whose presence prevents this. We repress this desire and feel guilty about it. Christianity thus turns parricide into a religion; Paul teaches, according to Freud, that human unhappiness results from our wish to kill God the Father, and our redemption comes from the death of the Son who sacrificed his life in expiation. Fear of the primordial father is a constant thread in Christianity.[52]

While such a theory does seem fanciful, nevertheless it has been influential. The notion that the Father God is one who oppresses and removes opportunities for living, rather than being the generous giver of life and of recreative possibilities, has become a common criticism of Christianity and other mainline faiths, especially by the New Age movement. Such a father needs to be removed for repression to lift, and for the whole agenda of guilt to dissipate. The Father has at times come to be seen as the abusive father rather than the loving father, and the feminist criticism of patriarchy has some roots here. Theologically such a view of God the Father has been implicitly resisted in the Christian tradition, although at times spirituality has strayed perilously close to this kind of picture of a nasty Father and a nice Son. The Arian controversy in the early church raged over the issue as to whether there was a 'unity of being' between the Father and the Son, and the Council of Nicaea (321 A.D.) affirmed that indeed there was. The Arian alternative, that there was a distant and unknowable Father, left a question mark over character of the real God, the Son not sharing his essence. The Nicene theological instinct was that God was 'Christlike' in every respect.

Pastorally, such a debate has its reflection in much spirituality. The person for whom Jesus is a friendly and approachable face, but the Father is the frowning face of providence always dealing the unkind blow when least expected, effects a similar split of Son from Father and gives a foothold for the Freudian critical analysis. All this falls infinitely short of the trinitarian prayer: 'the grace of our Lord Jesus Christ, the love of God, and the fellowship of the Holy Spirit be with us all'. This concern, crucial to the Christian gospel, takes us back to the theological contribution of Irenaeus we have already considered, with his insistence on the Old Testament and its God as being integral to the New Testament and the God of Jesus. There are not two principles or two gods, a capricious creator of this evil world and a principle that saves us from it. It turns out that the character of the Father is decisive for the identity of the Son and *vice-versa*; to hold the two together remains vital, and to allow them to be split asunder destroys the heart of both redemption and creation.

This theological insight should be enacted pastorally in many ways, and notably in worship and personal morality. But it has to be said that a correct trinitarian theology does not necessarily work itself out into a mature Christian spirituality. By the Middle Ages, Jesus Christ had become the 'Pantocrator', a kingly figure of remote glory and power. This led to an increased cult of the Virgin Mary who became the humane, friendly figure needed to 'put a word in for us' to her exalted Son. The paradoxical truth seems to be that God and the stories of the historical Jesus must be held together for a right understanding of each. It seems to be a tendency of human religiosity to push God upwards and away, whereas the incarnation concerns the self-giving of God in our human historical conditions.

7. Acknowledging the Father

Freud's projection theory and his interpretation of the Father as a guilt-inducing figure does have a certain cultural fit with what seems to be the irrational suspicion and hatred of God in Western society. This inversion of the attitude of thanks and praise, taught by Jesus of the heavenly Father, into a culture of complaint and cynicism, not only spreads to a scepticism about a good God; it also leads to a suspicion of the human mind which is making the supposedly false projection of God. This mind is unreliable, controlled by our unconscious drives, and suspicion therefore spreads out to erode all confidence. As Hardy and Ford put it, this extends

> . . . to engulf justice and ethics, the human self, all the arts, the objectivity of knowledge, and much else. Theology is not the only discipline challenged by projectionism, and the responses across the disciplines have had many family resemblances.[53]

By contrast, to pray 'our Father in heaven' orientates us to the identity of God and of ourselves. God is this particular God, known of Jesus who focuses the Hebrew experience of the creator and redeemer. We are, most deeply, children of God: that is, the self-image we have and through which we are conscious of being in the world. This self-awareness of being sons and daughters of the sovereign Lord who wishes to be known as Father bestows true freedom, a freedom rooted in the love of the creator and not in a rebellion against an oppressive external authority. God is the bestower of personhood, not a repressive mechanistic higher power. God therefore is personal in some way, and in particular is personal love.

Simply addressing God as bidden by Jesus opens all these paths of wonder and truth about God and ourselves. The depths of being, divine and created, are found as we say the first phrase of the prayer. We meet with pure reality and truth as we acknowledge the Father in heaven, in wonder, awe, and joy. We pray as it were with the figure of Jesus beside us, pointing us to his Father, and aware of the Spirit evoking our worship.

Notes to Chapter 2

[1]See, for example, Matthew 5:17-18.

[2]Schleiermacher, *The Christian Faith*, pp. 19ff, 377ff. See above, pp. 4-5.

[3]See E. C. Hoskyns and N. Davey, *The Riddle of the New Testament* (Faber and Faber, London, 1931) on this theme of the link of the Old Testament with the New Testament portrayal of Jesus, a presentation which remains stimulating.

[4]Martin Buber, *Moses* (East and West Library, Oxford and London, 1946), p. 52.

[5]Ibid., p. 54.

[6]Ibid., p. 28.

[7]Sydney Carter's hymn.

[8]Luke 10:21; Matthew 11:25 omits the rejoicing in spirit.

[9]E.g., I Corinthians 1:18ff.; 2:6-10.

[10]Luke 4:18, quoting Isaiah 61:1-2.

[11]In Luke 7:18, for example, where Jesus replies to John the Baptist by citing Isaianic prophetic texts.

[12]Vermes, *The Religion of Jesus the Jew*, p. 210.

[13]The famous phrase of David Jenkins, Bishop of Durham, uttered on television and mistakenly taken as denying the resurrection.

[14]A. T. Hanson, *Grace and Truth* (SPCK, London, 1975), p. 92.

[15]Hanson, p. 94.

[16]Stuart Hall, *Doctrine and Practice in the Early Church* (SPCK, London, 1991), p. 21.

[17]C. S. Lewis, *The Four Loves* (Geoffrey Bles, London, 1960), pp. 12-13.

[18]See Charles Taylor, *Hegel* (Cambridge University Press, Cambridge, 1975), p. 392.

[19]Hardy and Ford, *Jubilate*, p. 119.

[20]See, for example, Desmond Tutu, *The Voice of One Crying in the Wilderness* (Mowbray, London, 1986).

[21]The title of Grace Janzen's book, *God's World, God's Body* (Darton, Longman, and Todd, London, 1984).

[22]Hardy and Ford, *Jubilate*, p. 119.

[23]Karl Barth, *Church Dogmatics*, English translation ed. G. W. Bromiley and T. F. Torrance (T & T Clark, Edinburgh, 1936-77). Henceforth cited by volume

number, part number, and page. References to Vol. I/1 are to the second edition, trans. G. W. Bromiley, 1975.

[24]Barth, *Church Dogmatics*, I/1, pp. 371-73.

[25]Augustine, *Confessions*, Book 13, chapter11.

[26]Jürgen Moltmann, *History and the Triune God. Contributions to Trinitarian Theology*, trans. J. Bowden (SCM Press, London, 1991), p. xiii.

[27]Ibid., p. xiv.

[28]Ibid., p. xv.

[29]John Passmore, *The Perfectibility of Man* (Duckworth, London, 1970), p. 312.

[30]Elizabeth Achtemeier, 'Female Language for God: Should the Church Adopt It?' in Donald G. Miller (ed.), *The Hermeneutical Quest: Essays in Honour of James Luther Mays on His Sixty-Fifth Birthday* (Pickwick Publications, Allison Park PA, 1986), p. 109.

[31]Janet Martin Soskice, 'Can a Feminist Call God Father?', in Alvin F. Kimel Jr., *Speaking the Christian God* (Eerdmans/Gracewing, Grand Rapids/Leominster, 1992), pp. 88-93.

[32]Moltmann, *History and the Triune God*, pp. 21-23.

[33]Barth, *Church Dogmatics*, II/1, pp. 220 ff.

[34]Ibid., p. 230.

[35]Ibid., p. 229.

[36]Barth, *Church Dogmatics*, I/1, p. 55.

[37]John Zizioulas, *Being as Communion* (Darton, Longman, and Todd, London, 1985); see esp. pp. 44-49.

[38]Anthony Freeman, *God in Us* (SCM Press, London,1993). Freeman, a clergyman, was asked to leave his parish ministry by the Bishop of Chichester, having been given a year to consider his theological position.

[39]Ibid., p. 9.

[40]Ibid., p. 25.

[41]E.g., Don Cupitt, *Taking Leave of God*; *The Sea of Faith. Christianity in Change* (BBC, London, 1984); *The Long-Legged Fly* (SCM Press, London, 1987); *The Time Being* (SCM Press, London, 1992).

[42]Ludwig Feuerbach, *The Essence of Christianity*, trans. George Eliot (repr. Harper and Row, New York, 1957), pp. 33-37.

[43]Freeman, *God in Us*, p. 25.

[44]Karl Marx, 'The Critique of Hegel's Philosophy of Right', in *Karl Marx. Early Writings*, trans. and ed. T. B. Bottomore (Watts & Co., London, 1963), p. 44.

[45]Hardy and Ford, *Jubilate*, pp. 108-12.

[46]Peter L. Berger, *A Rumour of Angels* (Penguin Books, Harmondsworth, 1970), p. 64.

[47]Dietrich Bonhoeffer, *Letters and Papers from Prison*, enlarged edition, ed. E. Bethge, trans. R. Fuller, F. Clarke, J. Bowden (SCM Press, London, 1967).

[48]E.g., *Letters and Papers*, pp. 325-29, 361.

[49]E.g., Romans 8:12-17; Galatians 4:6-7.

[50]Tatiana Goricheva speaks of the difference as she became aware for the first time of 'the living personal God who loves me and all creatures, who has created the world', as she used a mantra that was the Lord's Prayer; Goricheva, *Talking About God Is Dangerous* (SCM Press, London, 1984), p. 17.

[51]See, for example, Sigmund Freud, *The Future of an Illusion*, trans. E. Jones (Hogarth Press, London, 1928).

[52]Don Cupitt offers an exciting account of Marx, Freud, and other 'projectionist' thinkers in *The Sea of Faith*, pp. 37ff, 139ff.

[53]Hardy and Ford, *Jubilate,* p. 109.

3

'Hallowed be your name'

1. The Holy God as the wholly Other

Opening ourselves to the person of the Father brings us before his quality of holiness. The Lord throughout the Hebrew Scriptures is called 'holy', which is the root of the word 'hallowed'. Geza Vermes links this phrase of Jesus' prayer to Isaiah's vision of divine glory in the temple: 'The sanctification of the divine name by the worshipper echoes on earth the "Holy, holy, holy" song of the Cherubim in the heavenly Temple (Isa 6:3)'.[1] This phrase, says Vermes, 'restores the transcendental dignity to the familiar anthropomorphic image' of the Father, the basic image that evokes trust and confident approach.

The holiness of God in the Hebrew tradition contained several emphases. God's holiness implied his uniqueness, and this was particularly shown in the Temple cult and the priesthood. The holy is set apart and awe-inspiring in an almost physical way so as to be dangerous to the trespasser over the boundary into the holy. In Exodus 19:12 we read that the people and their animals were banned from contact with Mount Sinai on pain of death. Leviticus 8–9 tells of the ritual laid down to transfer priests from the realm of ordinary life to that of the holy, so that they can serve as mediators between the divine and human. When the unfortunate Uzzah, watching the Ark of the Covenant being transported on a cart, 'put out his hand to the ark of God and took hold of it, for the oxen stumbled', the anger of the Lord was kindled and he died there (2 Sam 6–8), as if having touched a live high voltage cable.

The message of this quality of holiness is that God is not common, to be taken for granted, part of the furniture of life and somehow manipulable. Traditionally this aspect of the Old Testament has been taken as part of the education of Israel about God's uniqueness and transcendence. God is not simply part of the causal network of the world, not even the central matrix we can learn to 'work'. There is a mystery and an otherness about God. An absolute respect must be maintained towards this God and the things set apart by him.

Having already argued that the creation of humanity in the 'image and likeness of God' means that there is a commonality between creator and created,[2] nevertheless this motif of holiness speaks of the radical unlikeness between them. God is holy and removed from the 'everyday'. The sacrificial cult, with its mass slaughter and bloody rituals, expressed just this quality of God's absolute claim on our attention and obedience;

God is not simply part of ordinary life, he is the awe-inspiring giver of all life and death. To have contact with God is a matter of ultimate concern, of utmost gravity, and includes the tension of the unlikeness as well as the commonality between God and his people. There will always be a tension for theology in relating these aspects of God, his link with his creation and his radical difference from it.

This otherness of God was the dominating theme in Rudolph Otto's book *The Idea of the Holy*, written in 1917. God is the *mysterium tremendum et fascinans*, both utterly mysterious and awe inspiring, yet also gripping and binding our attention. God is 'wholly other', the numinous, in whose presence we are aware of our creatureliness and finitude.[3] The year 1919 saw the publication of Karl Barth's *Romans*, followed by the even more radical version of 1922, in which another theology of the transcendence of God was stated in an attack on the liberal theological approach of the previous century. Metaphors of the lightning striking the tree, leaving it burnt and smashed, were used to illustrate the sovereignty and judgement of God over against the world in its sinfulness.[4]

The domestication of God was one of Barth's targets, meaning the failure to distinguish the divine from human aspiration and value. God in us, or God as our own moral and aesthetic cultural productions, was not God, according to Barth, but the human being writ large. Like Otto, Barth was protesting against a view of God which lacked the quality of the holy. Significantly, Barth wrote these early works from the context of the pastorate in which he felt expected to lead the faithful to the transcendent God; so the pastoral factor, and probably the factor of worship also, comes into the theological revolution begun by Barth after the First World War. Otto and Barth certainly make a central point about divine holiness, the 'infinite qualitative distinction', the sheer deity and purity of God.

Whether their corrective to easy-going, mildly moralistic, liberalism is fully biblical is another matter. In the paradigm stories of Isaiah's vision, for example, or that of Moses at the burning bush, the recipient of the vision is not left in a state of frozen terror. Nor does the vision render the disciple, albeit acknowledging sinfulness, dead, equivalent to the heap of ashes left after the lightning bolt strikes the tree. When the Lord has engaged Moses and Isaiah, they are indeed filled with awe, but energized for the sake of repentance and of purposive discipleship and mission. This is the renewal of the creature, not its paralysis in trembling, nor its negation. Moses and Isaiah emerge as God's co-operative workers, not as disgusting vermin full of self-hate. Biblical spirituality always upholds creation: humans are not divine, but have a place in relation to the divine. Humans have sinned and fallen short of the glory of God, but God, in his holiness, desires not the death of a sinner but repentance and purposive life. Reflecting on this points us to the immense wisdom of the initial phrases of the Lord's Prayer, with 'hallowed' and 'Father' balancing the otherness and care, the purity and love, found in God.

The holiness of God, as underlined in our age by theologians such as Barth and Otto, is an otherness and majesty which affects worship and prayer in the life of believers. God has not been experienced in the Judaeo-Christian tradition as warm and cosy, but rather as a burning fire of love. God is known not on conditions we lay down, but solely on his own terms of an absolute claim. The nineteenth-century theologian Friedrich Schleiermacher, although criticized by Barth, did seek to develop his theology from the actual religious sense of 'absolute dependence' on God, working from the reality of experienced faith. God is defined as the one on whom we depend utterly.

2. Prayer as thankful resignation in the face of holiness: Friedrich Schleiermacher

The debate that Barth holds with Schleiermacher might be said to turn on the nature and content of 'absolute dependence'. Both these theologians teach that we are dependent on the divine generosity, defined through Jesus, and upon the empowerment he brings to our consciousness through the church, the community of faithful who bring the message of Christ to us. Schleiermacher tries to work from the faith experienced by the community, the bond with God which has the structure of a one-way street, a strict dependence of humanity on God. This dependence embraces the freedom felt by adult human beings, and the limitations known to all finite creatures. The sense of dependence on the divine is felt in other religions, especially the more mystical, and reaches its peak in the faith of Jesus, *Christus Consummator*.

Schleiermacher believes in an innate sense and taste for the infinite we all have, before we have recognized it. This sense rises to the conscious feeling of utter dependence. In Christ, the union of the divine and the human taste for the infinite reaches its climax as we participate by faith in Christ through membership of his church. Schleiermacher does not regard feeling or emotion as a bad thing; indeed it is part of our created human nature. In this he has something important to say to the church when it strays into either cold dogmatism or arid rationalism. Faith is living faith, and God is *felt* just as validly as he is *known* about. How we feel, and feel about God, at a particular time is a matter to be included in our prayers and brought before God, not to be bracketed off as unworthy or unreal.

Schleiermacher works from a base in spiritual God-consciousness. Our God-consciousness palely reflects that of Jesus and depends on it to rise from its lower levels. The analysis of our God-consciousness includes our sense of being sinners who are forgiven and therefore something of the holiness of God by implication, since we sense the need for forgiveness and help. The sense of unworthiness weaves into the feeling of absolute dependence, along with the sense of security and trust, echoing the evangelical sense of being both a sinner and yet accepted through the mediation of Jesus. Gratitude colours this God-consciousness and may even be the foundation for prayer:

> Now as the consciousness of the Church thus moves to and fro between the present and the future, it enters in a twofold way into combination with the God-consciousness. In view of the fact that every success attained is due not solely to its own activities but also to the divine government of the world, it becomes thankfulness or resignation for what in the present is the outcome of previous exertions, according as the average result of human effort is surpassed (thankfulness) or unachieved (resignation). But for that which still remains undecided it becomes prayer—i.e. the inner combination with the God-consciousness of a wish for full success.[5]

Prayer is defined, in a thoroughly Reformed fashion, as a combination of resignation and thankfulness for the events which occur and their relationship to our God-consciousness and our hopes. This describes intercessory prayer and may also sum up what Schleiermacher wishes to say of praise and adoration; that is, have a grateful heart for all that happens! In the case of Jesus, this state is called 'blessedness', and 'The Redeemer assumes the believers into the fellowship of His unclouded blessedness, and this is His reconciling activity'.[6] According to Schleiermacher, the redemptive activity of Christ complements his reconciling act by assuming believers into the power of his God-consciousness, and this is the act of his sinlessness, a powerful regenerating influence.

The feeling of absolute dependence expresses itself in worship as gratitude and resignation for the God-consciousness and blessedness known by the community of faith. But it is very hard to find the note of praise and worship of the *God* on whom we are absolutely dependent. The focus constantly falls on the middle term, the coming together of God and humanity, the consciousness of the faithful, corporately or individually. We look within ourselves at the feeling of absolute dependence and find it to be the very condition for our capacity to speak of God at all. The blending of the divine and human takes on a mystical tone, which is considered to provide a middle path between the 'magical' supernaturalist and the one who wants to reduce everything to what can be observed and tested.[7]

The warm-hearted, Jesus-centred piety of the Moravian Brethren has been given a rather academic reformulation by Schleiermacher, and this has made it light on the sense of awe and wonder, which should be an important factor in defining the Christian feeling of absolute dependence. This is surely characterized by the feeling of bowing before the holy God, but in a way which flows over with adoration rather than passivity and resignation. The spirituality of Schleiermacher's feeling of absolute dependence bends back on itself, working indirectly from the self-awareness of our implicit God-consciousness. We have fellowship with Christ and his God-consciousness, an unclouded blessedness which has power to sanctify, through his community the church. So the focus returns to the middle term, the union of divine and human, not sufficiently rising from that to contemplate the divine itself.

Prayer for Schleiermacher is what happens when our God-consciousness and our hopes or fears meet. If we did not pray, he says,

> that could only be due to a disappearance either of our interest in the kingdom of God, which evokes these ideas of an advantageous but uncertain future, or of our God-consciousness, which keeps present to the mind the absolute powers of the divine world government'.[8]

We notice that there is no mention here of the sheer worth of God to be worshipped and adored as the basic motive to pray. Indeed, when we look at what Schleiermacher means by the holiness of God, we find this definition:

> The holiness of God is the divine causality that legislates in the corporate life of man, and since the law, especially as traced to its inward source, is always for us absolutely holy, and the whole historical process

is ordained by this divine causality, no exception can be well taken to
our regarding that causality as a distinctive divine attribute, or to our
designating it exclusively by the name 'holiness'.[9]

This definition comes very close to Kant's theory of practical reason and
its postulation of the concept of God as a basis for the moral experience
of humanity. It is a moralizing view of divine causality, and the religious
aspect of the God who inspires awe and wonder and worship is missing.

Is Schleiermacher focusing on the awareness of the *sense* of dependence, rather than on the *God* who is the object of the awareness? This
may be the reason why the content of his 'feeling of absolute dependence'
seems to have lost the spirit of praise and adoration that should suffuse
this feeling. According to Daniel Hardy and David Ford, 'Schleiermacher
has moved away from the world and history to their meaning, moved
from knowledge and duty to the pre-reflective and intentional, and from
the being and activity of God to man's consciousness of them'; this
results, they suggest, in a kind of 'formalism of the affections'.[10] Schleiermacher's stated aim of tracing the dynamic of faith experience has somehow turned back on itself.

This may be too severe a judgement, but there is a lack of the feeling
of overflowing joy and worship in the kind of feeling of absolute dependence articulated by Schleiermacher. There is, to be sure, a sense of peace
and 'blessedness' or serenity in the hearts of the faithful, mirroring imperfectly that of Jesus, who even at his passion (according to Schleiermacher)[11] did not have this serenity ruffled. But serenity and peace, while
splendid spiritual qualities, are not adequate as the high point of Christian
prayer and praise. This is a mystical union of the divine and the human
consciousness, reaching perfect poise and harmony in the mind of Jesus,
and derivatively in his church. Mystical harmony, atonement in its most
literal sense of at-one-ment, blurs the identity of the worshipper with the
divine. This has a historic place in Christian spirituality, where worship
can be a matter of 'lost in wonder, love and praise', but the creator-crea-
ture distinction should still remain sharp in the sense of rejoicing in *God*.

Schleiermacher's mystical tendency has an importance for Christian
spirituality, and is perhaps a neglected dimension in the Western Church.
Indeed his combination of this mystical emphasis with the Reformed
stress on the government of God in the world, to which our prayer life
must conform by way of resignation or thanks, bears further development
and exploration. But his omission of the vision of the grandeur and

majesty of the holy God and the corresponding lack of an emphasis on praise and worship is serious. Is it necessary to say that Schleiermacher's method entails this omission? That is, by deriving his doctrine of God from an examination of the God-consciousness as a latent category of the human spirit, does Schleiermacher inevitably miss the note of worship evoked by the objective God? This question resolves into asking whether Schleiermacher is speaking of human religiosity or of God. When he speaks of the feeling of absolute dependence, is this simply a human feeling arising from the human condition, with no root in a reality to which it refers, God?[12]

One of the drawbacks of constructing theology from experience is that it will inevitably reflect primarily the author's own experience. Schleiermacher was no Pentecostal, for example, but a German with a pietist background deeply involved in the culture of the Romantic movement, keen to articulate the faith to the 'cultured despisers of religion'. The mysterious sense of the beyond in our hearts serves as a base for apologetics and also as a test bed for statements about God by Christian theology. We can gain access to this sense and taste for the infinite, but we can tread no further into God himself; we are restricted by our limits of knowing. Therefore, concludes Schleiermacher, 'All attributes which we ascribe to God are to be taken as denoting not something special *in God*, but only something special in the manner in which the *feeling* of absolute dependence is to be related to Him'.[13]

In the case of 'the divine causality', for example, Schleiermacher argues that our feeling of absolute dependence implies the universal causality of God over the whole of nature, as the ground of this feeling. The match between this divine causality and all of nature amounts to what theology has called divine 'omnipotence'; divine causality in contrast to the finite, natural world is called by theology, 'eternity'.[14] As the 'whence' of our feeling of absolute dependence, God is not therefore an object given from outside ourselves. God is that divine causality in which we live and move and have our being. The spirituality and the notion of prayer which arises from this theology, or rather that is experienced prior to this theology, seems then restrictively passive. The feeling of absolute dependence rules out any freedom over against God, although it does allow for our human freedom in relation to the world.

God relates to us as the 'whence' of our feeling of absolute dependence, and as such God cannot be simply a subjective or even corporate psychological feeling generated from ourselves as a projection, according to Schleiermacher. But God cannot be classified as an object somehow 'face to face' with us, or even a personal reality in that relation. Schleiermacher states a subtle Christian 'panentheism' ('everything in God'), but not pantheism ('everything as God'), almost two centuries before it gained currency in modern theology. Prayer appears then to be predominantly fitting in with the purposes and conditions of the kingdom of God, conforming to the divine causal 'omnipotence' or kingship; in this it echoes the later phrase of the Lord's Prayer, 'your will be done.'

Prayer in the name of Jesus, embracing as it does the full vocational activity of each individual Christian, is a reflection of Christ's kingly activity, both as it is in itself and as his rule relates to that of the Father.[15] Prayer involves submission to the Father, the feeling of absolute dependence; but included in that is the partial freedom we have in the world, and that partial human freedom is for the Christian informed by the God-consciousness of Jesus, so that we can take pathways of purpose into the world which are Christlike. This can also be put in terms of the priesthood of Christ who represents us to God. Christ appears before the Father to 'establish our fellowship with Him and to support our prayer before the Father';[16] prayer to the Father at the bidding of Jesus means that it is prayer in his name and therefore a form of co-operation with Christ 'which hallows our prayer by purifying and perfecting our consciousness of God', and so makes it acceptable to God.[17] Jesus remains the great high priest, the representative of the whole human race since 'he brings our prayer before God and conveys to us the divine blessings,' all this being based on the content and dignity of his personality in relation to God and us.

The human consciousness of Jesus thus supplements the passivity of the sense of total submission and surrender that otherwise seems to melt away any sense of freedom in relation to God. At the same time as we sense this utter dependence and passivity, we also have our minds oriented to the needs of the kingdom, and these become part of our prayer. Schleiermacher's subtlety surpasses very many of his modern theological heirs. God is taken to be other than us by the very fact of the 'whence' implied in the feeling of absolute dependence; but what can we say of this 'whence' in its mystery and ungraspability? We can only speak of how we experience the world in the light of this feeling, or how we experience our feeling in the context of the world. God himself is not given to our experience from the outside, but we do experience this sense of utter dependence and submission. We feel the 'noumenal' supporting our 'phenomenal' experience—to use terms developed by the philosopher Immanuel Kant —but we have no way of talking about this divine being except by talking of *our sense and taste* for the infinite.

We must again place the test of worship and praise against this theology and spirituality, for such is the test Schleiermacher desires. Clearly we have a strong description of a Christian relaxation into the ocean of the infinite, and the experience of all the blessings that brings; there is a sense of pure acceptance, of serenity and blessedness as both active and passive sides of human experience are taken up into the unity of divine consciousness. Here is an authentic form of worship and warm well-being in God, one with close links to the Romantic movement. This emphasis seems important especially to the Evangelical wing of the church, and coming from an 'Evangelical' (German Protestant) theologian it needs to be recaptured today. The sense of being settled in God must form something of a brake on modern fevered activism.

We can and should rejoice in our consciousness of the sustaining and supportive ground of our being. We do not call across a chasm to God, but rather we find him present ('immanent' in the world) as the one in whom we live and move and have our being. But can this particular working out of the sense of absolute dependence on God give room for robust praise and worship, a praise which is thoroughly creaturely and free and directed *to* the Father? We need to develop our doctrine of God and our practice of prayer with both divine immanence and transcendence ('otherness from us') in mind.

3. Prayer as resting in the mystery of holiness: Immanuel Kant, Martin Heidegger, and John Macquarrie

The way of thinking about God that we find in Scheiermacher, together with its accompanying spirituality, was stimulated initially by the philosophy of Immanuel Kant, who taught that we can examine the conditions of our knowing and draw some conclusions from these concerning the objects of our knowing, but we cannot know the objects of our sense experience *in themselves*. We cannot escape the processes of our own thought. For Kant, we 'construct' the material world around us by the use of our mental categories, and scientific and critical reason works in this realm of the phenomenal.[18] But faith and morality, value and meaning, belong to a different kind of realm, which is not open to scientific enquiry, and which is the area in which 'practical reason' operates.[19] Our human spirit, in both its aspects of scientific enquiry aspect and the moral will, perceives itself as having its root in this transcendent reality. Human free- dom of spirit is the highest aspect of reality; we are free to rise above our- selves and to reflect on ourselves and the conditions of our knowing and our willing.[20]

Schleiermacher works similarly in his theology. We have a sense of the divine in our hearts, and we need not doubt that this does refer to something 'real', although what that reality is *in itself* we cannot know, for we cannot escape the processes of our minds and hearts to float free of them. Kant's treatment of our moral experience gets even closer to Schleiermacher's method, since Kant recognized the sense of 'ought' within us and tried to postulate from this the *concept* of God as important in making sense of our moral experience. Schleiermacher, however, speaks of not just the *concept* of God, but of our *consciousness* of God. It is the character of this consciousness from which statements about God are to be extrapolated indirectly. The presence of the divine comes to articulation, to cognitive form, as we reflect upon our God-conscious state in relation to that of Jesus. The resultant understanding of God emerges as a kind of 'Logos' theology; the divine reason (Logos) perme- ates all things, and we come to the awareness that we live and move and have our being in the divine being and sense our dependence on this ground of all being sustaining all life. The divine breathes through the universe, and humanity is sensitive to this infinite presence in the finite.

God is the mystery of the universe, and so 'beyond' or 'transcendent' in terms of our knowing; we catch glimpses of this presence in our expe- rience, and in the consciousness of Jesus we see such glimpses reach con- sistent insight. The literal meaning of the term 'understanding' is useful here; we 'under-stand' more clearly the supporting divine being that 'stands under' everything as we reflect on our feeling of this sustaining presence. John Macquarrie[21] has articulated this move in theology in its most accessible form with his 'new style natural theology' as a base from which to unfold a Christian view of being, seeking to get behind ratio- nalist debates about faith to actual human faith experience.

The catalyst to this enterprise in the twentieth century, which gives it a different tone to the early nineteenth century and its context of roman- ticism, is the thought of Heidegger who influences modern transcendental theologies. Heidegger's *Being and Time* seeks to analyse our experience by way of minute description of life experience as lived, not bracketing out such ordinary and unintellectual feelings as the fear of death, and by asking the Kantian question about the necessary preconditions for the experience to be as it actually is.[22]

Therefore 'the world' emerges as a field of happening, since our self-consciousness would be inconceivable without a sense of something happening. Likewise our consciousness is involved with the happenings, is concerned with them. The passing of time is also a crucial item of life experience, as is the death we all face with all kinds of responses. The prospect of death sharpens our sense of the banality of much of life and of the need to focus on its significance and mystery. The question of being itself 'grazes'[23] us. We must not hide ourselves from it with 'everyday' busyness, but we must ask about fundamental 'being' as we live it out in the world, in all the fear, distress, and alienation of our experience of being 'not at home' and worried, for some weird reason, or non-reason.

The experience that we are both *free* and *restricted* at the same time, that we act on the world while the world impinges upon us, also prompts John Macquarrie. He speaks of God as 'Being', and creation as 'beings' who are continually supported by Being.[24] Being is the condition of all there is, and human beings act in the world as shepherds for Being.

Humans 'stand out', 'ex-ist', from the background of the generality of beings in the world and are aware of this standing out. In this sense, humanity 'transcends' (goes beyond) itself by being able to reflect upon itself. A human is a being, but one that raises the question of Being itself, is grazed by it, and gains awareness of the great sustaining presence of Being.[25] Thus Being is 'the ground of being', or 'letting-be'. If we simply refuse the question of Being and are content to live evading the question, in our shallow busyness, then we become mere objects, one of the herd.[26] The human quest for meaning reaches out into the future and finds itself already meshed with the supportive Being sustaining all life, which religious people might call grace or 'holy Being'. We call Being 'holy' because we trust Being and find it trustworthy; we find that Being is 'for us.'

Like Schleiermacher and Heidegger, Macquarrie cannot separate God from the world as if God were another 'object' over against the world. God cannot be classified or be given boundaries as 'a being' always can, however superior a being it might be. Being, rather than 'a being', therefore commends itself as the best kind of description of God. We must, urges Macquarrie, remove the borders and allow God to be the everlasting context and condition of all that is, the 'incomparable who is present and manifest' in all beings through the sense of holiness or wonder that occasionally comes through the experience of our being in the world.

In this kind of theology the 'wholly other', and the sense of holiness, is closely associated with the mystery of the universe, the unknown which makes itself felt and sensed as good ('on our side') rather than evil. Yet there is still a threat that constantly presents itself to human 'being-in-the-world'; it is an awareness of hostile 'nothingness', of the 'non-being' that confronts us in a sense of meaninglessness or the approach of death, and which indicates the possibility of lack of supportive Being, or its withdrawal or indifference. *Angst* [anxiety], the vague feeling of worry as a general state rather than as specific fears, pervades the human condition. Macquarrie argues that this forces the choice between taking life as absurd or meaningful, between nothing and Being. Even having staked one's choice on Being, the onset of *Angst* remains, alongside hope.

The image conveyed is that of a pulsing centre of Being, continually pouring forth life and being. But the sense of *Angst* felt by all humanity mirrors the alienated conscience, the unhappy consciousness of beings who have drifted from their source in Being, and who sense the need to return and yet are fearful of this since it may threaten their freedom. Our self-transcendence, our ability to think about our own situation, leads us to false choices and commitments as we live selfishly and defensively, inverting the generosity of Being. Since Being indwells and sustains all beings, however, and indeed is revealed through beings, it seems that in reality beings cannot dismiss Being, although they seek to do so.

Holy Being means the self-giving, self-outpouring God, symbolized in the doctrine of the Trinity,[27] in effect, life in total fulness, sheer letting-be. Old-fashioned natural theology, using rational arguments, cannot prove the existence of Being; but a 'new style' of natural theology, working from how we *feel* about existence, can point us toward the beyond. We feel oriented towards our context and source, and we feel alienated and frustrated in refusing to acknowledge Being. Being is around and within us; we catch traces of it and sense its presence from time to time.

Accordingly, prayer and worship are interpreted in the contemplative mode by Macquarrie, as by Schleiermacher, with a similar emphasis on the community as the context of prayer. We find ourselves in the tension between non-being and Being. We need to be open to Being so as to reunite with Being. We advance and slide back. 'It is unitive Being (the Holy Spirit) that moves us to prayer, in response to the self-communication of Being, a communication that is possible because Being is immanent in every being'.[28] We can also turn inwards from openness and so slip back towards selfishness and idolatry, such as that of consumerism.

Macquarrie says that 'those prayers that have an inward and meditative character can be fairly well understood in terms of the description we have given . . . But what are we to say about the kind of prayers that are directed outward . . . ?'[29] Prayer that is meditative and mystical can be said to 'go with the flow' of the energies of Being in a feeling of absolute surrender, absolute dependence, on 'holy Being'. Relaxing into the ocean current of the infinite, rather than struggling against it, worry and *Angst* dissolve in at-one-ment with the source of all Being.

This fits in well with the need to overcome alienation and merge our beings with Being in a more complete fashion. Although in reality Being is always present and manifest in and through all beings, the sense of *Angst* persists; hence we seem to be deluded in our fears that are, fairly literally, groundless. Unification with Being therefore brings us to an awareness of our true state, that is, our groundedness in Being and our absolute dependence. We have an unhappy consciousness, which needs again and again to be made aware of its real state of being in Being. In prayer our consciousness harmonizes with the surrounding context of Being.

It seems important here to harvest this insight that prayer counteracts the corrosive fear and worry common throughout our culture, by steady contemplation of the source of all Being, traditionally 'Our Father in heaven'. This orientation of the self to holy Being, in praying 'hallowed be your name', opens it up afresh, effectively dispensing with the attitudes of cynicism and despair which afflict the Church as well as the 'world'. To pray in this regard, sinking one's will again into the divine life, deliberately giving up one's idols, refocusing on the generous love and holiness of God, is to go more deeply into the springs of trust and honesty, away from hardness of heart and hiddenness. This is certainly a vital dimension of prayer.

The medieval Church recognized a form of sin they called *accidie*, which is often translated as 'sloth'. This translation fails to bring home the subtlety of the condition which is that of both cynicism and lack of action, a pessimistic negativity towards the endeavours of others, rooted in a hidden negativity about oneself. A certain paralysis of spirit sets in, preventing honest effort and fostering a critical spirit towards that of others. Prayer was said to be the main way of overcoming this sin, and perhaps *accidie* can be equated with the phenomenon of debilitating modern fear that also undermines positive effort and engenders self-doubt and criticism of others. Sarcasm (literally cutting the flesh), suspicion, and lack of 'respect' for others, all melt as we contemplate divine loving holiness.

The quiet orientation of the self to the source of all being as the total priority of life, a focusing on what is truly worthy of worship, counters the chaos of competing claims upon the attention. The thinker Søren Kierkegaard, who was highly influential on this tradition of theology, probed deeply into the modern distractedness; he examined the inability to settle and focus, flitting from one insignificant task to the next, ignoring the one thing needful, which is attending to God. This alone, Kierkegaard proposed, could counter the modern fragmentation of the self.[30]

This account has worn well in describing the effect this aspect of modern life has on peace of mind, or on what the Hebrew tradition calls *shalom*, or wholeness. Concerns which are really secondary and yet establish themselves as primary or ultimate take a hold as idols in the mind. Their grip is broken by the influence of Christ and repeated orientation towards and into the kingdom of God which he embodied. Worship of this kind, quiet reassertion of trust, contributes strongly to a wholeness of attitude. Divine holiness evokes from disciples a dedication, a fixing of our ultimate concern.

Such meditative worship is not turned inwards on the self, nor is it centred on the still centre of the self. It is oriented to God or towards 'letting be' in Macquarrie's terminology, the source of being. Authentic selfhood goes out beyond itself and finds its fulfilment in letting-be. 'It does this not of itself, but by letting itself be caught up into the movement of Being'.[31] This type of meditative worship therefore focuses on Being, not on nothingness. Further, the self in worship 'concentrates' the movement that goes on throughout the whole realm of beings; such worship mirrors the cosmic process of creation, reconciliation, and consummation, according to Macquarrie.

Macquarrie admits that his theology of God and the world finds it easy to accommodate a mystical and contemplative spirituality, and difficult to give a place to the more robust outwardly oriented prayer and worship. Prayer expresses our deepest moods, but, he asks, 'can prayer communicate?'[32] He does not think that prayer does communicate with God, although it certainly refers to God. Communication is ruled out for Macquarrie, since he agrees with Kant that as humans we have no shared background of ideas with God. Prayer cannot therefore be a kind of dialogue with God. Likewise Macquarrie denies that our experience of revelation is anything like the 'I-Thou' experience of communication we have with other persons. There is a huge difference, an asymmetry between God and ourselves, so that there can be no true reciprocity between us and God.[33]

Denial that prayer can communicate with God is a serious theological and spiritual claim. After all, much Christian spirituality is based on the assumption that we do communicate with God. Macquarrie must surely be commended for resisting a childish view of prayer as a conversation between two entities that have an equivalent reality. God is indeed beyond our being. Likewise God is not the supplier of consumer goods. But is not this caution overdone when Macquarrie insists that no mutual communication is possible? Is the 'Beyond in the midst' deaf? To answer this, we need to return to the sense of the 'holy' and what this tells us about our point of contact with God. Holy is the most characteristic adjective applied to God, and Macquarrie agrees with this when he names God as 'holy Being'. This refers to the mystery (*mysterium*) of God, but also to our *response* when this mystery impinges upon us. As Macquarrie puts it himself, 'The response is twofold—the experience of the holy as demanding, judging, overpowering (*tremendum*), and the experience of the holy as granting, saving, empowering (*fascinans*)'.[34] Here we do have a field of shared experience between beings and Being, and this seems to contradict Macquarrie's own assertion that petitionary prayer is improbable because of the lack of such a common background.

However, in Macquarrie's account the link between 'Being' and 'beings', between the source and the derived, between the One and the many, is always a one-way flow. Macquarrie speaks of the 'penitential' way of spirituality, together with the 'illuminative' way and the 'unitive' way,[35] but the priority of praise, issuing forth from the faithful outwards to the glory of God, cannot find a place easily in his theological framework. Prayer for Macquarrie focuses inwards on the co-ordination of being in Being and the need to be ever more transparent for Being. The worshipper is essentially passive, seeking a mystical atunement to the mysterious flow of Being. Opening oneself to Being is to be an opening for Being in the world. In Heidegger's vocabulary, Being (*Sein*) gains a clearing or presence in human beings as 'being there' (*Dasein*).

This gives us a sense of the holy as what is uncanny, or mysterious; such a feeling is already a *response* in itself, perhaps because 'unitive spirit' takes the human spirit into itself, so bringing about something akin to 'irresistible grace'. This sense of the mysterious, uncanny as it is, overcomes the sense of *Angst* and alienation from Being, while at the same time the sensation of 'holy Being' contains within it a degree of alien-ness, otherness, so as to render the human afraid as well as glad.

The flow of being from holy Being to beings is the flow of creation and of grace simultaneously. We become aware, again and again, in our worship, of the everlasting and holy, which gives us our true identity. Spiritual orientation is inwards, to the realization that we participate in the flow of Being, and the place of prayer is to describe and focus the movement of Being in and through ourselves. As a Christian theologian, Macquarrie understands this movement as a trinitarian one. There is the 'primordial' movement of Being (the Father), which pours itself forth generously and everlastingly through 'expressive Being' (the Son), bursting out into the varied and rich life of creation. The alienation of created beings from Being is healed by the third movement of 'unitive Being' (the Spirit), which reintegrates fallen beings into harmony with Being. Human beings thus share in the movement *from* primordial Being, *through* expressive Being and *back* in unitive Being.

There is truth in this understanding of communion with God as resting in the movements of the divine holiness. But taken on its own, it makes prayer merely passive, a mystical self-opening, a seeking to be transparent to the flow of Being. Holy Being is immanent in creation, while creation rests in holy Being. The type of theology we have been tracing from Schleiermacher to Macquarrie thus defines the holiness of God in terms of a sense of mystery and strangeness that somehow gives us a sense that Being supports everything.[36] Faith chooses to believe that there is meaning rather than absurdity, and that Being is the context or condition of life giving it final meaning. God, or Being, is the meaning of life, the final overarching horizon making sense of things often despite how they seem.

4. Prayer as personal encounter with the holiness of God

The point at issue here is how such a theological framework might do justice to the 'personal' aspect of the God to whom our worship is directed. Prayer by its very nature addresses God as personal. In Macquarrie's thought we take part in a circular movement from primordial, through expressive, back to unitive Being. We are in the trinitarian flow between the Father, Son, and Holy Spirit. Our worship is *in* this movement of divine life, which may be thought of as personal by analogy, although God is to be more accurately described as 'Being'.

According to Macquarrie, Being is not a person any more than it is 'a being'; as unique, Being cannot be contained in such categories. Being itself cannot be a person, but since Being lets all beings be, Being 'may well be most fully manifested in . . . personal being.'[37] Being knows no confines, but it always exists through beings, and so is most fully disclosed through the richness and complexity of human, personal beings. Worship is therefore personal insofar as our personal prayer is taken up into the movement of the divine movement, the structure of the movement being the one-way-street of grace through nature, prayer being a way of adapting to the divine flow of Being.

Macquarrie seeks to offset the inference that such a view renders prayer enclosed and solipsistic, self-therapeutic and mystical, by appealing to the community benefit of prayer and arguing that 'the prayers of an individual or group afford a way of ingress for the unitive Spirit into a closely knit texture of human society'.[38] So the effects of prayer spread far and wide by the transforming influence of the Spirit, now given greater access into the minds and hearts of human beings through our praying.

But does this view, taken in isolation, do justice to the personal dimension in prayer? Should not a Christian doctrine of God and of worship include the 'I-Thou' experience of encountering the transcendent Lord? Macquarrie thinks not. In revelation, he argues, 'we do not know another being, but simply being'.[39] Holy Being lets all beings be and has the power of creating persons, so it is quite appropriate that as personal beings we should worship Holy Being using personal metaphors such as 'Father'; yet when we think carefully, urges Macquarrie, what we are worshipping is nothing less than holy Being. However, we must say in response to this that the fact of worship demands that 'holy Being' should have a focused *identity*, to avoid its evaporation into an abstraction, an ideal or an energy. To say that we pray 'in God' plainly relates to classical Christian theology, as long as in the movements of divine being there is included one *to whom* worship is addressed.

In the kind of theology Macquarrie is commending, to pray 'hallowed be your name' is only to pray in a movement of holy divine life, and not also *to* a holy divine identity. Now, the argument for saying that God cannot be defined and transcends all categories is very strong. Even personal language for God will be analogy, and so fall short of the reality of God. But this surely does not exclude a divine identity to which the words 'your name' point? The word 'identity' stems from the Latin *idem*, meaning 'the same'. Even if we cannot think of God as a person in the sense of 'a being', he is surely Personal Being in the sense of remaining 'the same' for us, having an identity for us we can praise and worship and find to be holy. Worship depends on the fact that God is 'the same yesterday, today, and forever'. Worship is addressed to the holy one, who does not become unholy and unworthy of worship. From this fact seems to flow the identity of the God who is worshipped, trusted, and adored, even if the being of this God cannot be put into a category. The prayer 'Our Father in heaven, hallowed be your name' seems to be a way of holding together the transcending being of God with the identity of God.[40]

This *identity* of the divine, utterly worthy of praise, would have to be invented were it not given by the biblical tradition, since human communication needs someone with whom communication takes place. To argue that humans need an object to whom worship is addressed is not to establish the point that such a concrete object exists as the outcome of a logical argument. But theologically, from within faith, the reality of Christian worship punctures any notion that the Church merely affirms a set of values or an abstract idea. 'Hallowed be your name' goes beyond such a celebration of what is right and good.

A value, or an idea, can endure through time; in fact, it needs to do so if it is an idea capable of being shared by people across space and through time. But praise and worship are not addressed to ideas. Christian language is not, according to the reality of the Christian experience, merely picture language for what is really a philosophical concept. Worship breaks out of this definition. Nor is admiration precisely the same activity as worship, although there is an interesting point of comparison with the human response to beauty. The beautiful is always a concrete beautiful thing, while the *idea* of beauty is an abstraction from actual objects of beauty. It is not 'beauty' in abstract but the beautiful object or scene (or even concept) that attracts admiration for its excellence and worth, in that respect reflecting the worth-ship of God.

Worship of God, however, *always* contains the element of 'real' contact, which is not inevitably the case with the appreciation of beautiful things. A person can be beautiful and admired without giving back any reciprocal response, positive or negative. Such admiration in effect refers to the beautiful person as an object only. Truly 'personal' relationship always entails more than the acknowledging of worth in a person *as* object. If there is a truly 'personal object', some kind of response will be given back to the admirer, even if it is deliberate coolness, even if it is the decision to treat the admirer as a thing rather than a person! In the case of a morally good person, and especially with those whom we are inclined to regard as 'holy' persons, that response will be perfectly attuned to the needs of the admirer.

Christian experience of worshipping the holy God knows that worship, as acknowledgement of goodness, beauty, and sincerity, goes beyond the mere admiration of a wonderful scene or work of art. This kind of extreme objectivity is certainly *included* in the Church's adoration and praise, since the sheer holiness of God must be praised independently of any relational benefit to us. But the God worshipped is the covenant-giving Lord who loves to evoke the praises of his people, knowing this is right and also truly good for them, making them holy as he is holy.

While personal language for God thus remains an analogy, it is the analogy running throughout the Scriptures of the Jewish and Christian communities for this relationship of worship. God is not like a work of art in receiving adoration, as pure perfection in detachment; rather, God is the superb artist. Another way of putting this is to say that worship reaches God in a way that has similarities with the praise of persons. This is recognized by the writer of Genesis 1:23 when he describes human beings as made 'in the image and likeness of God'; if modern biblical scholarship is correct in suggesting that the writer is a priest, it is surely significant that the idea of 'likeness' comes from someone steeped in the patterns of worship in Ancient Israel.

In opposition to the idea that there is no 'common ground' between holy Being and beings, the creator God is quite capable of making a field of communication with those 'made in his own image'. In all aesthetic experience there must be a common area of appreciation between object and admirer, and this is all the more so between us and the ultimately beautiful object, God. If humankind is made in the divine image, there is something of real worth inherent in the created human. But all the more is there worth in the divine creative artist who is worshipped and praised by humanity. Some dimension of personal reciprocity seems unavoidable then in describing the Christian experience of worshipping the holy God. We may agree with John Macquarrie that there can be no 'equal reciprocity' between human beings and holy Being; but a reciprocity is there nevertheless, even though vastly unequal. It is assumed in the doctrine of creation and in worship, which is the highest activity of the created order, the aim for which we were made, an aim fulfilled 'in heaven' as 'on earth'. Moreover, worship is the way by which the created order will become truly itself, fully at one with the creator and therefore sharing the characteristic holiness of God.

Worship for the Church assumes a theology of God who really is addressed by the prayer of the faithful, God for whom it does matter that worship takes place. God is not pure mind, contemplating himself and uninterested in the creation he has brought into being. Such an understanding of God offends the Christian experience of worship and of the divine holiness. The holiness of the biblical God entails a radical claim upon his people, a 'jealousy' for exclusive loyalty. This tradition portrays a God who cares passionately about the true worship of his people. This relationship is often likened to a marriage in which the divine partner expects absolute fidelity from his partner Israel, an image continued by the apostle Paul in picturing the relationship between Christ and the Church. The holy God gives a covenant relationship to a people who will also be holy in responsive obedience. Straying after other gods, or unfaithfulness, is not a matter of indifference to God, who is anything but aloof and uninterested in this covenant relationship. In short, we not only relax into the God who underlies all life (as Macquarrie proposes), but we also encounter the God who oversees all life.

'Our Father in heaven, hallowed be your name' addresses no vague life force, principle, essence, or majestic object of beauty indifferent to inferior creatures. On the contrary the Father in heaven cares deeply and his holiness is to be communicated, not simply admired and adored. This holiness is a relational quality, certainly personal, defined in terms of being set aside for God, consecrated. Holiness is not a thing or substance, but works out personally as love and holy relationships, stemming from commitment to a holy God; holiness is communicated, or 'caught', from faithful relating to him.

New Testament theology calls this divine self-communication of generous outgoing holiness, the Holy Spirit. Personal relational language is always used in describing the Holy Spirit and his work in the lives of the Christian community in the New Testament. Holiness is not a thing or substance; it is personal. We recognize this in life: to know holiness in real life is to know a person of sanctity and dedication whose life demonstrates holy relationships, or in other words, demonstrates love. Worship of the heavenly Father at its most profound is worship of awe-inspiring holiness, but in a personal kind of mode. Ultimately this truth reaches its clearest point in the incarnation of Jesus: God reveals his holiness in a definite life, death, and resurrection of this scandalously particular man.

5. *Prayer as finding holiness through Christ*

'Holiness', for Christian theology and worship, is not a vague sense of being in the presence of something mysterious. It has a definition given in flesh and blood. God has actually spoken to us in our own terms to lead us back to true worship and appreciation of the divine. 'Spirituality' has a definition and form; Schleiermacher and Barth in their own ways were quite correct to tie it to the historic person of Jesus Christ.

The kind of spirituality espoused by John Macquarrie has many merits, with its stress on a contemplative bathing in Being. In this there is an outpouring of balm for hurt minds and a restoring of the quiet calm often needed by Christian disciples who are tempted into self-justificatory activism. Macquarrie's type of theology of the holy leads us to the God in whom 'we live and move and have our being', whose flitting manifestations we fleetingly detect in life and deliberately cultivate in moods of worship. The aspect of holiness he stresses is that of mystery, the unfathomable. We rest in the underlying deity, rather than encounter the overseeing deity. But surely we need both aspects for Christian spirituality, in what we might call a 'catholic evangelicalism'.

The call to contemplate, to remembrance (*anamnesis*) that we are rooted in the divine being, is very necessary as a part of spiritual life. Macquarrie's emphasis may well be related to the biblical view of our being 'in Christ' and of Christ being 'in us'. Put in biblical terms, prayer is in Christ, to the Father. The Church stands always in Christ, who is her advocate with the Father, the propitiation for her sins. The lines of a well-known communion hymn express it well:

> Look, Father, look on his anointed face,
> And only look on us as found in him.[41]

Recalling this facet of worship would help erode a common evangelical spiritual heresy whereby the 'prayer time' is regarded as the restoration of our link with God, as if outside this time the link is broken. The Catholic equivalent of this is the notion that there is a sort of 'real absence' of God outside of the 'real presence' in the sacraments. As a matter of sheer being ('ontologically'), the Christian is always 'in Christ', however much feelings may say otherwise at times. We are not intermittently in Christ. Neither are we alone, but bonded together in our prayers. Our holiness is indeed partial, but we are becoming what we truly are, members of the body, the royal priesthood worshipping the Father in Christ. We pray with and in the Son who says 'Our father . . . hallowed be your name'.

Such a biblical amendment to Macquarrie's approach corrects a tendency towards lack of focus and vagueness of identity in worship that would otherwise be present in 'sharing in the movements of Holy Being'. Worship is offered to the Father, rather than to Being. A focus on the place of Christ in the contemplative approach to the Holy also safeguards any use of spirituality as a kind of narcotic, sapping our own personal identity or energy by being absorbed into a mystical 'whole' in a monistic absorption. Isaiah's vision of the holy Lord has many aspects, one of which is the lostness in, and wonderment at, the divine. But it produces no narcolepsy. It is an invigorating encounter and challenge. Rudolph Otto's description of utter fear at the 'tremendous and fascinating mystery' indicates a frozen terror that paralyses the astonished disciple.[42] But the Holy One of Israel, as given supreme definition by the teaching, spirituality, and destiny of Jesus Christ, is holy in many ways that elicit various aspects of prayer. The church knows it can 'approach the throne of the heavenly grace' in joyful awe and sombre repentance, in wonderment rather than fear, in total honesty and trust that our lives do actually matter to God, the God who cares in holiness. There is a deep particularity about holiness, both of God and ourselves, and this is bound up with personal identity, both human and divine. The divine identity is that of the Father to whom the worship of the church is directed, in the midst of our participation in the trinitarian movement; in the words of the apostle Paul, 'God has sent the Spirit of his Son into our hearts, so we cry Abba, Father!'

The biblical theme of the holy personality, consecrated to God, reaches its climax in Jesus' self-dedication before his death. Holiness is revealed primarily in personal life and relationships. Paradoxically then, holiness for the Christian does not mean poised spirituality and a still centre, unblemished by the taints of the world. Rather, holiness and getting involved in the midst of the unpleasant and vicious aspects of the sinful world seem to coincide, both in the ministry of Jesus and in church experience. True holiness involves 'getting our hands dirty' in sacrificial fashion, rather than withdrawal from the problems of the world, however overwhelming and distressing these may be. Holiness reaches out trans-formingly. The fullest act of worship was enacted on the hill of Calvary, and this is what gives meaning to the message of Easter; joy and renewal come through the 'blood, toil, tears, and sweat' of discipleship, of being for God.

The communion of the holy God with his people through prayer and worship means that the church is holy, set aside for this relationship, pro-foundly privileged. In worshipping the utterly holy one, the church knows that she is the first fruits of the renewed creation, the restoration of the divine image of creation. Offering worship to the creator in the body of Christ is the priestly task of creation and of the faithful. To pray 'hallowed be your name' embraces all aspects of divine activity and being. It addresses the transcendent Lord of Isaiah's vision, high and lifted up, as well as the immanent movement of Being that we find has been there all along, sustaining and supporting existence with constant faithfulness and forbearance. The creator whose power gave the created order its being and rhythms of seedtime and harvest, the redeemer who calls us to repent and respond: God is worthy of all worship, to be adored as the heart of all things.

Thus 'the holy one' encompasses the divine immanence suggested by Macquarrie's 'holy Being' sustaining all life secretly, and the transcen-dent one who 'faces' us. The Jewish philosopher Emmanuel Levinas uses the image of the 'face' of another to express the universal human experi-ence of ethical responsibility; the demand we feel upon us comes from the other person, whose very being lays a claim on my freedom.[43] The other person, facing us, breaks open our ego-centrism. This goes far beyond the argument of enlightened self-interest, which bases responsibility in a mere calculation that we owe each other rights. Levinas regards the other as 'transcendent', placing a claim on my freedom independently of any reciprocal rights I might have. This insight fits perfectly into this phrase of the Lord's Prayer, since the ultimately transcendent one with whom we come 'face to face' is utterly holy, ensuring that good will triumph.

God, the heavenly Father, who desires us to urge the hallowing of his name in all the earth, has therefore given us the 'space' to side with divine purity, to identify ourselves with it, and to consecrate ourselves sacrifi-cially in response. If the heart of worship is unconditional adoring sacri-fice of ourselves to God, our worship will colour our character and our life in the world, in the likeness of Christ who prays himself 'your name be hallowed.'

Notes to Chapter 3

[1]Vermes, *The Religion of Jesus the Jew*, p. 16.

[2]See above, pp. 25-28.

[3]Rudolph Otto, *The Idea of the Holy. An Inquiry into the Non-Rational Factor in the Idea of the Divine, and its Relation to the Rational*, trans. J. W. Harvey (Oxford University Press, London, 1925), pp. 5-11.

[4]Karl Barth, *The Epistle to the Romans*, trans. from the 6th ed. by E. C. Hoskyns (Oxford University Press, London, 1933), p. 331.

[5]Schleiermacher, *The Christian Faith*, p. 669.

[6]Ibid., p. 431.

[7]Ibid., p. 434.

[8]Ibid., p. 669; my italics

[9]Ibid., p. 344.

[10]Hardy and Ford, *Jubilate*, p. 194.

[11]Schleiermacher, *The Christian Faith*, pp. 435-36. This is a rather docetic interpretation, in which the humanity of Jesus seems to be an illusion.

[12]In theory there seems no reason why Schleiermacher should not be allowed to expand his spiritual register so as to include what I have suggested is missing. If the God-consciousness of the Church does include a dimension of praise welling up inside its heart, then this could be claimed as another 'religious affection' that ought therefore to be 'set forth in speech' and linked to an aspect of God. The aspect of God found missing here is that aspect of the 'holy' as the divine danger and awe, the 'wholly other' which yet is still within the scope of human contact in worship. Such worship would go beyond self-negation in face of what could be taken to negate the merely creaturely, but that in fact attracts devotion and praise as the utterly positive.

[13]Schleiermacher, *The Christian Faith*, p. 194.

[14]This distinction between the divine equivalence with the natural world and the divine distinction from it derives from the antithesis of the receptive and active way our self-consciousness works, according to Schleiermacher's analysis. We experience ourselves in a twofold way, the ego and the aspect of ourself that is over against ourself, making self-consciousness possible. The highest state of our self-consciousness is the feeling of absolute dependence in which the sense of freedom and of limit are taken up and united in the highest form of self-awareness, which is God-consciousness. God is the whence of the feeling of our passive and active experience. The feeling of absolute dependence cannot, says Schleiermacher, arise from the influence of anything *given* to us, 'for upon such an object there would always be a counter-influence, and even a voluntary renunciation of this would always involve a feeling of freedom' (*The Christian Faith*, p. 16). This translates theologically into the statement that 'any possibility of

God being in any way *given* is entirely excluded, because anything that is out-wardly given must be given as an object exposed to our counter-influence, however slight this may be' (p. 18).

[15] Schleiermacher, *The Christian Faith*, p. 590.

[16] Ibid., p. 464.

[17] Ibid.

[18] Immanuel Kant, *Critique of Pure Reason* [1787], trans. N. Kemp Smith (Macmillan, London, 1933); see, e.g., pp. 41-51.

[19] Immanuel Kant, *Critique of Practical Reason* [1788], trans. L. White Beck (Bobbs-Merrill, Indianapolis, 1956); e.g., pp. 44-50.

[20] Kant distinguishes the 'transcendent', which is unknowable to our minds, and the 'transcendental', which is the logical apparatus of concepts and princi-ples that organizes experience and so is logically prior to it. The transcendental aspect of our mind's working can be brought out by our philosophical explo-ration of the conditions of knowing.

[21] John Macquarrie, *Principles of Christian Theology*, rev. ed. (SCM Press, London, 1977).

[22] Martin Heidegger, *Being and Time* [1935], trans. J. Macquarrie and E. Robinson (Blackwell, Oxford, 1962); e.g., see pp. 279-85.

[23] Martin Heidegger, *An Introduction to Metaphysics* (1953, repr. Yale University Press, New Haven and London, 1959), p. 1.

[24] Macquarrie, *Principles of Christian Theology*, pp. 107-22.

[25] Ibid., pp. 60-62.

[26] 'Das Man' in Heidegger's vocabulary, thus making humanity neuter and impersonal.

[27] Macquarrie, *Principles of Christian Theology*, p. 216.

[28] Ibid., p. 494.

[29] Ibid., p. 495.

[30] Søren Kierkegaard, *Purity of Heart*, trans. W. Steer (Collins Fontana, London, 1950), pp. 41-6.

[31] Macquarrie, *Principles of Christian Theology*, p. 292.

[32] Ibid., p. 493.

[33] Ibid., p. 93.

[34] Ibid., p. 209.

[35] Ibid., p. 501.

[36] It is implicit that Being is good, seeking the best for beings, although the sense of the uncanny and weird might indicate otherwise, as might the experience of many who suffer.

[37] Macquarrie, *Principles of Christian Theology*, p. 115.

[38] Ibid., p. 497.

[39] Ibid., p. 94.

[40]Even on Macquarrie's own argument, the self-transcending capacity needs to be exercised by a self, a centre of being and thinking, a communicative spirit.

[41]W. Bright, hymn: 'And now, O Father, mindful of the love'.

[42]The early Barth cannot escape such a suspicion.

[43]Emmanuel Levinas, *Totality and Infinity*, trans. A. Lingis (Duquesne University Press, Pittsburgh, 1969), pp. 195ff; cf. *Outside the Subject*, trans. M. Smith (Athlone Press, London, 1993), pp. 45ff.

4

'Your kingdom come'

1. The kingdom in tension

The angle of sight in the Lord's Prayer, which to this point has been sharply focused on the identity and character of God, now widens as we pray for the coming of the kingdom of God. Now we speak of earth as well as heaven, the confusion of history as well as the care and holiness of God. We consciously think of the contradictory situation in which we pray. How do we conceive of the kingdom? The kingdom of God means the reign or rule of God, and we have therefore moved from the identity and nature of God to his act.

The theologian Wolfhart Pannenberg points out that the kingdom of God and the Fatherhood of God are integrally related: '[The fact] that the nearness of God's kingdom includes salvation in itself establishes the confident nearness of God himself expressed in addressing God as "Father" '.[1] God the Father is this sort of God in relating outwardly. The kingdom of God is revealed and enacted in Jesus. God is the creator whose kingdom will triumph, however much this prospect seems to contrast with the state of things, a contrast revealed finally between Good Friday and Easter day.

Jesus preached the kingdom of God and announced its presence in his person and activity, which included his prayer life and handing on his 'pattern prayer' to us. 'If it is by the Spirit of God that I cast out demons, then the kingdom of God is come among you', he said; the kingdom of God is 'at hand' as Jesus acts and teaches the kingdom. He is the sceptre of the king, and his presence 'implements' the kingdom.[2] In the prayer Jesus taught his disciples, the phrase 'your kingdom come' almost certainly refers to the coming of the rule of God at the 'end-time', that is, the end of this present world age, an eschatological hope long cherished by the Jews for the divine vindication of God's suffering people.

Christian belief has sharpened this tension between present and future by interpreting the coming of Jesus as the *arrival* of the kingdom, with its *climax* still to come. The biblical narratives oscillate between two views of the rule of God; they tell of the divine hand working out its purposes during the course of history here and now, and they await divine vindication in the future after people have endured the evil of events. Jesus' ministry brings both strands together, living the life of the kingdom, finally clashing with the kingdom of this world, and inaugurating his overlapping and transforming kingdom in time.

'Your kingdom come' calls upon God to act in a decisive fashion to end the ambiguity of the world's sin and confusion. The previous prayer, 'hallowed be your name', may also be interpreted as calling on God to act so as to vindicate his name in the sinful world and reveal—even enforce —the true holiness of his identity. In other words, here we have a distinctively Hebraic prayer, centred in God, and summoning divine action, for the glorification of the divine name and purpose. 'Your kingdom come' is the reverse of a prayer centred in human activity. It clearly calls upon the divine to act. This is not a request to God to *help us* to implement the kingdom, but plainly asks for the coming of the kingdom that only God can bring. The request has a robust confidence about it; there is no doubt that the prayer comes from within the family of God, perhaps even from the persecuted faithful awaiting salvation from oppression.

We live in the tension of the kingdom; it *has been* inaugurated by Jesus' life, death, and resurrection, but is *yet to be* fulfilled. The church believes herself to be firmly in the kingdom, *and* prays for its coming in the latter sense of total victory over all that works against God. If, however, she imagines herself outside the kingdom, then she has lost her grip on one side of the tension, the fact that the people of God are in Christ and are walking in the Spirit. This confident sense of living in the kingdom seems foolish in terms of secularized society, since it looks more like weakness and defeat than rule of any sort. It stems from the actual ministry of Jesus that announced the kingdom in many ways, including eating with the outcast and the notorious sinner. The holiness of the kingdom extended into all society. Fellowship (*koinonia*) was for Jesus with the impure or common (the *koinos*); contact with him was saving, making the impure clean. In this respect his touching of the leper, ritually unclean and 'untouchable', enacted the same kingdom.

The kingdom is full of sinners aware of their failings. The parable of the Pharisee and the tax collector shows that Jesus thought in this way (Luke 18.9-14). The religious man thanks God for his own religious performance. The tax collector, a tool of the occupying powers, beats his breast and simply prays, 'God be merciful to me, a sinner'. It was this man who 'went down to his house justified, rather than the other', in Jesus' view, according to Luke. Justification by grace through faith means precisely this, the approach to God on the basis of divine mercy, mercy ultimately focused in the cross of Calvary. Worship in the kingdom rests on this divine grace and has the pattern of joyful praise through the tears of moral failure. The kingdom of the Father rules over the lost prodigal children.

Worship in the kingdom of God therefore cannot be rooted in moral effort, although that may be an outcome. Christian worship certainly cannot be regarded as a 'good work' in the sense of a good deed for the day, a moral credit. To regard the act of worship in this way reduces it to the satisfaction of a religious duty. That is not to deny that duty is often an essential strand of motivation in initiating worship, but worship itself goes beyond duty, rooted in covenant love rather than in contractual obligation. Another of the tensions of the kingdom may be that it passes judgement on our moralistic endeavours while it also rejoices in finding traces of sacrifice for others, as Jesus commended the poverty-stricken woman putting her money into the Temple offering.

Making worship and prayer into a good work or into a penance or minor punishment, a religious act of sorrow for committing sin, as if worship were a painful chore, loses the Christian spirit of prayer. The idea of prayers as exercises to be 'got through' for accreditation of merit to cancel out sins or for exercise in self-discipline, has no foundation at all in biblical faith. It is certainly an aid to worship when we seek to establish a pattern for our prayer life, and to take advantage of such corporate practices as saying the daily office. But to make the meeting of such a timetable the end in itself falls below what the church means by worship of the heavenly Father. Charles Elliott laments the tragic paradox that 'love which is offered to make people free is so overpowering that it is quickly encased . . . this institutionalization takes many forms . . . ritualization of a relationship . . . commercialization . . .'[3] Christian prayer must constantly purify itself by reference to Jesus and the particular kingdom he brings.

God's grace as described in New Testament writings is associated with heartfelt worship and communion between God and his people. Mary is 'highly favoured' or 'graced' (Luke 1:28); the 'grace of our Lord Jesus Christ' is linked by Paul with the 'love of God and the fellowship of the Holy Spirit' (2 Cor 13:14), indicating some common relational bond by the term grace. John Henry Newman has been rightly criticized for writing the lines:

> And that a higher gift than grace
> Should flesh and blood refine,
> God's presence and His very self,
> And essence all divine.[4]

This surely understates the free love of God poured into our hearts. Any gift 'higher' than this is hard to conceive, as grace indicates the communion rooted in the costly love of God that is given to us.

Prayer stands on the ground of the kingdom, and the fact that it addresses 'Our Father' emphasizes the personalistic character of the praying and of the kingdom, both of which go beyond the merely institutional while requiring human forms as supportive structures that are necessary but not sufficient. 'God is Spirit, and those who worship him must worship in Spirit and in truth', although the forms may change with time. But this is just another of the tensions introduced by the kingdom and its inaugurator.

2. The Spirit and the kingdom: true freedom

In the writings of Paul and John in the New Testament, the theme of the Holy Spirit seems to have taken the place of the topic of the kingdom. The Spirit, who is also a major theme in the Synoptic Gospels, now becomes the present context in which the believer lives, the dynamic that bonds the church together in love and service. Kingdom and Spirit are two sides of the one coin. Both indicate the end-time is somehow come ahead of time, released by the work of Jesus.

The miracles of Jesus were not contradictions of creation, but liberation for creation so as to bring it to the state of its true destiny. The healing of the sick is an obvious case: creation is here freed from the distortion disease brings. This chimes in with Paul's claim that creation groans for redemption, as if knowing its state of decay is not the fulness of destiny intended for it (Rom 8:22). Likewise the other miracles are signs of the kingdom and simultaneously of restored creation, the same creator being the king restoring perfect harmony to creation by his rule. Raisings from the dead clearly establish victory over the last enemy of creation, death, and destruction. Exorcisms indicate the military kind of conflict by which Jesus drives out the forces of negation and evil, reclaiming the ground of the good creation for the kingdom of God. The nature miracles of the New Testament indicate that Jesus stands in the place of the creator of the heavens and earth, sovereign over the winds and the waves that obey him.

The end-time recreation ushered in by Jesus thus affects reality in all aspects, subjectively and objectively. The disciple testifies to the renewal of the heart and will, the opening up of the personality to worship. Both 'the kingdom' and 'the Spirit' are not only 'within' individuals, however, but extend to all areas of life since God wishes to reclaim all for his rule.

This insight has been claimed by the 'liberation theologians' of our day, who use the term 'kingdom' a great deal in their concern for the practical impact of the message of Jesus as lived out for the good of people, especially the poor. 'Kingdom values' have come to mean a priority for the poor in Christian *praxis*, especially over issues of social equity and peace. Prayer in this context relates especially to the amelioration of poor socio-economic conditions; God is the God of history who brings liberation to the oppressed, as was the case with the exodus from Egypt. The New Testament scholar Tom Wright even argues that to pray 'Our Father' was a kind of Old Testament way of referring to liberty, echoing the Exodus.[5] Similarly, Charles Elliott shows the resonance of Old Testament liberation throughout the Lord's Prayer.[6] The kingdom of God has social and political relevance, involving us and our prayer.

By contrast, the connotation of the 'Spirit' in Christian spirituality is often that of inner piety, almost the reverse of the very practical activist emphasis of the category of 'kingdom'. The very term 'spirituality' conjures up personal devotions and private prayer life. This can convey the unfortunate impression, if pressed too far, that spirituality is other-worldly and mystical, an escape into a different realm altogether. It can even move from a Christian understanding into a Platonic kind of dualism, whereby this world is bad and the realm of the spirit is good, a dimension to which we must seek mentally to ascend, putting aside all creaturely emotions and concerns. But spirituality cannot, for Christian faith, be 'other-worldly' or escapist; the Holy Spirit empowers the faithful for service in the world. Neither the kingdom nor the Spirit can be 'privatized'.

Pannenberg has recently suggested an analogy for the Holy Spirit, which may be useful in bringing together the Spirit and the Kingdom of God as theological categories. He suggests that the scientific notion of a 'force field' may be an apt way of regarding the Spirit,[7] although seeking also to protect the personhood of the Spirit. The image of a 'force field' points to the Spirit as the *context* for Christian life and worship, and this is certainly a biblical idea, since believers are urged to 'walk in' the Spirit as well as to be 'filled with' the Spirit. Here Pannenberg criticizes much Western theology for linking the Spirit too exclusively with mind or thinking, as if the Spirit were confined to helping us understand revelation. Drawing on Psalm 139, he suggests that Spirit is the force field of God's mighty presence, the creative life-giving dynamic in the world.

This notion of the Spirit's presence as the church's milieu of new life comes close to the notion of the kingdom of God in which we live, whose rule conditions the life of faith. This is so especially when it is remembered that the rule of God, the power of God, is revealed in Jesus and his death. The omnipotence of God is that of love, which has not conquered unless it has attracted free response of faith and love. Such is the kingdom of God revealed and enacted by Jesus.

Prayer in the Spirit means prayer that is oriented to Christ and uttered in Christ. It does not mean, necessarily, worship in a specially emotional tone, or unreasoning worship. It is worship flowing from the relationship of being 'in' the Spirit and 'in' Christ, hence worship coloured by the nature and person of Jesus. It is worship arising from an ethical community, not worship which is a spirituality divorced from lived holiness. The idea of a force field holds good here, as does that of the kingdom, pointing to a wholeness about worship and life that admits no dualisms of sacred and secular.

The New Testament associates the Spirit with prayer very clearly. According to Paul, even when we are too overburdened by care to pray, the Spirit intercedes for us and with us. The Spirit gives life to our spirits creatively, and the Spirit 'helps us in our weakness; for we do not know how to pray as we ought, but that very Spirit intercedes with sighs too deep for words' (Rom 8:26). Worship seems to be close to the very essence of the Spirit's activity, that is, taking the offering of the created order before the face of the Father, in the trinitarian movement. This role of the 'the go-between God' is that of communication and appreciation, as through the Spirit the worship of the creature acknowledges the majesty of God. The fact that this a trinitarian movement is underlined by continuing the passage from Romans: 'And the one who searches the heart, knows what is the mind of the Spirit, because the Spirit intercedes for the saints according to the will of God' (Rom 8: 27). In another epistle Paul writes that 'the Spirit searches everything, even the depths of God' (1 Cor. 2:10). To live in the Spirit is to live and move in the divine life and understanding. Moreover, the church has received the Spirit of adoption, whereby she can call God 'Abba, Father' (Rom. 8:15). Intercession from the weary and heavy-laden person of faith is brought to the Father by the deeply empathetic Spirit.

John V. Taylor floats the suggestion that the notion of divine substitution, getting into our life situation and acting for us, happens in this way by the Spirit.[8] Being in Christ means that the Spirit intercedes for us when we cannot, a kind of vicarious praying, making good what our basic intention wishes to happen. Nothing will be able to separate us from the love of God in Christ Jesus (Rom 8:39), and the Spirit secures this bond in every respect. A deeper hold on this truth would deliver many evangelicals from the grip of a secret legalistic bondage, according to which failure to pray brings ostracism or excommunication from the family of God, necessitating a kind of re-conversion. But on the contrary, the New Testament stresses the care of the Spirit for the tired and struggling disciple. This guidance removes the temptation to import an alien 'justification by quiet times' into evangelical spirituality. The Spirit 'knows the deep things of God' and also our innermost state of mind, will, and heart, that whatever our failings, we are indeed committed and oriented to God. A bruised reed he will not break; a dimly burning wick he will not quench. Here lies the message of true freedom, that God the Spirit even upholds us in our fear, failure, and unfaith.

Love and strength are mediated from the Father to us by this 'go-between' dimension of God. This love and strength, it must be remembered, has been redefined in the life, death, and resurrection of Jesus. The intercession we make needs to be conditioned by being in Christ, as in the Spirit. The suffering servant of God prophesied in Isaiah 53 both suffers and intercedes in priestly fashion, becoming the sacrifice and praying for sinners. The revolution of Jesus' kingdom has roots here; transformation will come through self-giving and prayer, not through violence and force; in their comments on the Lord's Prayer, Elliott and Wright both stress this when they consider the political liberation the kingdom brings. Intercession for others, for release, coupled with life decisions for others, is God's way of implementing the kingdom: God is the God of freedom and not coercion.

To live and worship in this context is a mode of being, being as communion. To be in the divine supportive presence, the divine understanding is to be in the most substantial dimension of life conceivable. For the Christian, this is being at its most real, this is ontologically foundational: the Spirit of the Father and the Son providing the environment of life and thought, even supporting us when we are beyond coping ourselves. When we worship, therefore, we are in God's ambit already. God is not periodically brought into the midst of the worshipping assembly by some particular act, either of a highly charged emotional kind or a ritual sacramental kind. Rather, the Spirit evokes our worship, and in the Spirit the people of God wield their only means of power, that of prayer.

3. Perfection is not yet

'Praying the kingdom', to use Charles Elliott's phrase, means sharing in the divine project that is focused in the ministry of Jesus and empowered by the Spirit. This vision avoids false emphases, for example, those which identify the kingdom with politico-economic improvement and those which identify spirituality with psychological or mystical improvement or poise. Both aspects belong to the work of the Spirit and the rule of the Christlike God, but alone cannot be said to constitute that work and rule. The best of the liberation theologians root their concern for economic justice in the values and way of Jesus, linking in the way of prayer with the way of social amelioration. This has long been the case in the history of reform worked for by Christians.

The vogue for plumbing the depths of the psyche in the name of Christian spirituality, an equal and opposite error if absolutized, can become an in-turned enterprise, insufficiently conditioned by the kingdom and its imperative to look outwards at the pressing needs of the world. Interestingly, a certain perfectionism can be seen in the extremes of the two types of error under discussion. Politically, we live in a sinful world and will always be dissatisfied with the failure of socio-economic systems to match up to the eschatological pictures of harmony in the reign of God. One danger of a perfectionism or utopianism is that massive human sacrifices may be made on its altar now, to secure that absolutely desirable goal for the future generations. Such ruthlessness with present humanity cannot have a place in the kingdom of God.

Likewise a perfectionism of Christian spirituality and psychology is a temptation. We are never going to iron out all our personal flaws which cause us anxiety and fear. To think that re-enacting our birth experience will achieve this kind of healing, for example, by enabling us to confront unfortunate events during our passage into the world from the womb, seems highly speculative and misleading.[9] To attach this kind of psychotherapeutic technique to the work of the Spirit seems to risk entrapment by suggestive and well-meaning practitioners of a certain theory. When such procedure is associated with the Johannine text, 'you must be born again', we are entering the world of 'never-never land' in terms of biblical exegesis.

The real danger relates to expectations. Is there a psychological utopia accessible by such therapeutic channels, into which the Spirit is invited, or should we regard our psychological health in the same way as our physical health? We will remain imperfect, but are on a path to new-ness. The issue of psychological health has become a matter of huge concern in Western culture generally, and many new forms of spirituality have sprung up which focus on the need for poise, harmony, and balance. Such moments of serenity are certainly much to be desired; and when we find them, we give thanks for them. But to identify such a sense with spirituality sits uncomfortably with the Christian way. The current Western cultural preoccupation with counselling has apparently got out of hand and may be reflected in a spirituality marked by the quest for a continual sense of harmony and well-being. The tensions of life, especially life in the kingdom which will be struggling against the powers and principalities over many things, must be acknowledged. The Western secularized world is based on the consumer society, with expectations ratcheted up to high levels, hence the increasing culture of litigation by way of compensation for even minor inconveniences. In a recent case in America, for example, a customer whose hot coffee spilled on him from a tray provided by a fast-food establishment claimed millions of dollars in damages.

One huge difference between life in ancient and modern societies is this matter of expectation. Now life is expected to be smooth, and compensation is looked for if not; then life was a difficult and rough path in the nature of things. Life is not, of course, a constantly smooth way, despite the virtual-reality world constructed by the advertising industry. Counselling is therefore resorted to as a means of enabling people to cope with the shocks of the inevitable accidents, bereavements, and blows encountered in any normal life. It may be that this phenomenon of state-funded counselling in the West has arisen at the same time as the breakdown of the family unit is in full flood, for that was the context by which care, counsel, and indeed the rituals that coped with death and illness, were formerly given. This having weakened, the citizen expects a listening ear to be provided, as a matter of consumer rights, to help reorient the person to normal trouble-free existence. The West has become an analgesic society, even a saccharine society, expecting sugary substitutes to soothe away the intrusion of difficulty.

It just may be that the Western Church has not escaped the cultural effect of consumerism and expectations of normal life being free from problems. This conceivably may have fed into discipleship and spirituality a certain false expectation of perfection or at the least a smoothness and a 'centredness' which bring harmony and inner peace. Many forms of aesthetic and therapeutic techniques are available to foster such sense of well-being. While the Spirit can indeed be seen as working in and through such channels in the created order, whether focusing so much upon them is characteristic of the kingdom of God is quite another matter. Of course, those who genuinely suffer from mental illness need all the help available, just as the patient with a broken leg. But as a matter of normal spirituality and pastoral practice, the furthering of the poise of the disciple seems to be a side alley, and a possibly distracting one.

The 'peace which passes understanding' comes from the pursuit of the kingdom. Walking in the Spirit relates to following Jesus. Peace in the eye of the storm is not to be easily equated with psycho-dynamic balance. If the latter becomes the primary focus of spirituality, then it has parted company with the classical gospel tradition of life and worship in the Spirit, and been led into a form of 'self-actualization' and away from the kingdom-actualization inherent in being in Christ. Self-fulfilment is indeed seen in the life of the ardent disciple, but this comes indirectly, as a spin-off from discipleship, rather than being the main aim of spirituality. No doubt some of this tendency comes from a misinterpretation of the gospel along consumerist lines; the notion that turning to Jesus will remove all one's problems is simply unbiblical. In many ways, problems (in the world's terms) will increase, but the joy of being a disciple far outweighs this fact.

The need to achieve perfect inner peace can also become a goal to be attained by other means than the therapeutic or mystical. It can be felt to be an end accessible through suffering itself. So the infliction of pain on oneself as a means of mortifying the flesh and the senses, of fleeing this world of pleasures and cares into the realm of the spirit, can also become a primary goal. But suffering and pain for its own sake is not a Judaeo-Christian principle; it rather has its roots in the Gnostic tradition of escape from the created world of the physical and the senses. The injunction of the apostle Paul to put up with suffering for Christ's sake concerns brave discipleship and witness; suffering is not a primary aim in itself, but a consequence of working for the kingdom. Suffering in the apostolic tradition is purposive in an outward looking way, rooted in love for God, other people, and creation. Jesus prayed that if the kingdom could be founded without his brutal death, his Father might take this cup from him (Matt 26:29). He was no masochist seeking suffering for its own sake. Spirituality based on the ascetic practice of self-inflicted pain for its own sake looks like the equal and opposite error of the consumerist spirituality; in both the goal is spiritual perfection, but by quite contrary means.[10]

Spirituality concerns not primarily myself, whether in modes of what I can gain or what I can learn to suffer, but the kingdom. Part of Christian spiritual health is an acknowledgement of imperfection, and a determination to carry on as a limited but faithful servant. The notion of the constantly serene and poised spiritual master is not necessarily a Christian one. Jesus in Gethsemane agonising about his life gives the Christian an important model of an inevitable point in the life of a disciple. The theologian Schleiermacher was in danger of docetism, the ancient heresy in which Jesus only appeared to be a human being, when he portrayed Jesus continuing in an unclouded blessedness of unbroken God-consciousness as he faced and endured the anguish of crucifixion[11]; so we, too, risk a psycho-spiritual docetism if we yield to the mirage of perfectionist expectations.

The reverse, in fact, appears to be true. The deeper one's discipleship, the deeper one will know of Christlike suffering, in the depths of spirituality lived out in the world for the kingdom. Holiness, one might argue as a Christian, comes indirectly through discipleship, that is, following Christ in building the kingdom, rather than through self-conscious religious and psycho-therapeutic exercises. Prayer is part of this loyalty to the kingdom, the orientation of the believer to the king and to the particular quality of the kingdom, marked out by the cross of Christ. The coronation of this king took place at Golgotha, and the victory of this kingdom over all others was that of crucifixion.

Worship in the kingdom of God naturally praises such costly love and goodness which has liberated humans from the disorientation of the Darwinian principle of the law of the survival of the fittest, and replaced it with the way of care and love. The power of this rule is within; the omnipotence of this God works through love and freely given loyalty. The kingdom has conquered none through force, inquisition, or cultural manipulation, despite the demonic attempts well known to church historians. Such is not the way of Jesus, nor is it the way to freedom. The kingdom is implemented by the Spirit in its impact on the world's events and structures, demonstrating that the kingdom of God is indeed wider than the church.

4. The kingdom of joy and suffering

God is the God of creation, a universe of galaxies of matter and energy, of particulars as well as of universal structures. The creation of humanity, such a tiny reality in the vastness of things, as the medium through which God discloses himself and with which he interacts most deeply, speaks of humour of scale as well as of the most tender care. Creation, which is a prior reality to salvation, contains laughter, joy, and humour. Creation contains play.[12] The created order embodies 'disorder' or 'non-order',[13] that which seems pointless and not functionally useful for anything else except to attract wonder and joy.

A magnificent butterfly fluttering in the summer's breeze, settling for a moment with its brilliantly coloured wings spread out, such is 'non-order'. The absurdity of certain human sporting activities, hitting hard leather balls around beautifully mown grass fields, for example, also illustrates something beloved, harmless, and part of the 'non-ordered' experience of creation. Swimming and dancing, again utterly pointless in terms of anything but themselves, show a delight in being in creation, feeling movement and rhythm, the sense of wind and water against the skin.

These examples may well prompt the accusation of triviality in the midst of a serious subject, the kingdom of God. But God fashioned this creation with such experiences of the non-rational and non-functional as part of life. The free Spirit can and does communicate through all kinds of experience, including such as these. They evoke our praise to our maker, infinitely more subtle in relating to us than we often take him to be. This too is part of the kingdom of God, as well as the planned campaigning for justice and for conversions. Simply to ponder in wonderment at the non-ordered beauty of creation and its creator is a rich act of worship.

A related question perhaps worth risking here is whether God has a sense of humour, or anything divinely equivalent, and accordingly whether this finds an echo in spiritual experience. Perhaps the nearest one can get to an exploration of this question in modern times is in the form of story, in the *Chronicles of Narnia* by C. S. Lewis, but the wisdom tradition of Ancient Israel gives some grounding for the suggestion; its writings contain a sense of playfulness in creation[14] and a sense of divine pleasure when the wholly unpredicted comes to pass and excites our gladness, often at the same time as a melting cynicism.[15] Somehow the underlying divine presence, the 'holy Being' of Macquarrie's thought, is manifested as more than a neutral reality, and instead flits past us as intimately concerned with the minute fretwork of our life story. God the Father 'knows'. It may even be that the resurrection of Jesus from brutal death and the accompanying human despair, contains an element of divine laughter and sheer gladness, in which we can be caught up in our worship.

Having said this, however, we must instantly acknowledge the inexplicable suffering and misery, which is the other side of our experience of the world and of the kingdom, and which is indeed specifically predicted by Jesus as something to be expected in the kingdom. Suffering as a mark of the church[16] seems plain in the New Testament, but has disappeared from the famous definition of the four marks of the church as 'one, holy, catholic, and apostolic'. The kingdom was inaugurated at Calvary, and it will bear the marks of the way of the cross this side of the new creation. The distinctively Christian note of joy in worship and prayer is precisely that of sensing the divine promise *in the midst of* suffering, the risen Christ at a time of pain and helplessness. This is in continuity with the Hebraic tradition of worship, confident in the sheer reality of the good God, in the face of all kinds of misery and disaster. This reality makes no sense at all to the non-believer, for whom Christian faith is the cry of the oppressed, or—according to Marx—the opium of the people, a narcotic which neutralizes the misery of life by projecting our wish for happiness onto an imaginary God.

As we have already seen,[17] there is no *intellectual* proving whether Marx or the believer is right. In a sense, the eschatological joy in historical pain is indeed a 'projection' in Christian teaching, but a double one. The divine reality first reaches into the world situation, and then the faithful reach to the heavenly Father in the confidence of Christ. It remains a fact of Christian worship and spirituality that times of hardship are sometimes linked with times of irrational security and even joy, when the future hope seems to break into present miseries and bring fresh courage. Christian prayer happens not simply as matter of reaching up, but forward to the future consummation and victory.

Jesus' resurrection, as Pannenberg reminds us,[18] is an end-time event come in advance. We might even develop this idea as P. T. Forsyth does, and say that the death of Jesus was the last judgement come in advance.[19] The kingdom of God, initiated by Jesus and made present by the Spirit, involves its members in this proleptic mode of life which brings divine love into the now, inevitably involving clashes with the way things are in many different ways, but also bringing inscrutable depths of joy from time to time, depths not reducible to socio-psychological factors.

The situation of suffering, both in creation and in the church, under the rule of God gives us another tension. We live in the Spirit who bridges this age and the age to come. In this age, according to Paul, creation groans with the aches and pains of age and decay, somehow aware of a future release into a liberation. This is the context of 'the sufferings of the present time' for Paul, who considers that they 'are not worth comparing with the glory that is to be revealed to us' (Rom 8:18). Creation itself has been groaning as has humanity within it, and we wait for the 'redemption of our bodies'. The Spirit is present in this time of mysterious waiting and frustration and pain, bridging us into the *eschaton*, or the 'final reality' of the future new creation. So the Spirit empathizes at the deepest level with us in the bewilderment of suffering, 'the Spirit helps us in our weakness, for we do not know how to pray as we ought, but that very Spirit intercedes with sighs too deep for words' (Rom 8:26). From the other end of its tensioned context, the *eschaton*, the church receives ongoing love and grace in the pain of this world. In another epistle the apostle tells his readers that while 'even though our outward nature is wasting away, our inner nature is being renewed day by day' (2 Cor 4:16), as the continuing presence of the Spirit renders love and power to cope Christianly.

The sympathy or empathy of the Spirit could hardly be expressed more radically by Paul. The Spirit prays for us when we are beyond praying, at the end of our capacity, at the end of *our* 'spirituality'. The Spirit is the 'Go-Between God'[20] who constantly links us to the Father, and in ways beyond the merely cognitive. The Spirit stands in our shoes and, according to Paul, really does feel as we feel, somehow 'ghost writing' our emotional response when we cannot cope, keeping us orientated to the Father in the midst of grief. 'The Spirit searches everything, even the depths of God' (1 Cor 2:10-13), and this searcher and sympathizer mediates to us the Christ life, binding up the broken-hearted, blessing the meek, encouraging the poor in heart, the kingdom community as described in the beatitudes of Matthew's Gospel.

This interplay of prayer, not merely evoked by the Spirit but expressed, breathed out, for us when we could not, is surely eschatological, a real relation of the believer to God, a genuine link kept and maintained through good times and bad. The Spirit is the 'paraclete' of John's Gospel, the one who comes alongside, bringing to us the things of Jesus and his spiritual mode of being. In the Spirit we live an end-time life in the here and now with all the ambiguities and fractures and failures of human history.

The eschatological life, heavenly life, struggles to exist within fallen time, and the Spirit bridges between 'that day' and the current life of 'wars and rumours of wars, famines and earthquakes', the bumping along of history as described in the Book of Revelation and in the Synoptic Gospels in passages such as Mark 13. The message of the famous 'four horsemen of the Apocalypse' (Rev 6:1-8) is that current history is a matter of war, economic disruption, and famine, on a significant although limited scale, and that the church cries out for God's judgement and vindication for the saints waiting 'under the altar' (Rev 6:9-11), suffering and martyred by the oppressors. 'How long O Lord?' is the cry of the church, awaiting the final establishment of the kingdom of God in triumph over evil. It is probably this implementation of the kingdom, the final vindicating judgement and rule of God, which is spoken of in the Lord's Prayer.

While the context of church life in the affluent Western world does not often press Christians to pray this prayer for the fulfilment of God's reign, the inbreaking of the kingdom to save from oppression can be an overwhelming prayer request for those undergoing persecution. According to Jesus in Mark's picture of apocalypse, the Holy Spirit will enable disciples under persecution to know what to say and how to conduct themselves (Mark 13:11), precisely the same 'advocate' role of the paraclete in John's Gospel and that of the deep empathy given when the disciple is utterly exhausted. The context of Christian life is one of stress, stress between the fulfilled reign of God and life in the world as it is. To be citizens of heaven and of human history is a tension, and the Spirit is the go-between in the stress. If Christians sense no stress, then perhaps they have settled down rather too comfortably in the social customs of the day, the consumer kingdom of this world, and need to hear the prophetic word cutting into history.

5. Prayerful struggle for the kingdom in history: Karl Barth and Christ, the Servant-King

The structure of the inbreaking kingdom, Karl Barth teaches, is focused on the person of Christ. Critics of Barth's theology have called this a 'christological constriction'[21]; but does this have the effect, as they charge, of freezing the one who receives revelation into an identity with the divine and eternal realm, rather than creating a covenant partner with freedom and motivation to work for the transformation of this world? This was indeed the case in Barth's early theology, usually called 'dialectical' because of the stark contrast between the world and the Word of God. But even in Barth's developed phase of thought, where a relationship between God and humanity can and does exist because it exists in Christ, the church relates to Christ by *waiting* in faith. Does Barth (and can we) think of it as existing in a way in which it might wrestle with the actual problems of the world, and seek to transform the world according to the kingdom of God?

Christians should indeed rejoice at the fact of redemption, of the contradiction between God and humanity being overcome, and should worship the mystery of the Father as revealed in the Son and imparted in the Spirit. Barth stresses a structure of life in which we wait for the Spirit to enliven the church. The church repeatedly *becomes* the church, while already being the visible church. Perhaps we might say that the church is more the church as it lives out the kingdom, yet the initiative remains very much with God who acts at the moment of faith. Modern criticisms of this position focus on the concentration of salvation in Christ, and the lack of focus on the significance of God's involvement in history since A.D. 33. 'Not until Jürgen Moltmann published his work *Theology of Hope*', says Stephen Neill, 'was the German theological world prepared to take seriously the idea that the world is there to be transformed and not merely to be endured . . .'[22] We should add that the quite different theological school of thought about God as Being, which we explored earlier,[23] also falls under this criticism.

The mature Barth continues the one-way-street pattern of grace and seems to emphasize our knowledge of God through revelation in Christ. God can, of course, reveal himself through all manner of things in creation, since he is God and supremely powerful. The main point is the fact of God's having revealed *himself*, enlightening our understanding, giving a knowledge of God in trinitarian form. The kingdom is known and acknowledged as having come in Jesus. Jesus, the priestly king, declares the message of his saving love to the world in his prophetic ministry. Reconciliation has happened in the act of Jesus Christ, God has united humanity to himself, taking responsibility for sin and unholiness by the cross and resurrection. The continuation of time after the resurrection of Jesus is a space for the human race to say 'yes' to this act of divine grace, space in which grace finds 'its correspondence in a voice of human thanks from the depths of the world reconciled with Himself'.[24] This era since the resurrection of Jesus, 'a history which is a postscript', gives us room to give praise to God for such a great salvation. God wills the church since he wants 'a body, an earthly historical form of the existence of this Head'.[25] This marks a shift in Barth's thought from his early 'dialectics' to a stress on 'analogy', whereby the contact between heaven and earth brings about a 'correspondence' between them; grace takes up nature and ordains it for service and worship.

This kind of theology might be suggesting that the kingdom has come in such a way that there is no need to struggle together with God to implement it in the world. Jesus Christ's reconciling work has been achieved, and it only needs to be proclaimed and responded to in worship by the faithful recipients of the revelation. God has acted in Christ by assuming humanity to himself decisively, once for all. But would that leave any room for the transformation of human history by the faithful who are responding to the gospel? The revelation is complete, and so the reconciliation is also complete. At-one-ment has been made in Christ, and the Spirit is imparting this truth to human hearts and minds. Can such a theology allow sufficient room for the struggle that, for example, the liberation theologians argue is necessary on behalf of the poor?

On Barth's behalf it should be said that he conceives the revelation of Christ imparted by the Spirit as stabilizing the recipient in an act of responsive worship, and that this is a response in which the whole range of human subjectivity is taken up; so it is a genuinely human response. The point to be pressed, however, is that the kingdom of God is somehow enacted or forwarded by disciples as they live and pray their way into the future. Approaching this problem through the dimension of spirituality and worship may be of some help. The great concentration of Barth's theology is that of 'revelation'; the church waits in faith for the divine act of revelation through the mediation of word and sacrament. It may be that what is usually understood by 'revelation' at this point may prove to be too narrow for Christian theology and practice. For Barth, and surely rightly, revelation means the disclosure of *the very self of God* to the church, not merely the delivery of information. The response to divine self-revelation for Barth is one of obedience and worship, acknowledgement of God, acknowledgement of being bonded to God in Christ. The awaited moment of revelation brings this renewed sense of divine presence, and the church again becomes the church in the fullest sense. Might then the category of 'revelation' be improved by adding to it that of 'presence'? And might this also correct any notion of the absence, or lack of presence, of God, which might be implied by the need for his renewed revelation?

Worship of God should continue whether or not the Lord in his freedom renews the revelation of Christ to the church in the power of the Spirit. The given revelation of the person and work of Christ also always remains true as the object of worship. The word does not have to 'come alive' as if it were dead beforehand, or somehow less than true. God remains God for the church, and therefore she can praise and thank this God in confidence. God who is present hears the praises of his people, hears the confession of their sins, their petitions. God is present, whatever the spiritual state of the individual worshipper. This seems to be the assured message of Pentecost, that the Spirit, the Paraclete, is with us. The church does not need to wait again for the coming of the Spirit for the self-disclosure of God, for that disclosure has been made and the Spirit has been given. The church is always in a position to repent, to praise, to intercede, and to thank the living God who is constantly present.

Michael Ramsey regards Protestant Christianity as deficient in its sense of devotion, missing 'the deep emphasis of Catholic Christianity upon adoration'.[26] He may be mistaken in terms of individual piety, where evangelicals place great stress on the discipline of daily prayer, 'the quiet time'. But in terms of corporate worship he may have a point, and it may relate to the need to focus on the *presence* of God. Ramsey speaks of 'an ontological element in the New Testament as utterly essential for New Testament Christianity', and by 'ontological' here he means the sheer 'isness' of God.

The Old Testament story of Moses asking God for assurance and gaining the reply 'I am who I am' confirms this theology. Martin Buber, the great Jewish exegete and philosopher, translates the phrase as meaning 'I am present',[27] the promise to the people of the continuing faithfulness of God. Behind this self-revelation, argues Buber,

> stands the implied reply to those influenced by the magical practices of Egypt, those infected by technical magic: [God replies that] it is superfluous for you to wish to invoke me; in accordance with my character I again and again stand by those whom I befriend.[28]

Ramsey makes a similar point in his criticism of the Protestant ethos when he says:

> In the experience of salvation existentialism may seem to suffice, for the Saviour is definable as 'what he means to me'. But in the experience of worship the Christian was and is concerned with *One who is*. The worshipper forgets his own being and experiences in the adoration of One who is, and the 'isness' of deity is there, behind and before, now and for ever. The 'isness' of deity—prominent in the Old Testament—is reaffirmed when it is revealed that Jesus shares in it'.[29]

Martin Buber's theology of the divine name, the promise to be present, stands at the heart of this insistence on the presence of deity as the focus of worship, which for Ramsey as a Christian theologian is mediated through Christ.

God is present to be worshipped in all the forms of prayer and praise known to the church. But this focus on the present God entails worship 'not only with our lips but in our lives, by giving up ourselves to Thy service', in the words of *The Book of Common Prayer*. Worship in the community of Jesus will entail an ethical and 'horizontal' aspect. Love for God and love for our neighbour go hand in hand, according to the Ten Commandments. The holiness of God is not primarily revealed to us in detachment from the world, but in incarnation into this sinful and dangerous world. Holiness is shown by getting hands dirty, as well as by piety. The presence of God as the continuing context for his self-revelation means that the disciple is always called to prayerful struggle for the kingdom.

Praying for the kingdom to come means praying for the final climax of the kingdom, the unambiguous rule of God. But praying in the name of Jesus, given the attitude of Jesus to the poor in every sense, means that such a petition cannot be offered from the stance of a ghetto walled off from concern for the world and its confusion and misery. Prayer for the final kingdom, the unqualified rule of God, feeds back into our prayer life, fuelling prayer for the world. It simultaneously conditions our mindset towards the world. Christian prayer is from the standing of Jesus and his kingdom.

The very structure of the Lord's Prayer shows how the focus on the holy God draws us down to earth and its needs. Here Barth's detailed Christology is relevant, and was found to be so by a South African theologian, Charles Villa-Vicenzio, prior to the dismantling of apartheid.[30] Barth develops a Christology which embraces in the one person of Jesus both the divine condescension and sacrifice and the exaltation of humanity. To worship the God of Jesus is to worship the self-giving Lord, and so to take on the character of serving others, with no barrier of separation. Since the Lord is the servant king, his people will inevitably take up his towel and serve likewise. Paul's image of the Second Adam (1 Cor 15:45-49), a new humanity forged in the life, death, and resurrection of Jesus, may help the connection between Christology and the struggle for the kingdom here and now. The church prays in the mind of Christ, who humbled himself and became servant for all (Phil 2:1-11). Rather than human response being frozen by the inbreaking of the eternal moment, the Spirit therefore liberates and releases the people of God to serve others in the Christlike mode of life.

Prayer for the coming of the kingdom embraces the tension between the present and the future, and also the tension between the divine command over history and human effort demanded of disciples. These tensions can be held together by classical trinitarian theology, especially if worship remains central to the church as Ramsey insists. The 'light of the world' embodied the sacrificial self-offering and service to God that was at the same time sacrificial service to humankind as a whole. The faith and humanity of Jesus is the model for all disciples, concentrated on worship of the Father whose will is to spread his kingdom of love outwards into the darkness. The tension of worship and social concern is no contradiction, since worship is directed to the holy God of creation and redemption.

The church contributes best towards society's needs not by becoming another think-tank or social services department, but by bringing her distinctive message and action of Christ-centred care. The dualist approach of much Christian social thought and practice, bracketing the 'spiritual' from the temporal as if the two were separable, leads to moralizing and unconvincing postures being struck. Sermonic addresses to the government of the day about housing policy, for example, sound very hollow from church leaders if their churches are doing little practically, or sacrificially, to help the homeless, apart from haranguing politicians. The specifically Christian note of care for the individual as a person precious to God needs also to be sounded in forwarding 'kingdom values'.

The spiritual and the temporal coincide in the kingdom of God, and the prayer life of the Christian confirms this in experience. The worship by Isaiah of the transcendent holy one in the Temple led to his acceptance of the call to 'go' for God (Isa 6:8). The figure of Jesus, the suffering servant and the glorified Lord, crystallizes this double movement of worship and service, self-offering to God and self-offering to our neighbour. The title of a modern hymn, 'The Servant King',[31] aptly sums up not only Barth's dynamic Christology, but the particularity of Christian worship. The exalted holy Lord is this Lord who for our sakes became poor (2 Cor 8:9). Barth's insight into the self-revelation of God must be included as necessary to worship, for it is worship of God who discloses himself to be like this, and such worship has to control our lives as a whole.

6. God's rule and the world:
Process theology and divine persuasion

The paradox that God wishes us to pray for the kingdom of God to be completed raises sharply the question of God's relationship to the world. What can it mean to ask for God's kingdom to come? This prayer could be simply good for us to pray, God having predetermined the climax of the kingdom, the praying therefore having no real significance to God or to world history beyond the calming influence on the worshipper. Such a prayer may express trust in the fact that, in the end, God will vindicate both himself and those who suffer in world history. But prayer for the coming of the kingdom seems to fit best into the general scheme of the gospel if its context is that of active struggle for the kingdom here and now by disciples, prior to its climactic fulfilment.

Not adopting this pattern would effectively exclude the impact of the person and work of Christ and the Spirit in history as a decisive, but not final, implementation of the kingdom of God and assault on evil and suffering. Oscar Cullmann's analogy of stages of warfare remains useful; while the overall war has been won in principle, smaller battles within it still remain. The less military example of the final creative act of the artist, 'the finishing touch', also gives an insight into the prayer for the final coming of the kingdom. The work of art as a whole is completed by the final action of the artist, making that act significant in a way surpassing all the previous actions except perhaps the very first one that began the work. The climax incorporates all the intermediate labours, but with the climax the work itself is simultaneously finished and its full meaning can have expression. The final action is the moment of bringing to birth of the 'new creation'.

This concept is complex, bringing together two notions that are usually distinguished, those of continual gradual development and of a decisive act or event. The work of art develops and yet is an act which finishes with a burst of creative energy at its climax. Creation itself, according to Romans 8, groans until its final climactic redemption. Disciples of Jesus live in the work of redemption and pray for its completion, the great moment, 'that day', when the picture will be completed, when the child is delivered, when 'Christ shall be all in all'. The purpose of creation will have been totally fulfilled, and joy will be complete.

The church which prays for the coming of the kingdom is involved in this process and knows that the nature of the kingdom being established is a reign of love and holiness, not force and violence, for this kingdom 'is not of this world'. So the establishment of the reign of God will happen through the omnipotence of love, when the spirits of all are won over to worship, to free love for God the Father and acknowledgement of his purposes. Worship of the king by the church and prayer for the culmination of this kingdom is linked inseparably to the final reign of God, and so is a foretaste of it. In the Spirit the church gives herself to the Father in full openness and glad service, knowing that this is a pale form of the richness of the kingdom in total reality.

The life of the church is meant to reflect the kingdom of God, a life of self-giving, the way of *kenosis*, the way of Jesus who did not count equality with God a thing to be grasped but humbled himself. This is the pattern found in Paul's theology of the 'body of Christ', a new way of mutual respect and the inversion of worldly power. Such is victory over the world. Christ is the head of the body; therefore, the worship by the church is from a body grafted into the life of the Son of God. Prayer for the kingdom arises from the body of Christ, from those knit together in Christ by the Spirit, and hence constituted into a new mode of being. Praying for the kingdom is itself part of being moulded into the kingdom in the hands of the divine artist. God works his creation and recreation through the hearts and wills of his people, desiring that all join in this great enterprise. God creates in such a way that creation creates itself and develops as the work of art.

The analogy of the playwright and the play, or the novelist and the novel with its world of characters, has been made several times in the history of theology, notably by Dorothy Sayers in her *The Mind of the Maker*,[32] but prior to that by William Temple.[33] 'Dramatists have declared that when once they have set their several characters in motion, they have no further control over the conduct of those characters' says Temple.[34] Sayers testifies that this is so, that the characters of an authentic novel or play are not mere puppets to be manipulated from outside the context of the movement of the plot; when this artificial control of characters does happen, it ruins the quality of the work, turning them into ciphers or mere cardboard cut-out figures. The dramatist has to work with the sinew and substance of each character, allowing the dynamic of each to take its own course.[35]

Temple wishes to combine this analogy with that of a father and his growing children:

> He gave them being; to a great extent he shapes their circumstances; perhaps his influence over them is so great that they will never knowingly act against his wishes; yet they are free to respect his wishes or not; if they do so, it is because it appears to them good to do so; when he controls them, he does not coerce them, because his control is effective through their wills and not either apart from or against their wills.[36]

The analogy between the dramatist and God breaks down because the characters are not real, and the analogy of the father fails because he is as much bound into successiveness as are his children. Both kinds of relationship, however, illustrate the purposive and benign relationship of the kingdom with its junior partners, with the latter being totally respected in regard to their freedom. These analogies avoid the mechanistically causal notions of control in favour of personal influence and working through freedom of the will, and so express the omnipotence of love. Divine rule is coloured by this kind of self-limitation and respect for created freedom.

The school of modern thought called 'process theology' stresses this point, that the whole process of the world is 'lured'[37] towards the good and needs to choose it for itself. Human beings freely decide and do what they want, and God exists within the process as that part of it that seeks to attract them to act positively towards maximizing the greatest pleasure for the whole process. God is defined as the influence within the process, not as controlling it in any sense.[38] There is an aspect to the process that persuades it towards maximizing happiness for all, and this we call God.

This insight of the process theologians is at least necessary if not sufficient for Christian theology. History shows the freedom of individuals to act for or against what is beneficial for the human race, and the grace of God is never experienced as overriding the freedom of the will. The power of God is that of love and self-giving, as is revealed in the death and resurrection of Jesus. God completes his creation through the joyful consent of disciples. The 'process' vision of creation comes very close to the Pauline view of the church as the body of Christ, each item of the body subserving the other and as a whole incarnating Christ who is all in all as that body. In this process the power of God is made perfect in weakness, as viewed from the eyes of those still needing to be conformed to the mind of Christ. To pray for the coming of the kingdom of God is, for process theology, to pray for the ongoing influence of God to maintain the lure towards perfecting the bliss of creation. This prayer, for such a theology, orients the self to God and asks for the ongoing beckoning of God.

The prayer must envisage the intensification of the world's orientation to God into a grand climax of joy.[39] Process theologians are 'panentheists' (believing that 'everything is in God'), regarding God as the heart and soul of the process and not separable from it, any more than the mind can be separated from the body in a human being. For process theology the word 'universe' means what it says, a single entity encompassing all; nothing is outside this cosmic unity. Joy in any item of the universe is actually experienced somehow by God as joy, and the goal of the process called for by the prayer 'your kingdom come' entails a climax of joy for God simultaneously as for all other items of the universe.

The coming of the kingdom means, then, the self-actualization of God, the rule of divine being through free consent, a rule which will have come to triumph despite all appearances to the contrary—in the late twentieth century, for example. The joy felt by the component items of the universe, that which is non-divine, will be shared by the divine 'nervous system' of the whole body of the world. Praying for the coming of the kingdom, according to this view, is praying that we in history may complete the kingdom by attending to the lure of the divine will, not that some decisive act of God will supervene to end history from 'outside' the world process. The process view does not have a place for a final *end* to the process, but rather a burgeoning of temporal happiness which will grow and grow, even through a climax, as the lure of the divine is accepted.

The process reinterpretation of the Hebrew calling upon the Lord for the in-breaking of the rule of God may not end up as far from the traditional view as may be thought at first. According to process thought, the rule of God *does* come about, and as a result of the persistent power of the patient persuasion of God acting as an influence on the wills of created entities. This is what is prayed for. God is honoured as triumphing through persuasion that respects the created order and brings it to the fulfilment of its destiny. A kind of millennium, in the form of the 'earthly' rule of the saints of God and the victory of their values over other negative ones, will be inaugurated, if the prayer for the full implementation of the kingdom comes to pass.

The prayer itself, in the process vision of the world, supports the divine influence in some way. The kingdom is hardly that of a king in the sense known at the time of Jesus; rather, it can only represent a constitutional monarchy effective through its attractive qualities, not by any coercive force. Prayer for the success of the allurement of the divine towards universal pleasure is a hope and a renewal of self-commitment to this aim. Perhaps the fact of the prayer itself is a signal that the lure of God is being taken seriously by items of the cosmic process, that it is being incarnated in the lives of people.

From the creaturely perspective this petition for the coming of the kingdom amounts therefore to an assertion of trust that the lure will remain strong, will not weaken, nor change into a different type of lure of a less than good variety. The critic of process thought might well think that this latter prospect of divine degeneration away from the absolutely good arises from the heavy emphasis on divine immanence and 'real relations' with the process; God experiences what the process experiences in a real way, and therefore must be vulnerable to change and suffering and temptation just as we are. The critic might then go on to conclude (against what process theologians themselves want to say) that this leaves open the potential for divine collusion with what we now would call evil, and for evil actually taking over as the allurement. Rather than evil being permitted as a minor discord within the whole symphony, what we now call good would foster a great carnival of bacchanalia, chaos, and corruption, to be enjoyed in the cosmic divine experience.

A reader of history might legitimately conclude that this could be the way events work out; the flashes of genuine goodness are there to fuel the main fire of corruption and wickedness, to deceive us in deepest consequence. This world process could be a massive joke by a cruel deity deriving vast pleasure from leading people to trust goodness and hope for it, only to be let down in the end into despair. Whether we could know this or not is a difficult question, since such a deity would inherently oppose genuine revelation, disclosure of the truth about his kingdom of deceit and cruelty. Simply examining the face of the historical record, or the history of the process, could lead an intelligent inquirer to such a pessimistic conclusion, rather than to atheism.

This possible scenario leads us to bring the test of worship to the God of process theology. Can, or should, adoration be offered to a superior energy that *may possibly* become degraded by the world process of which he is an integral aspect? The God of process theology is not, it seems, secure from temptation and may forfeit the moral claim upon us. Indeed this immanent deity may have enjoyed some of the evil experiences of the world process, forfeiting the traditional attribute of absolute moral purity. Such moments of enjoyment would not make any difference to the process deity, who like us could incorporate them into his life system and move on in time from them, perhaps repenting of them and learning from them, as we do. Is such a deity to be worshipped and adored, to be called 'king' and 'holy'? Should we give our total adoration and obedience to a deity who is fallible, perhaps morally and rationally, this pragmatic deity who muddles along with us as best he can?

At this point the process theologian deploys the doctrine of divine 'dipolarity' to defend God's constancy. There are twin 'poles' in God's being. Deity is indeed integral to the world process and experiences all its events directly, being affected by them and seeking to draw them in its direction. God, according to Charles Hartshorne for example, has an absolute pole and a relative pole, the former constituting the more active and the latter the more passive modes of divine being.[40] The obvious analogy again seems to be that of mind and body, the mind controlling the body while being constituted by it and experiencing everything felt through it. Mind can be said to exist as mind, as thinking and planning, as abstract. Mind can also be said to be dependent on brain cells, kinetic energy, pulses of electricity, and even to be constituted by these physical occurrences although not reducible to them; mind can also think about them.

The process God exists through his body, the world, and the world exists entirely in God. God is the source of the life of the process, sharing in its experiences yet simultaneously guiding these. The mental, intentional aspect constitutes the necessary pole of the divine being. The analogy is terminated at this point, however, ruling out any possibility of the divine becoming deranged or losing its identity. This seems to be a secret smuggling back into the system of what process theology wished originally to eject, divine transcendence which is protected from 'real relations' with the cosmos. However inconsistent the system may be at this point, the absolute pole of deity (or 'abstract essence')[41] may be the one to which worship is confidently addressed as the faithfully constant God. Christian theology must guarantee such a deity if it is to fit the needs of worship, and process theology, while failing at the point where it most loudly claims to succeed, does seem to provide for a deity who will not mutate into something less than adorable, to whom we can address the prayer 'your kingdom come' without the nagging worry about the dubious character that kingdom might assume, given time. Time changes things and people and their characters; according to process theology nothing escapes time, even God.

Process theology prays for a temporal kingdom, since none other can exist according to its tenets; indeed, the notion of an 'end' to time is impossible for that family of interpretation. The coming of the kingdom will inaugurate ever more intense pleasure for the world and its divine aspect; the process will flourish forever, somehow having left behind the negative dimensions of life. The lure of God will be fulfilled in the wills of creatures at every level of being, and so there will be a coincidence of being and will between the lower and higher aspects of reality. The divine will reign by virtue of the complete correspondence between the experiences of the allured (creatures) and the lure (God), and in this way the non-divine will share in the reign of God. Prayer to God by those who have become utterly plastic to the will of God must take the form of praise and joy. But we notice that this picture is not one of covenant, the divine and human in partnership; it is rather one of inclusion. Everything is in God ('panentheism'), and the climax of the process results in the utter transparency of the finite to the infinite. Can the climax of the process avoid the collapsing of the finite into the infinite and preserve the former in relationship to the latter? Such is the problem of the process vision of the world, and of any immanentist metaphysics.

In any event, the coming of the kingdom will mean the victory of God only in the sense that finite spirits have made their free choices at the persuasion of the infinite, and the anti-divine dynamic has been transformed into faithful obedience. The acts of obedience to the lure of the divine persuasion are acts of concrete personalities who are *creating themselves* in the image of the invisible persuader. Such persons, conformed to the mind of Christ in their sacrificial mode of life, reaching out in real relationship to others, attain unity with the lure of God and are at one with the spirit of the universe. But such people die out of the stream of temporality, and since there is no other realm of existence than this temporal one, any after-life of union with God can only exist in the divine memory. The existence of the human person falls from the temporal process, and its only possible mode of continuation is as a fragment of the divine memory and experience. Applying the test of worship and praise at this point, vital to Christian eschatology, the notion of a memory in the divine mind worshipping the divine self, seems somewhat artificial and narcissistic. The finite self has nowhere else to exist, no other realm of being outside of this historical process. Therefore selves of the past cannot praise God other than in the imaginative speculation of the deity.

The eschatology of process theology thus seems hard to square with the biblical hope of transformed existence in the kingdom of God, issuing in 'wonder, love and praise' from the created order to the divine. Can the divine memory-bank project such praise and adoration to itself on the basis of past acts of worship by those now dead? This would amount to something like narcissistic self-worship of God by God. In other words the criterion of worship requires a creaturely order of being to be sustained past death, if it is to be an interpretation of the distinctively Christian hope. Buddhist anthropology may as easily be encompassed in this process eschatology, since the systems which compose the human being, including those of experience, relocate at the individual's death into new configurations, the enduring 'self' being an illusion. Ultimately, all experiences and systems are taken into the one great system, the single process.[42]

The process eschatology can claim to produce an interpretation of the millennium, that is, a period of history when those who have conformed to the mind of Christ will 'reign with Christ a thousand years'. A very literalist reading of this problematic text in the book of Revelation (Rev 20:4) has led many Christians, especially in the USA, to espouse the 'premillennialist' view of the 'second coming of Christ', that is portraying this millennium as predating the second coming. Most commentators regard this historical interpretation as a category mistake, in that the Book of Revelation comprises many symbolic ways of giving its message, rather than a linear chronology of literal events. What is interesting to notice here is that the ultra-conservative literalist interpretation of the 'millennium' ends up not far from the process view, with a stretch of temporal history in which Christ's will is at one with that of his people totally; this would be 'the kingdom' in full implementation. What the process view does not envisage is the element of battle between God and forces hostile to God's rule, although it does envisage the divine efforts to overcome the inertia of the human will and its failure to respond to the lure of deity.

7. *Transformation through the Trinity*

Process re-interpretation of the classical Christian theology of the rule of God and its final impact on world history offers the great gain of reinforcing the insight that God works through the freedom of created wills, not by brute force. The kingdom of God for which we pray will indeed not be one of cowering subjects under a despotic tyrant, but one of unity of spirit. As has been suggested, the process could culminate in something analogous to the Pauline metaphor of the Body of Christ, a picture of total mutuality suffused by the grace of God. This portrayal by the process theologians even, it may be said, has a sort of trinitarian language in a di-polarity of the Father and Christ, the latter being the life holding together the church which relates to the former: so the immanent pole relates to the transcendent.

Prayer by the church is rooted in Christ and aided by the Spirit, constantly oriented on God and the fulfilment of his reign. A new transformed order of being, stemming from this one but saved from the distortions and wrongs of human history, is envisaged in this hope and prayer. The strong implication of the prayer 'your kingdom come' is that the final salvation of history must come from *outside of its own process*, while to be salvation of history and humanity, it must be *internal to it*. Classical theology seeks to express this salvation 'from outside and inside' through the doctrine of the Trinity; the incarnation of the Son and the giving of the Spirit brings a renewed creation into communion with the Father. Process theology seeks a closer integration between nondivine reality and the pole of deity which is immanent in the world ('inside'); at the same time it tries to preserve God from negative change by way of the other divine pole, that of absoluteness and 'necessary being'. But it is clear that the process deity cannot exist without nondivine being. By contrast, the God envisaged in traditional Christian theology is free, and confers being on others from pure generosity; he retains freedom from being affected by the events and experiences of the world process, unless such vulnerability is *chosen*, as indeed it was in the incarnation of the Word.

The trinitarian doctrine grew out of the sense of praise for divine involvement in human suffering and redemption. God has reached into the human predicament in a costly identification, which evokes a depth of responsive worship going beyond that owed to a distant creator. The Christian gospel declares the overwhelming divine love, its constant presence in the world and invitation to participation. It also declares the majesty of God and the assured victory of his purposes. 'Thy kingdom come' is a prayer containing confidence in the fulfilment of divine rule through the omnipotence of love.

The climax of this kingdom will also mean a transformation of humanity into perfectly appreciative worshippers of God. The prayer of this petition looks forward to a new mode of being in which God the Father becomes so transparently glorious as to be wholly fascinating, absorbing, and joyful. The process view may be right to bring back the theme of joy to a central position in the purposes of God, with its keynotes of 'pleasure' and 'satisfaction'. But the experience of the redeemed creation and of God should not be confused as identical; God is the reason for the joy of creation, rather than an agent experiencing the common joy of the process.

When the church prays for the coming of the kingdom, she prays to the God of Jesus who conquers through the cross and resurrection, not through raw power exercised externally leaving a resentful cowed victim. The kingdom of God involves tension and challenge, but it remains primarily God's kingdom, with his people sharing in the implementation of the power mediated through crucifixion. Prayer acknowledges the self-giving God of Jesus as the one who reigns, and defines what true power is. The worship of the church is therefore priestly and sacrificial, and at the same time royal and powerful.

If there is any 'system' at the heart of prayer, it is that of self-giving into the hands of the God of Jesus. It is thus the reverse of a commercial system by which investment of time and money would reap dividends from the stock exchange of the kingdom of God. The kingdom is that of the Son who loves to do the will of the Father, even though it led to Gethsemane, and the prayer 'Thy will be done'; such a prayer points beyond our human possibilities to open up the final horizon of meaning.

Notes to Chapter 4

[1] Wolfhart Pannenberg, *Jesus—God and Man*, trans. L. Wilkins and D. Priebe (SCM Press, London, 1968), p. 229.

[2] The phrase used by Richard T. France in his *Divine Government* (SPCK, London,1990), p. 76.

[3] Charles Elliott, *Praying the Kingdom* (Darton, Longman, and Todd, London, 1985), p. 64.

[4] Hymn: 'Praise to the holiest in the height'.

[5] 'The word "Father", then, concentrates our attention on the doubly revolutionary message and mission of Jesus. It is the Exodus message, the message that tyrants and oppressors rightly fear.' N. T. Wright, *The Lord and His Prayer* (Triangle, London, 1966), p.19.

[6] Elliott, *Praying the Kingdom*, pp. 53-74.

[7] Wolfhart Pannenberg, *Systematic Theology*, vol. 1, trans. G. W. Bromiley (T & T Clark, Edinburgh, 1991), p. 383.

[8] John V. Taylor, *The Christlike God* (SCM Press, London, 1992), pp. 237-41.

[9] An example of this approach is Frank Lake, *Clinical Theology* (Darton, Longman, and Todd, London, 1966).

[10] In this regard the use of 'the discipline', 'a scourge of knotted cords for use as an instrument of penance', (see entry in the *Oxford Dictionary of the Christian Church*), as a spiritual aid to holiness, does seem questionable. St. John of the Cross instructs the prioress of Cordoba, for example, 'Do not give leave to all the nuns to take the discipline thrice weekly, in compensation for this or any other penance, without following the usual routine.' [*The Works of St John of the Cross*, trans. and ed. E. A. Peers, vol. 3 (Burns, Oates, and Washbourne, London, 1935), p. 282.] 'The discipline' was part of the spirituality of the Oxford Movement; for a time Gladstone, an Anglo-Catholic, used to scourge himself.

[11] Schleiermacher, *The Christian Faith*, pp. 435-36.

[12] Peter Berger, *A Rumour of Angels*, p. 76, makes the point that the phenomenon of play is hard to account for on purely naturalistic grounds.

[13] A point emphasised by Hardy and Ford in *Jubilate*, p. 96.

[14] E.g., Prov 8:22-31; 30:18-19, 24-31; Job 39:5-8; Ps 104:24-26.

[15] E.g., Prov 16:1-11; Jonah 4.

[16] See Jan Lochman, *The Faith We Confess* (T & T Clark, Edinburgh, 1984), pp. 202ff

[17] See above, pp. 39-42.

[18] Pannenberg, *Jesus—God and Man*, pp. 66.

[19] P. T. Forsyth, *The Justification of God* (Duckworth, London, 1916), p. 216.

[20] The title of John V. Taylor's book, which elaborates this theme: *The Go-Between God. The Holy Spirit and the Christian Mission* (SCM Press, London, 1972).

[21]Notably Hans Urs von Balthasar, *The Theology of Karl Barth*, trans. J. Drury (Holt, Rinehart, and Winston, New York, 1971), pp. 198-200.

[22]Stephen Neill, 'The Ecumenical Dimension in Theology', in F. G. Healey (ed.) *Preface to Christian Studies* (Lutterworth Press, London, 1971), p. 294.

[23]See pp. 61-68.

[24]Barth, *Church Dogmatics*, IV/1, p. 737.

[25]Ibid., p. 738.

[26]Michael Ramsey, *God, Christ and the World* (SCM Press, London, 1969), p. 56.

[27]Martin Buber, *Moses* (East and West Library, London, 1946), p. 52.

[28]Ibid.

[29]Ramsey, *Christ and the World*, pp. 56-57.

[30]Charles Villa-Vicenzio, *On Reading Karl Barth in South Africa* (Eerdmans, Grand Rapids, 1988), p. 22.

[31]By Graham Kendrick.

[32]Dorothy Sayers, *The Mind of the Maker* (Methuen, London, 1941), ch. 3.

[33]William Temple, *Nature, Man, and God* (Macmillan, London, 1935), p. 441.

[34]Ibid.

[35]Sayers, *The Mind of the Maker*, pp. 106-7.

[36]Temple, *Nature, Man, and God*, p. 442.

[37]See Lewis S. Ford, *The Lure of God. A Biblical Background for Process Theism* (Fortress Press, Philadelphia, 1978), pp. 15-28.

[38]E.g., A. N. Whitehead, *Process and Reality. An Exercise in Cosmology* (Macmillan, New York, 1929, repr. 1967), pp. 323-26; Charles Hartshorne, *Creative Synthesis and Philosophic Method* (SCM Press, London, 1970), pp. 238-43; John Cobb, *A Christian Natural Theology* (Lutterworth Press, London, 1966).

[39]See, e.g., Whitehead, *Process and Reality*, pp. 373-75, 530-33.

[40]Charles Hartshorne, *The Divine Relativity. A Social Conception of God* (Yale University Press, New Haven, 1948, repr. 1976), pp. 80-88; *A Natural Theology for our Time* (Open Court, La Salle, Illinois, 1967, repr. 1973), pp. 27f, 44f.

[41]This corresponds to Whitehead's 'primordial nature' of God, which is invulnerable to the world process: *Process and Reality*, p. 134.

[42]An alternative may be for process theology to adopt a view of the process as endless, interpreting biblical eschatology with some difficulty and producing an eternal dualism of finite and infinite. This could be seen as the logical outcome of the process view, remarkably akin to Plato's *Timaeus* in which the divine workman fashions pre-existent material into the world. In such an ontology, the prayer for the coming of the kingdom becomes a prayer for the moral improvement of the race.

5

'Your will be done on earth as in heaven'

1. The sovereignty and vulnerability of the divine will

The kingdom of God was ushered in by the crucified Lord whose rule inverts the power structures of the world order. He says: 'Whoever wishes to be first among you must be your slave; just as the Son of man came not to be served but to serve, and to give his life a ransom for many' (Matt 20:27-28). God chooses to work his will through the free wills of his created people, regenerating their selfish wills through the cross and resurrection. Divine choice settles this way of divine working, rather than necessity. As we saw in the previous chapter, God chooses to be conditioned by the wills of his created people while at the same time conquering these wills through the power of costly sacrificial love. Christian prayer arises from this spirit of self-giving, as a response to the self-offering of God in Christ and a sharing in it.

To pray that the Lord of the universe will do his will seems even more paradoxical than the previous petition for the rule of God to be implemented. At the heart of the paradox is the issue of divine purpose and of the character of the God who is revealed most fully in the cross and resurrection of Jesus. God is love, and his will is to be accomplished on earth, as in heaven, through the free and joyful hearts of his people. Hardy and Ford state the principle well in saying that God respects his creation partner utterly.[1] The creation cannot be rudely forced, but brought to acknowledge the sheer goodness and love of God. In this way creation is given the freedom to create itself, in and with the will of the creator.

As we have explored the view of modern 'process theology',[2] we have seen that it stresses this point to the extent that the divine will itself is made totally vulnerable to the pleasures of the world's experiences. This does not seem to fit with the sense of the Lord's Prayer as a whole, which points to the majestic stability of this will rooted in the character of God that will remain faithful and just for ever. Process theologians may argue to the contrary that precisely asking for the divine will to be done ('your will be done') indicates that this will is actualized through the wills of the worshipping community of faith, and not otherwise; so the will of God is simply the 'lure' of God, the divine wooing of creation to follow his way. The power of God's will thus consists in its appeal alone.

This argument flows from an insight into the person and work of Christ, the revelation that powerlessness discloses divine purpose and character, as opposed to the power that is 'of this world'. Process theology concludes, however, that the prayer 'your will be done' is not just a petition, but a form of moral support to the divine energy that is powerless over the finite order. The God of process thought has a will, the will to lure the world towards the divine way, but has no power to enforce that will. This God can only hope that the finite world will conform to his lure and succumb to his persuasion.

Prayer to this God is to the God who has no help to help himself, apart from a strong desire and hope that the finite world will eventually see sense and behave. This God is like the father of the prodigal son, waiting and hoping for the return of the one who foolishly wanders away, experimenting with what is dangerous and harmful. For those who are co-operating with the divine will, or lure, creation is a joint enterprise; God implements his will only through the will and activity of his faithful people. Prayer from the faithful for the implementation of the divine lure or will amounts to reaffirmation of the joint project of history, the project conducted together by God and the world at every level of its existence, from human consciousness to the smallest microbe.

Spirituality rooted in this understanding of God's will has the quality of shared endeavour to bring the world to its true destiny, a commitment shared together by the higher and lower aspects of reality, divine and non-divine. In such an understanding it really matters whether the believers pray and act for the will of God, for the very cause of the divine will depends on our efforts and our attitude of support. Indeed the divine somehow experiences directly the experience of the creation, sharing therefore the experience of prayer to strengthen the divine will. It is as if the goodness of the world even keeps the divine will steady and focused on the good. According to process thought, God is certainly maintained in his desire for the good by the 'absolute' (or 'necessary') pole of his being, but this is integrated into a 'contingent' pole which is vulnerable to the moral decline of the world. It seems that the divine will therefore needs to be empowered by the supportive action of those faithful to his aims.

In this process vision, God forms a collective mentality or mindset with the reinforcing worshipping community. As has been noted above,[3] the possibility exists that the noble divine and human project of history will fail, dragging deity down to the chaos of evil—or what we now call evil. The divine will may prove inadequate to cope with the negative reaction against it of the world process. The freedom of creation is therefore totally respected, and the will of God, or the desire of God, to promote maximum pleasure in the world is the only divine force. This means, however, that the process deity may lack freedom, being tied in to the world project and even potentially being its victim. This problem was what stimulated Wolfhart Pannenberg to develop his doctrine of the free God of the open future, a future not in any way controlled by the past history of the universe.[4]

More traditional Christian theology and spirituality differs from process thought in affirming the stability and freedom of the divine will. But it can endorse the sense of collective effort towards implementing the divine will and kingdom through the faithful obedience of the church. The way of the cross means precisely that, and the prayer for the divine will to be done must relate to the personal commitment of the worshipper concretely, rather than amounting to a pious wish. Also shared with process thought is the sense that prayer 'counts' for God, though not quite in the sense that it matters for the process God, whose very identity is supported and preserved by whether people are going with his lure and will.

Prayer for the doing of the divine will can fit well into the process system in that the divine will genuinely needs the support of the creaturely will. Tension then cannot exist between the divine and the human since both are pushing the same moral stone up the hill of history, with the same means, the resolution of moral effort to produce maximum joy in cosmic experience. Traditional Christian faith, however, maintains the tension, and so the paradox between the sovereignty and vulnerability of God's will expressed in the prayer 'your will be done'. The phrase 'on earth as in heaven' points to a distinction between a divine and a created sphere, co-ordinated yet different. Oscar Cullmann, in his recent book on prayer, says the phrase is 'probably to be understood more in terms of a parallel: what already exists in heaven is to be realized and prayed for on earth'.[5] God is God both with, and yet distinct from, the created order. The salvation of God exists and is to be realized on earth as it is in heaven; there is a security about this fact of the already existing divine will. While it could correspond to the 'necessary' pole of divine existence in process thought, it matches better the sense of divine majesty and security felt in traditional Christian spirituality.

The distinction between the earthly and heavenly will of God, and the terrible tension this can set up, is seen in the agonized prayer of Jesus prior to his death in the garden of Gethsemane. As Matthew tells the story, Jesus prays that the cup of suffering be taken from him, 'nevertheless, your will be done' (Matt 26:42), echoing the precise petition of the Lord's Prayer. The will of Jesus is to follow his Father's will, but it seems impossibly difficult in the face of the human historical conditions of violence and distrust. The kingdoms of God and 'this world' collide in Jesus' heart in Gethsemane. Jesus' prayer in Gethsemane reveals an honest human turning to God for help in desperate danger, far from a fatalist understanding of the divine will. There is a sense of co-operation with the divine plan, yet this does not exclude a faith that the desire for personal salvation can be brought before God. The prayer of Jesus is a struggle of the utmost honesty and urgency, certainly no experience of calm unruffled serenity, and it embraces the whole of his being. This prayer commits Jesus to the purpose and future of God; it is a life act. Christian prayer is part of the whole act of life in the world, a life oriented to the divine will.

The insights of the modern movement of thought which is often called 'existentialist' come into play here. Faith, for Sˆren Kierkegaard and his successors in this tradition, concerns what really matters in our existing; it entails total commitment, in which nothing can be held back from the divine imperative. There can be no cool rational reflection on the merits of faith; it is a matter of obedience to the divine summons, and this can be a calling to real sacrifice. When we pray for the will of God to be done, this takes our life forward into the future of God, something we cannot chart safely but must launch out into with the venture of faith.

Such a venture issues from the free will of the worshipper as, in face of the tension between heaven and earth, it seeks to be conformed to the mind of Christ. Kierkegaard provides a salutary caution against allowing prayer to become a ritual in the pejorative sense, a going through the motions out of cultural loyalty or habit or out of a need for costless reassurance. Jesus' prayer in Gethsemane makes the point sharply that what is involved is radical commitment. This message is reinforced when Christians recall that they pray 'in the name of Jesus', not merely obeying a historical command but sharing the very character of the life of Jesus and his self-giving to his Father.[6]

The petition of Gethsemane and in the Lord's prayer implies a divine will to which the human will needs to conform itself, but which can be disobeyed. The divine will is knowable in general terms and can be discerned always in the orientation to 'loving mercy, justice, and walking humbly with God' (Mic 6:8), the moral and spiritual ethos of faith. Jesus set his face steadfastly[7] to fulfil his calling to go to Jerusalem, a vocation he was clear had been given to him by his heavenly Father. Jesus wanted to conform his life and being to the divine will, and his Gethsemane prayer was the point of agonizing conflict between human well-being, freedom from pain and evil, and trust in the divine will. The cross of Calvary brings this conflict to its plain revelation, never without the Easter rising through the sacrifice of pain.

John's Gospel traces this conflict of will within a communion of wills in the life of Jesus by recalling the readiness of Abraham to sacrifice Isaac at the calling of God. Much later Kierkegaard picked this up when he told the story of Abraham and his disturbing act of faith.[8] The statement that 'God so loved the world that he gave his only son' (John 3:16) echoes the terrible story in Genesis of the patriarchal Abraham obeying the divine call to give up his precious, miraculously born, son Isaac. According to the Greek Orthodox theologian Agourides, the word 'only begotten' in the Johannine writings includes the sense 'he who is beloved in a unique manner'.[9] The Father suffers the loss of the son, while the son suffers the human process of pain and death in communion with the Father,[10] in the one act of divine and human self-giving for the human race.

Keeping to the divine will and calling leads to the terrible injustice of the trial and execution of Jesus. The will of God cuts into history, and into the inner will of humanity, in this event. 'Your will be done' bears the closest possible relationship to Calvary and Gethsemane. Just as the petition for the coming of the kingdom is not a plea for some external arrival of divine rule without an inner transformation of the heart,[11] so it is for this petition. The will sought is the will of this particular God, the God and Father of Jesus Christ.

The will of the Father is revealed and communicated through Jesus, a will suffused with love and strength, not subject to change yet infinitely subtle in achieving its ends through transformed personalities. In this sense both the sovereignty and vulnerability of this will must be affirmed. 'Your will be done' can then never be a quick and easy prayer, an alternative route around the rocks and deserts of human experience. The divine and human interweaving of purpose in the will of Jesus must be seen as continuing in the life of the faithful, the worshipping church. Prayer for the doing of this established will includes the commitment to invest ourselves in the implementation of this will and purpose. The plain structure of prayer is shown clearly here to be that of sacrifice in trustfully entering the will of God. This will is not unknown nor capricious: it is utterly manifest by Good Friday and Easter.

2. *Praying in the electing will of God*

The difficult doctrine of election concerns precisely the will of God in relation to humanity. The practical experience of praying the petition of the Lord's prayer, 'your will be done', may offer some help in understanding both the communion and conflict of the human and divine will, and so enable us to explore the mystery of election. Prayer to God presupposes a common field of moral purpose between human beings and God, as well as a sense of the radical otherness of God. This is because the otherness of God is a magnification of holiness and goodness, an extension of what we know to be good in our fragmented way. The petition for the implementation of the divine will takes the worshipper into the heart of God and his purposes, and since this petition is set forth by Jesus, the Christian believer feels encouraged to enter into this heart, which is love. The 'lamb in the midst of the throne' is also the life in which the worshipping community shares.

The will of God, as Barth so clearly saw,[12] and before him F. D. Maurice in the nineteenth century,[13] must be read through the lens of the life of Jesus. The notion that God wills anything un-Christlike or evil, such as for instance creating a mass of humanity for the very purpose of destroying them ultimately, cannot survive this test. Such a view would be to divorce the revelation of Jesus from God the Father. Absolute confidence can be reposed in God by those praying to him and worshipping him, since his character and will have been so definitely disclosed.

Election by God means that the choice of God is for humanity, and that God has bound himself to the cause of his creatures from the very beginnings of creation. Divine will and the incarnation of the divine word coalesce in the New Testament, at the start of such texts as John's Gospel, Hebrews, and Ephesians. Already in the Old Testament we hear God saying: 'I have no pleasure in the death of the wicked, but that the wicked turn from their ways and live' (Ezek 33:11)[14]; such is the divine desire and choice. It has been enacted decisively from inside the human heart and life by Jesus, in whose name we pray and petition for the further realization of this will.

There is no doubt about the fulfilment of this will and choice, for God cannot fail to bring about his purposes, however improbable such a statement may feel in our world. Jesus has pioneered and perfected our faith[15] in God and in doing the will of the Father, with the goal of saving human beings for communion with God. Creation was not conceived of without this deep will and choice, a choice that in the wisdom of God was always going to be a terrible one in terms of divine cost. According to John, the creative word spoken in the Genesis account of creation was in the very beginning with God, and without this word nothing was made that was made. The oversight of the divine Word and Wisdom was present throughout creation, as if a guardian figure, and the election of the world in Christ expresses the divine commitment to bringing this project to fruition.

'Your will be done' is therefore a petition flowing from the electing will of God in Christ; it has a wide angle and a narrow focus, just as the incarnation of Jesus made the creative word 'concrete' in a historical and temporal event. The particular desire of the worshipper is taken up into the whole desire of God for the world.[16] This desire of God has been fixed by his own act and decision, once and for all, but the divine will constantly seeks particular expression and fulfilment through the worship, by lips and in lives, of creation. This petition amounts almost to praying with God, and in God, for the fulfilment of his creative activity. It casts light on the passages in Ephesians and Colossians which link the pre-existent Christ, and his sacrificial ministry, with both creation and the church.[17] The cosmic Christ is at the centre of creation and the church, and has achieved atoning reconciliation by a costly act of *human* will which upholds the *divine* will for holiness and love. As with the whole tenor of the Lord's Prayer, this petition runs along the grain of God's plan and character, along the grain of divine election.

All who pray 'your will be done' identify themselves with the costly electing will of God as revealed and taught in the person of Jesus. Petitionary prayer when considered carefully should seek to do precisely this, to direct the desire of faith and love along the line desired by God, the line of divine choice or election. There should be a fit between heaven and earth, a fit which the Christian gospel believes happened perfectly in the person of Jesus of Nazareth. The church has the ministry of continuing this self-opening of the human will to the divine will, and accepting the revealed cost of this project of bringing creation into full communion with God. With the qualification that the divine will is not subject to possible alteration, this vision may accord with that of the process view we have been exploring.

The free God, the heavenly Father, created human freedom. The divine will created human will. Therefore, ideally, it is not necessary that there should be a *conflict* between them, despite the fruitfulness of *tensions*[18] and the potential for conflict. So a deliberate self-orientation to the divine will by the worshipping community fulfils rather than diminishes human freedom, providing a model of what God intended; in the biblical image, it is a 'first fruit'. This fulfilment, when extended into the culmination of history and divine purposes, is both the act of God and the activity of his obedient people, the free will of God and of his disciples. In praying 'Your will be done', we share the very vision of God's creative and re-creative purpose: the heavenly Father has entrusted creation, including our springs of action and motivation, to us: we acknowledge that and responsively offer ourselves for his kingdom.

3. The will and the person: The challenge of Nietzsche

The request for God's will to be done reinforces the personal character of the Christian God as the heavenly Father who is passionately interested in human history and in fostering disciples who share in his desires which are securely willed 'in heaven'. 'Our Father in heaven' is not a metaphor for inexorable fate or law that will happen anyway, but one who has chosen this creative and redemptive path and who draws his people into it. Here lies the priestly ministry of prayer, joining openness to the Father with openness to all in the world, and at times agonizing where the reign of God clashes with earthly power claims.

The Lord's Prayer sets out a principle of praying by placing petitions for the coming of the kingdom and the implementation of the divine will early on; this puts individual petitions (for bread, forgiveness, deliverance from evil) in the right context. Theologically it suggests an embracing of the divine will by the human, an identification, a kind of act of solidarity and absolute trust. The petition 'your will be done' does not suggest the abolition of the human will or its absorption into the divine. It is the self-giving of the lesser into the greater and the purification of the human by the divine. An act of will is needed by the worshipper to make the mutual identification with the choice and will of the heavenly Father, which is to actualize divine election.

The heavenly Father and his will 'in heaven' indicates a transcendent and yet somehow personal deity who chooses freely, by his sovereign decision, to create free wills. So he chooses to limit his own will in order to produce the richer work of art in creation. The prayer urging us to identify ourselves with the divine will can be seen as echoing the divine act of creation and its decision to condescend in co-operation with created wills. This co-operation seems radical; God decrees that he will act freely in such a way that the prayers and activities of humans play a part in the divine action. God works his free will out through the will and action of humanity, and creation generally. God freely limits himself to be affected by human will, desire, and action; yet the human will is most fulfilled when identified with the divine. Self-limitation by God does not remove the will of God, but does affect *the way that this is implemented* by somehow integrating human influence. In this sense the will of God is vulnerable, while it remains unshaken and active.[19]

'Your will be done', a simple sounding and familiar phrase, encapsulates just this mysterious tension within a communion of desire and purpose shared between two parties. Trinitarian theology has used the technical language of 'perichoresis' to describe the relationship of the Father and Son in the divine being; this indicates a mutual inter-penetration and mutual indwelling of the divine Persons. There is a close correspondence to this idea in the relationship between the worshipper and God in a total solidarity of desire and choice, with the crucial difference that the Father and Son are one in the divine being, whereas human worshippers in harmony with God are created from the divine will.

Christian worship, or appreciation, of God needs to reaffirm this commonality of interest, this shared aim for God's desire to 'come true' as the best and only outcome of the world order. God created the world with a dynamic to continue his creation not in the sense that the world is an emanation of divine being spread into a multiplicity of shapes and sizes, but in the sense that the will of the creator reigns and 'should' come about if things 'are working' properly. This is how things 'ought' to be in creation; the fact that the will of the benign creator is not obeyed and that things are not as they 'should' be is a problem dealt with by the theological tradition in terms of fall from what 'ought to be'. 'Your will be done' flows from the tension of the 'is' and the 'ought'; history is flouting the reign of God and when we know things should and could be otherwise, we commit ourselves to God's will—and should realize that this will mean re-baptisms of pain and conflict.

Will is a category attributed to a person; mere substances and processes do not freely choose. This is the precise point stressed by the family of philosophy called 'existentialist'; it urges that a person must resist becoming a mere thing or a cog in a process by making decisions which are authentic for that person. Failing to be bold enough to assert our choice is to subordinate ourselves to the social convention of the day, and in effect to depersonalize ourselves. The freedom of the will is crucial to personhood. The church pleads for the free divine will to be realized, and so for personal respect to override power and technique.

The person is not the product of a process but a creative centre of activity and decision, surely an aspect of the image of God in humanity. But it is doubtful whether this existential concentration on the free will alone as the defining element in a human being is sufficient for Christian theology. One reason for this doubt is the experience of worship and prayer. The divine will is not quixotic or capricious but is the will of the holy one of Israel, 'our Father in heaven'; in other words, the will of God is not experienced on its own, but as resting in the divine person with its own *character*. Its freedom is the freedom of this God and of none other. It is only because this is certain that God is worshipped unconditionally: there is no chance then that the will of God will change to something dishonourable, rooted as it is in the divine character.

Likewise, human will issues from a human being, and human beings exist in a context not in a vacuum, and not as autonomous units disconnected from others. Prayer for the implementation of the divine will preserves the will of the worshipper while freely offering it back to God in total trust. To the quintessential philosopher of the will, Friedrich Nietzsche, this is grovelling weakness and ignoble self-enslavement.[20] It is a failure to take oneself seriously, a kind of burial of one's talents in the ground rather than investing them into real life with confidence and boldness. For Nietzsche, the church invites humans to betray their own freedom and will. For Christians, baptism into the death of Christ (Rom 6:3-4), freely dying to live, brings true freedom, renewal of the will, and relationships that are integral to personhood.

Nietzsche should nevertheless be heard by the church on the subject of the human will, since the church is not a safe haven from the adventure of exercising freedom in the world. Christian life and piety is no escape from the divine will and its conflict with the world's resistance and sin. 'Your will be done' is no fatalistic mantra, nor an excuse for inaction or resigning oneself to being part of an inexorable process. The use of this prayer in Gethsemane illustrates that the divine will requires costly discipleship and courage. Self-offering is not to an impersonal process, beyond the personal, as in the Buddhist view of ultimacy.

Nietzsche's protest at self-enslavement, whether from secular social convention or religious self-denigration, teaches a kind of construction of the self by the self,[21] or rather by the will. The self is created by act of will. Following Nietzsche, significant twentieth-century thinkers assert the need for individuals to cut free from the grip of tradition and construct their own selves, whether or not the result be considered crazy or diseased according to the canons of convention.[22] Perhaps Nietzsche's puzzling later doctrine of the 'eternal recurrence' of the individual's life develops logically from his exaltation of the will. In his thought, life seems to be a kind of 'container' for willed experiences, and so the experiences of this life do not pass out of existence but overcome history as life repeats itself. The individual creates himself eternally, so that what has been willed is eternally real and cannot come to an end. But we are bound to ask whether such a doctrine leaves us with a person or with a set of experiences and decisions which need something to hold them together. This important question also touches on Buddhist ideas of what constitutes a person. But the question also usefully points to the need to root divine will in divine character or nature. An act of will, to be more than a spasm of nervous reaction, requires some rational direction and purpose behind it.

The exercise of the will springs from purposive personal being. The notion of a rootless will seems difficult in itself, and even more unlikely when applied to God. The divine freedom to will in sovereignty and majesty can be no unstable freedom to will; the Lord's prayer has already oriented itself around the heavenly Father who is holy.

4. God's will and fate:
The challenge of Spinoza

Philosophers have found the category of the personal difficult to attribute to God and have found it easier to interpret personal language as a vivid analogy. Baruch Spinoza (1632–1677), for example, was sure that personalistic language about God acting in history was simply a way of talking which the Hebrew people had developed to express what happens in life. God-talk is a way of talking about nature, what simply occurs, whether it is thinking or making money.

> I must premise . . . that the Jews never make any mention or account of secondary or particular causes, but in a spirit of religion, piety, and what is commonly called godliness, refer all things directly to the Deity. For instance, if they make money by a transaction, they say God gave it to them; if they desire anything, they say that God has disposed their heart towards it; if they think anything, they say God told them.[23]

Spinoza's view is that the biblical writers are merely using personalist language to express general causation in the universe, which in Spinoza's philosophy was an inescapable law amounting to a determinist system. 'Your will be done', on this analysis, refers not to any divine will of a personal kind, but to the unchanging law of nature set throughout the universe. Worshippers of God may utter such prayers, but they are forms of poetry and piety that refer to the causation in the cosmos already fixed for ever. Prayer, on this account of things, is purely therapeutic and non-relational in any sense.

Spinoza's God is not personal but rather the iron law of the universe. This, of course, cannot satisfy the Christian worshipper, but it should challenge us to ask what we mean by the sovereign majesty of God. God's will is stable and triumphant, not to be changed or moved; yet this is not a rigid system working itself out through the universe as a kind of inevitable fate. Against Nietzsche we must assert that will is not capricious but is grounded in nature. Against Spinoza we must affirm that God has a will and is not simply a nature working itself out. The one who prays the Lord's prayer asks that the will of the Father in heaven be done on earth as in heaven. This conflicts with the line of thought suggested by Spinoza, whose deity was the pattern of the cosmos of which we are all part and whose so-called 'will' is thus always unfolding second by second. If this were true, then worshippers would be merely worshipping themselves as part of the natural system, albeit a tiny part of the whole.

Capricious will and mechanical nature suggest two ends of a spectrum of view about God, and the category of the personal needs to embrace both the *will* and the *nature* that orients the will and purpose. In any Christian theology the freedom of God must be preserved; God must not be described as the victim of a system any more than as arbitrary and irrational in exercising his will. Here, the mystery of personhood alone supplies anything like an analogy for divine will and nature. Rational purposive will is exercised by a person who has the power to decide. The will of God proceeds from the heavenly Father who is holy and loving, whose nature is mysterious but certainly not less than personal.

The fact that a divine 'personal' nature underlies divine will is important for the Christian worshipper who is not simply submitting to the divine decree in a sense of reverential duty when praying 'your will be done'. God's will is not simply fate inexorably working itself out like some pre-arranged computer programme, demanding human submission. There is a majestic sovereignty about the will of the God of Jesus Christ, but it is a majesty defined by Jesus, who was therefore understood to have shared in the divine being and is rightly called Son of God.

The relationship presumed by the Lord's Prayer between God and creation is one of something like personal communion and mutual appreciation. If we just speak of 'the divine nature', then this has the connotation of an influence akin to the influence of the natural world, but at the higher level of mind, a pure mind abstracted from the context of decision making in life. Divine nature or divine being can be easily assumed to be such a spiritual substance, transcending the ebb and flow of the world. But this fits very uneasily with the Hebrew tradition of walking in communion with the God of Abraham, Isaac, and Jacob, a purposive being capable of responding to infinitely changing situations. When we pray 'your will be done', we are seeking the enactment of God's will, but we know that this is the will of the holy God, 'our Father in heaven', and so will always be reliable and good. This prayer is oriented to the God of Jesus, of Abraham and Isaac, the God who does know and care rather than a deity who is the logical necessity of Spinoza. Jesus tells the believers to pray 'our Father', the same Jesus who trusted a heavenly Father who even knew of the fall of a sparrow, and cared.

Is this invitation to pray compatible with the type of interpretation offered by Spinoza of the biblical texts? Is 'your will be done' really an acknowledgement of the fact of an inevitable system in which we are a tiny atomic part? I suggest that it is more natural to interpret these personalistic texts using personal analogies, rather than transposing them into impersonal ones. The interpretation of scripture and worship comes into a creative tension here for the community of faith: the experience of worshipping the living God must play a vital part in understanding texts and in translating them into the contemporary horizon.

Christians who pray for the doing of the divine will do not believe that they are in a mechanistic universe and merely setting their minds, by way of a liturgical formula, into the set pattern of things. Divine nature or the being of God does not act, somehow separably from divine personhood. An impersonal divine nature would certainly exert force or influence, but it would do so not just constantly but blindly. Nature and personal characteristics must be held together in considering human beings and God. A human being is never just an instance of a general 'human nature'; each human is unique and a person, an identity which endures through the changing processes of creaturely 'nature', which is nevertheless essential to personhood.

Jesus tells his followers to pray for the will of the Father to be done, and a hermeneutical choice needs to be made as to how to understand this. Should we regard this as picture language for a remorseless metaphysical system, akin to that developed by Spinoza? Or should we take it as a picture for 'non-realist' theism (see chapter 2)[24] which amounts to much the same in practice? Or does the language point to a relationship of trust and purpose with God who is in some sense 'personal'? The last option alone does justice to the religious experience of Christians which goes beyond that of human persons addressing a natural system or a cultural system of commitments. All the worshipper can say of the divine being or nature is that God 'is', in answer to the question 'what is God?' This God is revealed as a 'who', the self-naming and self-identifying God who invites worship of a free, rational, and personal kind.

The personhood of God does not arise from necessary nature or being, but from God's very self. God is not pure being, of a metaphysical kind, nor pure will, but the self-identifying and self-causing God. Form and freedom cohere, nature and will come together, in such a way that the self-constitution of the divine life can be reduced to neither. Even in this there is a parallel with human life, in that an individual person would hardly agree with the suggestion that his character and life had been determined by factors entirely outside his own self, that he had nothing to do with the formation of his character.

Decisions and moral actions taken in the past, stemming from genuinely free choices responsibly made, are vital, as we see it, in forming who we are. We have a nature, but we are more than nature, and we decide how to handle the nature which comprises us. When all is said and done, 'I am myself', however mysterious and unsatisfactory that may be. Similarly with God, God is God and is self-defining, self-constituting, not explicable in terms of any prior being or nature.[25] God *has* a will rather than *being* will. God has his own being rather than merely expressing a necessary being. Such is the mystery of person.

The worshipper, yielding everything to God in prayer, believes in the perfect integrity and truthfulness of God, and in particular believes that the revelation of God as one who offers communion to the faithful is genuine. In other words we must reject any idea that the injunction to pray is merely for human benefit, an arrangement for our good but detached from God in terms of real significance. God is, and God is personal in a way that transcends our fractured personhood. Personhood which is perfect, which can invite worship and total trust, does not deceive, manipulate, or crush; persons are treated as persons by God who is love.

5. *The two horizons of the divine will*

The will of God must thus be seen as personal in contrast to the mechanical, in which case it would return to the category of mere nature rather than will. An iron, predestinarian will which causes damnation to vast numbers of created humans does not equate readily with the personal goodness and fairness and absence of cruelty expected in a good human person. The heavenly Father desires not the death of sinners but rather 'that they may turn from their wickedness and live'. The will of God is faithful and constant, forbearing and forgiving in strong love, not in weak acquiescence.

Creation exists in its own right and its own freedom, not regulated in a direct fashion by God. Perhaps we might put this better by saying that creaturely life is not directly enacted or lived by God, which would after all be pantheism. Creatures are granted creaturely life. The overarching goal of creation is that it may come into full flower and be in harmony with the divine creative intention, and since this is the will of God, the church trusts and knows that this will be fulfilled in the ultimate destiny of all things. God has so chosen and willed. Creation issues from this source, the electing will of this God.

The divine will and desire are defined through the person and work of Jesus. Several New Testament texts do this with their vision of the world being held together 'in Christ' who is the divine focus of the world's destiny, the church being at its centre, and the cross of Jesus as the reconciling heart of all things.[26] The overarching will or desire of God is communion or covenant between creation and himself, an openness of the world to the divine love; the church is the first-fruits of this relationship, likened in the New Testament to that of marriage.[27] The moment of wedding is also used as an image for the culmination of history when the church as bride is finally joined to Christ, the bridegroom (Rev 19:7). This bond is the ultimate will of God for the church and for the whole created order.

To pray for the divine will to be done is to enter into this will, echoing the prayer for the coming of the kingdom in finality. The church, in Christ by the Spirit, enters into the intention of God's creative desire and will. This is the *great horizon* of 'your will be done'. This will of God was exhibited within the created order, including its aspects of distortion and disobedience, when 'we beheld his glory, full of grace and truth'; it was exemplified in the complete self-giving of Jesus, even to what the Evangelist John calls the 'glory' of Golgotha. The goal of the overarching will of God, disclosed in the behaviour of Jesus and anticipated in the Old Testament prophets,[28] is the fulfilled relationship of creation with the creator and thereby the attainment of the true being of the created order. This involves joy in God and in the world as his redeemed object of rejoicing; in this respect, the process theology view of joy as the goal of creation is very valid. The overarching horizon of divine will, the electing will of God in Christ, contains within it the history of creation and its creaturely freedom. The creaturely wills of myriads of human beings through time relate to the overarching will of God in detail as well as in general.

To pray 'your will be done' involves entering afresh into the divine project of creation, into its risk and into redemption as a finished whole. This means not only an entering in trust but in anticipation, a stance which can be taken not only because God is sovereign and must, somehow, bring about his will but also because this will has been enacted supremely in the resurrection of the crucified Jesus. In his risen life the will of God is supremely revealed and made real in transformed creation. The resurrection life is at work now in bringing the newness of the kingdom, the embodied will of God for creation, into being.

Within this overarching horizon of the will of God for all space and time, which is the will of God 'in heaven', there occurs real life and the contradiction of that will 'on earth'. The Christian praying 'your will be done' sees that will being flouted constantly, and yet maintains the eschatological perspective that God will not be defeated, and indeed will fashion ultimate victory from apparent defeat.

The sacramental pattern of the cross and resurrection, the baptismal dying and rising, remains normative and constitutive for the Christian disciple in praying for the will of the Father to triumph through the work of the Son in dying to sin and rising to righteousness. The Christian disciple 'owns' this baptismal 'label' as the primary human identity, the lens or mindset through which prayer is prayed and life is lived. Christian discipleship amounts to an increasing self-identification with this baptism, this dying and rising with Christ. Again we are brought close to the sacrificial core of prayer and its priestly character.

Human freedom within the context of the created order is real. Without it the phenomenon of sin would be meaningless, and sin is as real as the pavements, trees, and computers which fill our world. We are free to serve or to ignore the divine will, to fit into the order and wisdom of the creation or to reconstruct that order, temporarily, according to our own private preferences. 'Your will be done' is a prayer endorsing the moral wisdom of the universe, a prayer for the wisdom of God to endure and prevail and be 'owned' by humanity with loving enthusiasm. The over-arching divine will, reflected in the creative wisdom of the universe, gains respect as it is freely enacted and pursued by the people of God.

The fine details of the grand plan, the individual acts of men and women, are the narrower horizon of God's will; they cohere with his will in so far as they seek to do right. Each person responds to other people and circumstances in ways which endorse or reject the creative intention of God. God's will is worked in and through such decisions and deeds, despite as well as because of human will. The whole point of the gospel of Christ, to speak simply, is that the will of the Father may be done with the joyful consent of human hearts. Prayer for the doing of the divine will in the fine detail of human life is often discussed in terms of the meta-physical problems of 'divine will *versus* human will' and the action of God in the world. But at root it is a matter of the Gospel. A view of divine power frog-marching recalcitrant individuals by sheer force into divinely willed actions is not only plainly absurd, but conflicts with the good news of Christ. The power of God, as the election of God, is mediated through the Son whose character is disclosed in the life and death of Jesus. This God works his will through the consent of people. This God respects free-dom and does not manipulate human beings against their will.

Likewise, God is not *manipulated* by human religious activity which is not mediated through Christ. Christian prayer passes through the lens of Jesus to God, and God wins his victories in the detail of individual human lives through gaining acceptance in a costly fashion. He is the greatest and most persistent lover, or in the image of Francis Thompson's poem, 'The Hound of Heaven', pursuing the reluctant person who con-stantly seeks to avoid the attentions of those feet of God which follow.

In practical terms, it is often very hard to discern the will of God in the fine detail of life, and the need to discern this from moment to moment can lead to a dehumanizing of the creaturely person. The true story of the man who daily prayed to know which sock to put on first[29] shows that the link between the divine and human will is mediated through creation. The man of faith waking up and putting his socks on has the status of a created human being and a child of God. Does he not have the ability and freedom to choose his socks? He is not simply an empty channel, mere 'nature' for the divine will to fill, but a free, rational person with competence to undertake this exercise; to do so is not to declare independence from the creator, but rather to live as a creature should.

On the other hand, does this mean that God is wholly uninterested in the minor action of human beings, and that they therefore should not disturb the divine peace with ceaseless prayers about the fine detail of living? If a woman's goldfish is dying, if a man wants a safari jacket, should they be told not to bother God about such trivial things? I take these examples, as a pastor, from real life. We remember that God is the God who cares about small matters, and that 'not a sparrow falls' to the ground without his noticing it. If the believer practices the discipline of praying through the nature and name of Jesus, requests for safari jackets may well drop away as discipleship matures.

The fine detail of living is much harder to read than great events for signs of the will of God. Our choice of one brand of tea from another is hard to link with the will of God. This is an area of creaturely choice, of apparently little significance, so much so that total autonomy seems the appropriate understanding for the action. While prayer over this seems absurd, nevertheless all events, according to the New Testament witness, are under the care of the heavenly Father. Furthermore all events, small and great, are inter-related in the web of history. Modern scientific 'chaos theory' affirms much the same thing when it proposes that a butterfly moving its wings in China may cause a storm in Europe.

Common Christian experience of discipleship shows that the small apparently 'unspiritual', or morally neutral, choices in life are not detached from the care of God but entrusted to us as part of the regularity of the weekly round. We know the will of God sufficiently to conduct our lives with confidence—we tend to know when we are against the grain of divine intention. While the Christian would not pray before each moment of life to seek the divine will, without risking some kind of insanity, yet the routine moral way incorporates even the smallest decisions. The will of God is therefore present, as it is present to the vast tracts of uninhabited Polar ice-cap, present as given fact in an unproblematic situation requiring no hard decision. Buying a packet of tea might evoke a prayer of thanks, as might the sight of polar ice, but it is probably not relevant to discern the divine will in any specific way. Yet we should add that even such unproblematic occasions *can* become troublesome and matters for prayerful meditation on God's will. If we heard of virtual slave labour conditions for pickers of tea, for example, the situation would alter, and it would become a deliberately 'spiritual' matter.

Seeking God's will by praying for a knowledge of it in very particular and very minor events, and expecting to know precisely what is the conscious choice of God, for example over the colour of socks to buy, fails to realize that God has declared his will in the life of Jesus and the moral order. Our prayer for the doing of the divine will in the fine detail of our lives implies our own freedom in the Spirit to tackle life and take decisions with confidence, as we seek to live out the way of Jesus. That means a certain objectivity and looking outwards, rather than a worrying about our inner state, let alone a paralysis of living caused by waiting for some direct assurance of detailed instructions.

Guidance in the Christian life does include intercession for the big decisions; the story of Jesus in Gethsemane exemplifies the natural turning to God at times of crisis. But the whole context of discipleship, including the help of Christian friends, has to be taken as the living environment through which the Spirit works to lead us into acting well. The general disciplines and means of grace, including prayer, are the ways God mediates to us the path to take. This path, when we do come to the fork in the road, is often (even usually) by no means clear, and the Christian has to choose by objective rather than subjective criteria. The Spirit does not override our human faculties, so developing the Christian character which will face hard decisions and walk in the way of righteousness as part of a whole life of worship and service.

Discerning the will of God in particular decisions and actions is a matter of faith as we move forward in life; as we look back things can appear more clearly right or wrong, more or less in tune with the divine will, more or less in the Spirit. Donald Baillie speaks aptly here of a 'paradox of grace'[30]; it is our common experience that we walk ahead in faith and feel very much alone, while the retrospective view reveals the prevenient grace that was going before and enabling.

The horizons of God's will, the overarching covenant rainbow within which we take the particular choices of everyday life, coalesce and do not feel separate but part of the whole life in Christ. The experience of struggle and frustration in seeking to live out the will of God does not mean, contrary to the 'prosperity gospel', a failure in finding God's path. Indeed, almost the opposite might be asserted. The cross of Jesus was a way he felt called to take, but one he prayed agonizingly to be released from, and so represents the chaos of a world in which God's will is opposed. These

two horizons of divine will, the overarching and particular, find their theological definition in the New Testament through Christ as the one in
whom all things hold together, and the one who died at a particular hour
among certain human beings in a small province of the Roman Empire.
The two horizons of God's will come together there in a way which not
only speaks the final word to our plight, but provides the paradigm for the
mode of life in the divine will. The brutal death of the innocent Jesus does
not on the face of it seem to be the will of God.

The apparent failure and frustration of so much fine Christian work,
and the success of those who adopt the way of worldly power, demonstrate something of the mystery of tracing the will of God in sinful history. It needs to be read through the cross, the baptismal pattern of dying
and rising. The graceless death of Jesus was the reverse of what he deserved; it was 'all wrong', and yet somehow it was incorporated into the
heart of the will of God in relation to destiny of the human race. This
grubby act of betrayal and political accommodation links to the overarching will of God. This particular event contradicts all that we know of
the 'will of God' in terms of justice and care for humanity, and yet it
belongs within the grand horizon of God's purpose.

The will of God incarnate in human history, existing under human
conditions of freedom to sin, disclosed itself at Calvary and vindicated
itself there. That is the outworking of God's will. The Christian believes
that God himself was not merely an external agent manipulating or con-
niving at this event, but was actually participating in it as part of the created order surrendering its free will to God the Father. The result of this
was the resurrection of the created order in the person of Jesus, the pioneer and perfecter of our faith. The disciple, baptized into death with
Jesus and tasting in anticipation the resurrection life, thus prays 'your will
be done' in a new mode of being which coexists alongside that of the
world, with its success and power-driven agendas. 'Your will' must be
understood and lived through this decisive self-interpretation of God's
will by the cross. God reconciles the divine will with the creaturely will
by the cross. It is a moral act, not simply a matter of metaphysics, but
comes from the heart of the mysteriously personal God as a matter of self-
giving to bring about communion and make possible the enactment of
divine will 'on earth as in heaven'.

One aspect of prayer found historically among the people of God
which should gain a place in this context is that of lamentation. The
prayer of Gethsemane, 'your will be done', was uttered in agony and the

deepest possible distress. The collision of human sin and the divine purpose for creation meant such grief of spirit for Jesus, and final fatal aggression against his very life. The Old Testament has many examples of prayers of lament to God at times of disaster, bringing the horror of events before the face of God in sheer honesty. The great error of much piety is to feel that disaster has to be covered up, lest it be thought to let God down, to discredit him and cause unfaith. On the contrary, frank and open facing of harsh reality, bringing it before the face of the one who cares, is the way of truth and the way of Jesus.

How does the prayer 'your will be done' fit into this sharing of grief with God? Christian spirituality disclaims fatalism, a passive submission to the divine will as inevitably preordained and simply to be endured with resignation. God has a creative will and purpose, and this will be attained; within that, however, human freedom is a factor. The paradoxical prayer 'your will be done' entails the merging of the horizons of overarching divine desire and human action. The Christian is actively and worshipfully involved in working out God's will in communion with God, and so this prayer is actually part of God's saving project. The one who prays it becomes a crux where the two horizons meet, where the great electing will of the Father is 'owned' afresh by the disciple, as intended by the creator.

Notes to Chapter 5

[1] Hardy and Ford, *Jubilate*, pp. 74-81.

[2] See above, pp. 97-106.

[3] See above, pp. 101-102.

[4] Pannenberg, 'The God of hope', in *Basic Questions in Theology*, Vol. 2, trans. G. Kehm (SCM, London, 1971), pp. 237ff, 244f.

[5] Oscar Cullmann, *Prayer in the New Testament*, trans. John Bowden (SCM Press, London, 1995), p. 49.

[6] An existential emphasis can be fitted into a process type of theological system, the act of obedience corresponding to agreeing with the divine lure, although the process idea of this promoting pleasure seems distant from Kierkegaard's stark understanding of costly obedience.

[7] Luke 9:51. Compare what the Servant of the Lord says about himself in Isaiah 50:7, 'I have set my face like a flint.'

[8] S. Kierkegaard, *Fear and Trembling*, trans. R. Payne (Oxford University Press, London, 1939), pp. 5-11.

[9] Cited in Zizioulas, *Being as Communion*, p. 49.

[10]This is Moltmann's expression of the trinitarian dynamic in his *The Crucified God*, p. 243.

[11]Apparently this was the hope of the early disciples, according to Acts 1.

[12]Barth, *Church Dogmatics*, II/2, pp. 3-14.

[13]F. D. Maurice, *The Epistle to the Hebrews* (J. W. Parker, London, 1846), p. 29.

[14]Cf. Ezekiel 18:23, 32; also 1 Timothy 2:3-4, 'God our Saviour, who desires everyone to be saved and to come to the knowledge of the truth'.

[15]Hebrews 2:10-13, cf. 4:14-16.

[16]See Fiddes, *The Creative Suffering of God*, pp. 71-76 for an interpretation of God's desire behind the world process and the life of God in relation to that.

[17]Colossians 1:15-23; Ephesians 1:3-23.

[18]See here the comments above and below on the 'tension' between heaven and earth.

[19]This is close to the process theology interpretation of divine activity through luring the created will towards the values of the kingdom, but the divine will is to be more strongly affirmed as an active as well as a passive influence.

[20]Friedrich Nietzsche, *The Anti-Christ*, trans. R. Hollingdale (Penguin, Harmondsworth, 1968), pp. 114-20.

[21]This inevitably evokes memories of the joke about the 'self-made man, who worshipped his creator'.

[22]Michel Foucault, for example, in his analyses of health and sexuality; see his *Politics, Philosophy, Culture: Interviews and Other Writing 1977–1984*, ed. Lawrence D. Kritzman (Routledge, London, 1988).

[23]Baruch Spinoza, *Tractatus Theologico-Politicus* [1670], ch. 11, as quoted in Robert M Grant and David Tracy, *A Short History of the Interpretation of the Bible*, 2d. ed. (SCM Press, London, 1984), p. 106.

[24]See pp. 38-47.

[25]See Barth, *Church Dogmatics*, II/1, pp. 272ff.

[26]Colossians 1; Ephesians 1; 1 Corinthians 1:20-25; 2:6-9.

[27]The classic text is Ephesians 5:22-33, but see also Colossians 3:18–4:1 and 1 Corinthians 6:15-20.

[28]The harmony of creation is expressed in such language as the wolf dwelling with the lamb: Isaiah 11:6, cf. Isaiah 65:25, Habukkuk 2:14.

[29]Told in J. I. Packer, *Knowing God* (Hodder & Stoughton, London, 1973), p. 264.

[30]Donald M. Baillie, *God Was in Christ. An Essay on Incarnation and Atonement* (Faber and Faber, London, 1948), pp. 114-18.

6

'Give us today our daily bread'

1. Bread and life

The identity and character of God have occupied the hearts of those who worship beside Jesus in praying his prayer to this point. Now the theme turns to the staple diet of life, bread. The vast horizon reduces to the immediate detailed needs of life: 'Give us today our daily bread'. The petition for bread, apparently simple, involves some debate over interpretation. While modern exegetes clearly view the request as for ordinary material bread, the basic food needed to sustain life, it was in earlier times interpreted as meaning spiritual bread, Christ himself. The early Church Father Tertullian advises us:

> We may rather understand 'Give us this day our daily bread' spiritually. For Christ is our bread; because Christ is life and bread is life. 'I am', saith he, 'the bread of life'; and a little above, 'The bread is the Word of the living God, who came down from the heavens'. Then we find too that his body is reckoned in bread, 'This is my body'. And so in petitioning for daily bread we ask for perpetuity in Christ, and indivisibility from his body.[1]

Tertullian, the modern interpreter might say, spiritualizes the petition into some 'higher' request, as if merely asking for bread were unworthy or less worthy a cause. Tertullian internalizes the petition for the coming of the kingdom, that it might come within us, which we would not have expected from someone with the strong eschatology he has.

Some argue that the petition for daily bread refers to the eucharistic bread, answering the obvious objection that the Lord's Prayer antedates the eucharist with the idea that the feeding of the five thousand gives sufficient warrant for this interpretation. John McKenzie, in the Roman Catholic *Jerome Biblical Commentary*, does not raise that as a possible view in his commentary on Matthew 6:5-15. He discusses the difficulty of translating the Greek word *epiousios*, normally rendered 'daily'.[2] The phrase 'bread for tomorrow' would be an equally good translation to substitute for 'daily bread'. He points out that Krister Stendahl has raised the possibility that the petition may even be eschatological and refer to the messianic banquet at the end-time, in line with the eschatological prayer for the coming kingdom.

Cullmann translates the petition 'Give us today bread for tomorrow',[3] and regards the bread in question as ordinary bread for maintaining life. This seems to be the most obvious reading, given the placing of the Lord's Prayer in the context of the earthly ministry of Jesus. In the same chapter of his Gospel in which Matthew records the Lord's Prayer as asking for daily bread, or even bread for tomorrow, he also tells us that Jesus taught the disciples not to worry about tomorrow but to trust the heavenly Father who knows their needs before they ask. Cullmann reconciles the two ideas by suggesting that being *anxious* about tomorrow and *praying* for tomorrow's needs are not the same; indeed he argues that calm daily prayer may well be the antidote to worry.

The plain sense of the prayer is for ordinary material bread, from the hand of the creator, the caring heavenly Father. The petition fits in with the biblical understanding of God as provider and sustainer of the processes of nature and the harvest, symbolized by the rainbow in the story of Noah, the promise of God that seedtime and harvest will remain (Gen 8:22). God guarantees the conditions of life and sustenance for all humanity. Matthew's 'Sermon on the Mount', which follows Matthew's account of the Lord's Prayer, develops this theme for the little flock of the faithful; they are not to be anxious because the heavenly Father who clothes the flowers of the field will surely clothe them (Matt 6:25-34).

The creative promise to sustain the conditions needed for harvest, and Matthew's more personalized statement of the heavenly Father who cares about the fall of one sparrow, do not conflict with the need to pray for the wherewithal to sustain life: 'Give us today our daily bread'. The very preservation of the text of Matthew 6 shows that the earliest church did not think there was any contradiction between the divine promise to care and praying for our basic needs. Indeed, the fact of Christian prayer itself confirms the harmony between genuine prayer and covenanted promises. It is a delight to pray for what we expect will actually materialize. The Christian is no deist who regards the world as mechanically ticking along as a reliable system. God's provision for our needs is overwhelmingly generous. The world's continuities remain—its weather, its biospheres and regularities of growth cycles, the stability of chemical composition, of genetic identities, and the universal commonality through space and time.

These are facts, and usually regarded as scientific 'fact'. In our Western culture, scientific phenomena are divorced from spiritual significance, facts being supposedly value-free. Therefore, humanity can tailor nature to whatever shape or purpose yields the fastest immediate gain, and humanity itself is treated as mouldable substance, reconstructable into the image chosen by the individual. Harvests are a simply a given phenomenon to be exploited to the full. The Christian tradition knows that harvests are realities to be studied by natural science, itself a gift of God. But to reduce the significance of bread, of wheat ground to flour and baked into loaves through countless generations in countless ovens across the surface of the earth, to a cold and neutral statistical fact fails to register the fact in its fulness. The scientific analysis of wheat is vital and complements the human appreciation of its goodness and reliability, all part of the context of life that is fundamentally positive and generous.

The creator, the heavenly Father, is behind this order of nature which is so beneficent, reflecting his generous character in his workmanship. It is the will of God that this order of nature, this vast stability and fertility, should endure and not change; why it does not change, why the structures of matter are constant throughout the galaxies, is an insoluble question. The believer knows the deeper significance of this great universal fact of ordered and perduring structured life.

God created, and it was so, a world of plenty and of beautiful stability surpassing mechanical identity. The Sabbath, the day on which God rested on completing his work of creation, became the day of rest and of joy in the created order with its goodness and faithfulness. The resurrection of Jesus shifted the church's Sabbath to the first day of the week, away from the last day, so altering the perspective of rest after work done to looking ahead into redeemed, renewed creation. Praying for the continuing supply of the goodness of creation, in particular for the basics of life, is not to doubt the faithfulness of the creator and sustainer. God's creative promise is to maintain the cosmos and the universal order in all its productivity.

2. Praying in expectation

To pray for what we expect, especially for modern Western Christians, may be a very healthy discipline indeed, breaking as it does the sense of self-sufficiency of the economic system. In the days of Jesus no doubt people were closer to the edge of drought and famine, and prayers for daily, regular supplies of food were far from a pious artificiality. Regular prayer for expected, but not guaranteed, benefits of creation is genuine petition, but petition in hope and trust.

The Father in heaven is not to be taken for granted, as if the matrix of a mechanical system that simply ticks on. Neither is God one who needs to be bribed and teased into providing for the needs of his creatures. God cares; such is the plain message of the Synoptic Gospels and the context in which the Lord's Prayer is set. God is also free and sovereign in his sustaining of the universe, not to be manipulated by means of human approaches. The relationship is one of gladness to ask, assuming the divine gladness to give, and being prompted by God to express all our needs.

Modern secular attitudes find this very strange because an asker is reckoned to be weak and in an undesirable position, relying on the patronising goodwill of the giver. John's Gospel, we recall, talks of Jesus saying that he delights to do the will of the Father, as his meat and drink. That the Father loves to give good gifts to those who ask, is also a Synoptic theme. The context of the relationship is not one of contract but covenant, not one party screwing advantage from the other in a bond of suspicion and acquisition. That is more a picture of the devil and his victims than of God and his people. Praying to this God is praying in a rich context of pure trust and goodwill, of overflowing loving-kindness.

Jesus describes this context as being like a child-parent relationship, the child naively asking for what she knows will be forthcoming (Matt 7:9-11). Such is the kingdom of heaven. It may be objected that this is all strangely illogical and even irrational in that there is no need to ask if the benefit is expected without the request. But to think like this assesses the universe as system without the covenant bond revealed in the relationship of Jesus with the Father, and assumed in the manner of the Lord's Prayer. This petition amounts to praying into a generous and caring will, not working a system. Praying for what God wants to provide shows again the covenant relationship God bestows in such a way as to draw out from his covenant partner glad obedience and hopeful service. Both parties together join their energies in the project of enacting the divine plan for history.

This orientation of hope and of appreciating what God wants to achieve in the world is important in Christian prayer. While God is the holy and mysterious one to be worshipped and adored, he is also constantly working in the world, as John's Gospel registers.[4] As we have seen in considering the petition, 'your will be done', the Father chooses to work with and through the human will, centrally and crucially that of Jesus, into whose sacrificial self-giving the faithful have been bound and integrated in baptism. If the will of Jesus were that of humanity generally, then there is a good case for thinking that daily bread would be the lot of everyone without fail; the four horsemen of the Apocalypse would not be thundering over the wheat fields, making war and creating famine.

The tradition of praying for what will generally happen has become ingrained in the Christian tradition, as much as has praying for what seems impossible. This shows an objective view of prayer and the God to whom petition is made. God is not a mere system, although regularly what is requested does happen 'anyway'. Nor is God uncaring or removed from the scene, even when the highly unusual does not happen; for example, healings of incurables are extraordinarily rare. Whether prayer is for the harvest or for the healing of a child terminally ill with leukaemia, that prayer is addressed in the same spirit, to a loving God who does care and does provide. 'For I greet him the days I meet him, and bless when I understand'[5], as the poet Gerard Manley Hopkins found.

The care of the heavenly Father exists objectively, whatever conditions of life may be facing the praying disciple. Prayer is always heard by this caring God concerned for the fall of the sparrow; prayer is sought by this God as an act of trust and confidence and appreciation. Prayer for daily sustenance is not a 'penny in the slot' application to an agency requiring a special mode of approach before attention will be given or considered. On the contrary, this prayer, for the basics of life, is 'heard' and respected as from one in a relationship which can be described using the intimate analogy of marriage. Prayer is not a 'system' to be worked, but trust in a loving God sustaining all things.

The presence of our daily bread day by day is an answer to our prayer, and yet it is given to the just and to the unjust, since God has underwritten his creation as being fundamentally good; only when it is abused does it come into crisis and under judgement. Bread is a phenomenon that occurs regularly, while also being the gift of the creator; yet when bread is missing, we cannot say a gift has been withheld. Such is the paradox of grace when applied to petitionary prayer. Faith rejoices in the sheer gift when it is given, whether that is the gift of fresh air to breathe and water to drink, or the healing of a child from a terminal illness in a unique event.

Why the child should have contracted the illness in the first place, why a cluster of cells should have distorted themselves into a death-dealing disease, is a matter to be reserved for the petition 'deliver us from evil'; but any praying disciple assumes as axiomatic that God is good, that creation is good, that fundamentally life is good and suffering is a blot on that landscape. That does not minimize the very real problem of suffering and evil for theology and experience. It is, however, worth noting that there is only a problem at all because of the initial axiom of the caring character of God: evil would not be a 'problem' philosophically without the background assumption that the world somehow 'ought' to reflect care, justice, and kindness.

Praying for such basic stuff of human existence, be it bread or the rule of law and access to justice in the face of violent oppression, is praying with the grain of God's creative intention. 'Whatever is true, whatever is honourable, whatever is just, whatever is pure, whatever is lovely, whatever is gracious, if there is any excellence, if there is anything worthy of praise, think about these things' (Phil 3:8-9). Paul's insistence that disciples focus on the good matches precisely this point. To think of such things is to lock into the underlying substance of creation, into the truth, beauty, and goodness that God constantly desires and fosters. The expression 'original blessing'[6] holds good insofar as it describes God's fatherly caring intention for his creation. Creation was made, 'and it was good'; sin and fall are an overlay on this diamond reality. There is one sense in which people of faith walk as if in the garden of Eden, knowing the presence of the Lord and thankful in a childlike way.

'Give us this day our daily bread' therefore brings us down to earth from the heights of the divine will, but the earth to which we mentally descend is God's work, the theatre of history, a theatre which cannot ultimately burn down. The play will run its course and reach its end, in all its richness. The promise and the desire of God will be realized. The prayer is said with this view of creation and eschatology implicit in it, and with a sense of joy and confidence rather than bored fatalism. Creation is good, and evil will be ended: those are the book-ends of the history in which prayer takes place.

The Synoptic Gospels set the Lord's Prayer very firmly in this context. Disciples are to pray for what they need, but they are not to worry since the God to whom they are praying is both sovereign and caring. Prayer to the heavenly Father does not work a system, somehow external to the communion between God and us. Prayer is 'genuine', not a formality. Prayer for our daily bread works against the backcloth of optimism, not negative pessimism and fear. That is to say, Jesus' teaching on petitionary prayer in the Lord's Prayer and surrounding texts does not encourage an attitude of anxiety that the good will not happen *unless* we pray for it.

At the same time the parables of Jesus especially condemn attitudes of human self-sufficiency which trust selfish plans will work out, irrespective of contempt for God. The rich man who trusted to his barns full of produce and goods, was a fool, since that very night his soul was required of him (Luke 12:20). Complacently disregarding the good creator and sustainer of the universe while enjoying the fruits of creation is folly, in the biblical sense involving moral as well as intellectual error.

Praying for the goods of the earth rightly recognizes the ultimate provider, notwithstanding that such good things usually occur. The worshipper asks in a spirit of the gladness of the Sabbath, recognising the good creation as a garden of generosity established by God. The child asks the parent, in good faith, for what she needs for the day ahead, and the parent delights in supplying that, even if to do so is in fact costly and this cost is hidden. Luke's account of the Lord's Prayer comes immediately before the parables of the neighbour who asks expectantly for food for a guest, and that of the father who would not for a moment consider giving his son a serpent when he had asked for a fish, an evil thing instead of a good (Luke 11:5-13). A modern way of looking at the approach of the praying disciple and of the heavenly Father would be to say that cynicism, scepticism, and pessimism are excluded. A genuineness pervades the communion of praying. Naivety would be the wrong word. Childlikeness, in the sense of open honesty and unthinking trust that the good will be forthcoming from the parent, captures something of what is meant. The ghastly narratives of terrified Jewish children in gas chambers, running to clutch at the military overcoats of the guards, who were adults and so those who should help and be worthy of trust, describe precisely the betrayal of such trust.

The 'worthship' of God is a strong formative factor in Christian spirituality and theology, and it needs to be ingrained in the praying disciple. God is worthy, is not capricious, is not rigid, is not ashamed of creation or his providence. Despite the experience of life, therefore, worship remains right. God desires good, desires to supply every good thing, and all good is to be traced back to the heavenly Father. The problems of suffering and of evil, while they are inescapable primary data of experience, are secondary to the *theological* interpretation of reality. God is good, creation is very good, and the fact of pain and sin exists against this wider background.

Pain and deprivation can drive people away from praying for daily bread; but equally the Western consumer society with its vast glut of basic foods has the same effect, through producing complacency and confidence in humanly managed supplies. Why pray, if either you think that present suffering excludes a caring God, or if you take for granted the self-productiveness of the universe for your benefit? Both diversions from worship and petition arise from reading the face of the history and interpreting that reading anthropocentrically. The former misreading is more understandable than the latter; indeed, the fact that God himself enters into the experience of those who make it is the only guarantee that it *is* a misreading, and that the truth of God is disguised there.

The New Testament encourages trustful prayer, as a child to its Father who is able to provide and delights in so doing. Petitioning *should* be made to God; it is part of the interaction, the communion, between God and creation. It is as much a part of that intercourse as is praise and thanks and confession. It puts God under no obligation, does not manipulate the sovereign Lord, does not equate with working a sub-personal system nor seeking to strike it lucky with a moody potentate. Instead, petitionary prayer relates very closely to discipleship and choices in the Christian life. The apostle Paul's famous 'thorn in the flesh', probably a physical ailment, was the subject of his prayers, and he asked several times to be rid of it; the ailment continued, however, and Paul eventually concluded that it served the purpose of glorifying the grace of God which worked through his weakness (2 Cor 12:7). A kind of interaction took place, a kind of guidance, of which petitionary prayer was an important aspect. Although Paul, in this example, even speaks of Satan attacking him through this ailment, he still discerns a purpose that the thorn in the flesh be allowed to remain.

The situation resembles Jesus' Gethsemane prayer in the urgency of the asking, and the maturity of theological interpretation of a life with pain. 'Your will be done' precedes 'Give us today our daily bread', and more importantly the God whose will is implored is the God of Jesus Christ who enters into the tension of the experienced pain and the prayer for the good. Christian discipleship knows nothing of the consumerist view of God, banking on worldly benefits in correlation to personal piety. The judgement on any such understanding of prayer was given at Calvary. Would the consumerist view of petitionary prayer be compatible with respect and appreciation for this God?

3. God's response to prayer (1):
William Temple and divine 'adjustment'

Petitionary prayer asks from God, in the context of trust and mutual respect. The heavenly Father cares both for those who call upon him with sincere hearts, and for those who call with faith only as great as the grain of mustard seed. The heavenly Father makes the rain fall on the just and the unjust, the pious and the rebellious. But those who disregard God choose not to enter into the project of the kingdom with him, not seeking to involve God in life and experience by their prayers. Petition, with the other areas of prayer, is part of this joint project. Believers seek to crack open the impossible padlocks of human misery with prayer and action, the two in close relation.

From the angle of the disciple, petitionary prayer aims to bring about the good, whether the supply of staple food or the implementation of the kingdom. Requests in such prayer are not simply selfish, but for what is needed for oneself and for the goals of the mission of God; in that sense petitionary prayer is particularly 'apostolic', that is, part of being 'sent' into the world with the gospel. 'Being sent' means from that sphere of the world which delights in God to that which rejects him; the movement of mission is then between areas that are not so much geographically distinct as either open to divine influence or closed off from it.

In fact, the failure of the good to come about in life can be regarded sometimes at least as the temporary triumph of 'the world' over the kingdom of God; when famine strikes a land as a result of war, the galloping horsemen of the Apocalypse interfere with the good of creation and damage it—in limited but painful fashion. Petitionary prayer, always rooted in Christ, prayed in the name of Jesus, takes part in the battle for the good. If Immanuel is 'God with us', he is also 'us with God', and prayer lives out this purposive communion. To continue to pray in circumstances of depression and discouragement is somehow to continue to acknowledge God as good in face of the apparent victory of hopelessness, and this is to do what Paul called living out the sufferings of Christ in some important degree.

When we ask how God responds to our petitions, we find an important insight in the thought of William Temple. He suggests that the regularity of the universe is complemented by human freedom, which brings an aspect of indeterminism and variability into the web of reality. This is made clear by a simple illustration:

I am free to choose whether I shall stand still or walk across the room.
If I choose the latter, I effect a redistribution of the mass of the world
and shift its centre of gravity. That I do so to an extent negligible in the
most precise astronomical calculation possible to man, does not affect
the principle. And if I can do this to any extent at all, then God, if He
exists, can do it to any extent He pleases.[7]

Temple finds a correspondence between the indeterminacy that comes
through human freedom of choice and the Christian view of God as personal. To be truly personal means disciplined consistency on the one
hand, and deliberate self-adjustment and variation on the other; it is no
mere uniformity of system. 'There is in the world', according to Temple
echoing the ancient tradition, 'an immanent Reason—a Logos. If this is
impersonal, it may be only a principle of logical coherence. If it is personal, it must be a principle of perpetual adjustment according to "sufficient reason" . . . God immanent is a principle or energy of adjustment
and therefore of variation; God transcendent is the eternally self-identical
—the I AM.'[8]

Temple is insisting that God in his immanence in the universe is no
mere mechanism or law, but is personal as the indwelling *logos*. Because
he is present personally rather than as an impersonal process, God reveals
himself in various intensities and modes in different times.[9] He can
'adjust' himself to the needs and responses of the world. The model is not
so much the pulsing of logos as a neutral law of nature or energy of being,
but rather 'personal' purposive activity, with all manner of expressive
disclosures and strategies for fostering what is good.

This, explains Temple, is typical of personality, which is invested into
all its actions, but not always in the same *level* of intensity. Some acts are
performed on a semi-conscious level and are virtually automatic, with
differences between persons of no relevance or interest. How a person
brushes his teeth, for example, or changes gear while driving the car, does
not disclose much of his personality! How that person behaves towards
family and friends, or to a dying colleague, discloses more the character
of that person. A critical moment in life will bring to the surface the quality of a person, revealing the truth of the personality. 'Nothing reveals the
heroism of the one or the cowardice of the other until some crisis arises—
truly called a crisis because it is the judgement on their two characters...
the event discloses what each had been in the time when no difference
appeared between them'.[10] So it is, he suggests, with the immanent
presence of God in the world.[11]

God immanent as the Spirit blows like the wind as he will (John 3: 8), with vast purposes being brought about through the tiny events of the universe and in phases of varying intensity. 'There is ground for believing', in Temple's view, 'that there are infinite gradations of such adjustment and adaptation as find their climax in these alleged revelatory acts.'[12] God is faithful and stable, but mysterious; history has therefore both a consistency and also a total unpredictability and novelty. It is this combination, argues Wolfhart Pannenberg, which 'raises the question of God'[13] for the agnostic or atheist. Like Pannenberg also, Temple regards the factor of novelty or unpredictability in history as pointing to the personal character of God; Pannenberg stresses that these irregular aspects demonstrate the freedom and non-manipulability of God, Temple that they show the way God adjusts himself to varying circumstances.

This principle of infinite adjustment and variation, characteristic of the personal, applies to human religious experience in Temple's view. The way that God answers petitions seems to adjust to the spiritual growth of the one who prays:

> What is very startling to the philosopher whose mental habit is controlled by scientific interests is the abundance of testimony given by those who have had intimate experience of men's spiritual life to the conviction that in the early stages prayer receives literal fulfilment with great frequency; that later on this becomes less frequent, until it seems almost to cease, as though God at first gives encouragement of the most obvious kind and later withdraws this in order to evoke a deeper trust.[14]

Some reputable works on spirituality endorse this experience of the divinely graduated or subtly adjusted response to prayer.[15] If there is truth in this notion of divine adjustment according to our spiritual maturity, it can only highlight the fact that prayer cannot be regarded as a system to operate so much as a relationship to develop.

The 'God of the open future', to use Pannenberg's phrase, or 'the personal God who is immanent logos', to use Temple's, wishes his people to commune with him in adoration and action. Provision for creaturely needs is part of this practical project of life on earth and is what God desires, what generally happens. Famine is unusual in a world which has massive surpluses of food for the needs of the human race. The covenant promise to Noah, painted by the rainbow, holds good for the vast majority of humanity, with terrible exceptional spasms set against this background of consistent plenty.

God is a giver, not an exactor,[16] giving from the future in many and various ways, not amenable to strict taxonomy or systematization. He is the God who adjusts, and so aspects of novelty come to us in life in the microcosm of our individual circumstances, making life open to the future and largely, although not wholly, unpredictable. Into this future the Lord's Prayer bids us pray for our daily bread, bread for tomorrow, bread that will see us through, resources to cope with the present and the demands of tomorrow which we do not control. In dealing with the coming of tomorrow we deal with God, the God who deals with us personally and not as ciphers in a database. It is no surprise, therefore, that prayer does not work like inserting coins into a fruit machine, but is relational.

The writers on spirituality who tell us that the further discipleship develops, the less petitions seem to be 'answered' directly go on to say that the very petitions of such disciples no longer focus so much simply on getting things for themselves but for others, as prayer in the name and nature of Jesus and his kingdom. So the disciple adjusts and is adjusted as life goes on, and the heavenly Father is behind the evolution (as Temple puts it) of the soul's growth. This view of discipleship and prayer flies in the face of consumerist piety or 'prosperity doctrine', while still encouraging active dependence for the basics of life on the joyful Giver. What should a holy God wish to give to his more mature disciples? It makes sense to regard divine strategy as leading them on from the shallows to the depths. No doubt adjusting, and being changed can be a painful process as well a joyous one. It coheres with the meaning of Christian baptism into Christ and his death (Rom 6:3), which was one of Paul's models of the Christian life: so, 'though our outer nature is wasting away, our inner nature is being renewed every day' (2 Cor 4:16).

Transformation is occurring in the disciple, and this is linked to the way of the cross, participation in the death of the Lord and his risen life somehow at work in the lives of his people. Prayer life must be a vital part of this transformational journey with God to God. The action of the Spirit from God into our lives correlates with our taking of God into our confidence, in total honesty and openness, in praying about our needs and aspirations. The terms 'inspiration and aspiration'[17] usefully sum up this dynamic. With infinite delicacy the Spirit of God, immanent in the world and yet searching even the deep things of God,[18] relates to and transforms the life of disciples who seek the path of God's kingdom, to walk in the Spirit. The Spirit gifts individuals in the prodigal variety available to the

God who brought into being this world characterized by almost infinite variety and nuances of colour.

Temple stresses that the personal Logos constantly upholding the process of creation is the very same who died on the cross as a human being; there he entered into that which he did not uphold, the web of sinfulness, and so absorbed the tension between the holy and the unholy. The mysterious divine upholding of the universe in creation relates to human life as much as does the divine redemption with its blinding clarity:

> It is characteristic of God that He should usually act by what to us is uniformity (though the appearance of this may conceal variations too delicate for our perception and too small to affect our confidence in action), just as it is characteristic of Him to vary His action when the occasion is sufficient.[19]

'Ordinary' life, therefore, is under the guiding hand of God as much as those moments in life of supreme crisis such as the birth of one's children. Temple is saying that Jesus does not merely exemplify a process which is impersonally generated; rather the process is always personally guided, and the incarnation of the Word brings this out into the open at a particular time. Prayer fits into this whole environment of stability, variation, and adjustment. It is, as we have already seen, prayer for 'what usually happens' as well as for the unusual, and God responds by varying his presence and activity even when we do not notice it. The Spirit intercedes for us with sighs too deep for words, sounding our very depths and not simply echoing back to the Father, but co-operatively evoking our response to the Father in the same Spirit. Prayer for our daily bread, bread for today and tomorrow, will be needful always. Prayer in deep crisis is almost 'natural'; men in the trenches in 1914 prayed assortments of prayers, from cursings of God, to pleadings, to committal of the self into the care of God.

God desires such prayers, whether they be curses or blessings. Curses from the atheist are important, a bridge to the God who stubbornly remains in the world. Such curses imply the personal character of God, a God who can be cursed and blasphemed and blamed: no process can be addressed so. The personal quality of the prayer means that the Spirit is not Hegel's Absolute Mind *(Geist)*, but relates to our spirit in the most intimate way. The Spirit of God does not exist *as* human spirit, fragmented through time. God's Spirit exists *with* ours, in the deepest

intimacy and purpose, but there cannot be an identity of being. God identifies with our condition, and so draws forth our prayers and sighs that are
uttered in, but not as, the divine Spirit.

While not visible, the Spirit blows through the created order, using it
as a harp to play music attractive to the listening human ear. The life of
Jesus was the supreme instrument for the influence of the Spirit to play
upon and to introduce into the hearts of billions of people open to the
rhythm and melody. Human free will consents to follow this music, this
piper, drawing out the lost and unfashionable into the great company
transformed freely and willingly. Prayer takes place within this shaping
of the will and the whole person, who needs daily bread and needs to have
confidence in bread for tomorrow.

4. God's response to prayer (2):
the power of persons in history

Human personality is open to the personal working of God at all kinds of
levels and mediated in all kinds of ways. The operation of the gastric
juices on the bread eaten for breakfast mediates the strength-giving
resources of creation from God to us. God intends human beings to be
well fed and to grow strong. The power and greatness of God the creator
is felt in such an experience as eating bread, coming from the fields of
corn growing so liberally on the face of the earth. The impression of the
natural world on the heart, according to Paul in his epistle to the Romans,
is of divine greatness (Rom 1:19-20).

Likewise the impression of the incarnate Word, generous and open of
spirit to all who asked, was and is compelling. 'Follow me' was and
remains his summons, the voice coming through the impression of his life
conveyed through the narratives of the gospels. The disciple allows himself to be moulded and moved by this impression—ethical, emotional,
rational—of a great personality claiming total attention and respect. This
is how persons now present to us exert influence and a hold over us. We
freely and gladly follow. Marriages are made by the claim of one on
another and the final glad agreement to form a common life together, in
the expectation of mutual change and new paths of opportunity and
creativity opening up.

Christ and the church relate like this, according to Paul, so echoing
the image used by the Hebrew prophets of Israel and God her bridegroom,
notably in Hosea's message and ministry.[20] The heart is won, often

through a patient waiting, and the human yields to the divine approach freely; any other way of claiming loyalty and love than this respectful and courteous but bold summons would sink below the divine level of holiness. The claim made by Jesus, 'come follow me', to fishermen gainfully and usefully employed, entails a real moral self-confidence: how can anyone be confident enough to call others to follow his life pattern, to interfere with the nearly sacred bonds of family and even marriage, to drag people from their work and responsibilities? The call is clear, and has the compulsion of its giver, and that alone. No force is even hinted at; the power of the person suffices to reconfigure the lives of the fishermen by the sea of Galilee.

The Spirit moves us in our whole life, mental, ethical, emotional, and all these integrate in the physical dimension. Human beings develop and change, while retaining their identity, as they increasingly open their hearts to the prompting of the Spirit. Prayer is very much part of this discipleship of co-operation with God. Worship of God in the Spirit is evoked by the Spirit, and Christian theology has regarded it as a participation in the trinitarian dynamic of the love of the Son for the Father and the delight of the Father in the Son, in whom he is well pleased. The very purpose of the creation is the worship of the creator, not to satisfy a narcissistic divine appetite for praise, but because God is worthy of praise, and creation finds its true fulfilment in offering itself to God. Worship pleasing to God includes care for the poor and sick, a whole pattern of discipleship.

Mark presents the baptism of Jesus as a moment of ritual cleansing and self-dedication to the holy God of Israel, who declares Jesus 'the beloved Son' with whom he is 'well pleased'. The human Jesus enacts worship and consecration in his life, only to be driven into the wilderness and tempted by the devil rather than enjoying a time of pious contemplation. God's good pleasure in Jesus is a motif of the New Testament, as is the joy in God over the lost who return to the family of faith and praise. Acknowledging once more that all language about God is that of analogy, yet this analogy of divine joy displaces any analogy of divine remoteness and icy uninterest.

Given that God's holiness involves joy and love, that there is a holy responsiveness to the created order, how should the effect of petitionary prayer be defined? Such prayer may be therapeutic in itself, calming on the nerves for those in crisis, a steady rhythm of spirituality for those simply bumping along in life's 'mundane' phase of the 'normal'. As with all prayer, requests to God must be seen as within the continuum of an exist-ing relationship or covenant; the one praying is already in the Spirit, already being influenced and affected by the trinitarian movement from the Father to his people. Requests arise from the context of life given to us and somehow conditioned by God.

The God envisaged in process theology, we have already noted,[21] does not claim to change things directly, but does claim so to influence people by the attraction of goodness (defined in terms of maximizing pleasure in the cosmos) that they behave in accord with the divine 'lure'. Prayers of petition that God may act to achieve a particular end have to be rein-terpreted according to this view of God. The prayers most fitted to the 'process' God are those, often heard in churches, that request God to 'teach us' that something is so, or ask that people may 'know' something. These forms of petition throw the first responsibility onto the people, and call in God at second place. In particular, the formula 'help us to' or 'may we' displaces the calling upon God to act.

Such prayers have been criticized as Pelagian and didactic by some commentators.[22] They echo the view of Pelagius, deemed a heretic by the early church, that God's grace is simply an external prompting to moral achievement. 'Christ taught us this and that' is a common form of such prayer, or 'Give us grace to do this and that'; the congregation having lis-tened to this prayer as a kind of sermon is then expected to arise and do these good works. One critic of such prayer notes that Christ prays that the kingdom may come, not that we may have a heightened religious awareness. The tendency of some prayers is to ask for a change in our subjective state rather than making 'the confident, robust demands upon God which the biblical and early Christian writers were prepared to make'.[23]

But if one's doctrine of God does not have scope for such robust demands, then the more 'Pelagian', 'didactic', and moralizing form of prayer seems to be the only alternative. The one who prays asks for the strength and motivation necessary for the discipleship to achieve the requested aim of the petition. The one who acts is the one who prays, God coming in as an encouraging agent. The God of process thought is like this; he is not sovereign, but does care and exerts influence by allurement offered to the consciousness of the created order. We have observed, how-ever, that this God may change in the face of world history, and to pray to this God therefore entails a risk that such change may in fact have taken place.[24]

Petitionary prayer to this deity means communication with the 'consequent' pole of his being, that is, to the aspect of God which is immersed into the world. Petitions can hardly be more specific than seeking the maintenance of the divine lure towards goodness, and the promotion of further desire to pray and act. Prayer returns to the pray-er, or deepens communion between the consequent pole of deity and the faithful. Prayer affects God, or the consequent pole of God, and reflexively acts on the worshipper by way of deepening commitment to the joint project of creation. This might be said to equate to the reality of grace or the Holy Spirit at work in the heart of the one who prays and reflects on the character of the deity. Such a God is powerless to supply any bread, but may persuade humanity to grow and distribute it fairly.

The classical view such thinking seeks to replace stems from the ideas of Thomas Aquinas in the Middle Ages. Aquinas regards God as timeless, outside of the temporal process and so beyond the scope of our knowing. Strangely similar in this regard to its apparent inverse, the thinking of Kant following the 'Enlightenment' period, an agnosticism covers the deity of Aquinas. We know *that* God is, but cannot say much if anything as to *what* God is. We know that God is not in time or space, and that we can use words about God to say that he loves, creates, and is good; but since these terms are analogous, urges Aquinas, we cannot know *what they really mean* as they apply to God.[25] What can it mean to say that God acts, or that God gives daily bread, on such a view of God?

The timeless God of Aquinas's thought does not exist within the time continuum;[26] rather, all events are simultaneous to this God who is like the man on top of a hill who watches in one panoramic view the progress of the figures below. God thus knows the future. God knows that some things will happen by way of the petitionary prayers of some of the faithful, and that these prayers will duly happen; indeed, in the timeless or panoramic vision of God they *have* happened, as have the events or non-events to which they refer. That is the theological framework for the petition, 'give us today our daily bread'. This God 'acts' timelessly and spacelessly upon temporal events to answer our prayers, and so it is claimed that he can respond to our prayers without being changed by them. The timeless God, unlike the God of process thought, is immutable.

For this classical Thomist view, if a prayer is made that a relation be cured, and God does cure the person, then God acts timelessly to bring about this effect in time. It is not necessarily true to assume that because the passing of time was involved in bringing this effect about, then God must be in time, as some modern critics have argued.[27] As a matter of logic, it does seems possible to argue that God can act timelessly to bring about the effect in human history. But while this is a logically tenable position, it is difficult to understand since the terms 'God' and 'action' are shrouded in mystery, and do not represent concepts with content approaching the meaning common to humans. Augustine famously asked and answered the question concerning time and God prior to the created universe; he concluded that time only came into being at creation, and hence there could be no time 'prior' to God in which God is.[28] So God exists timelessly, argue Aquinas and Augustine, and does not experience the passage of events as a temporal flow as we do.

Peter Vardy questions the coherence of this view, asking us to imagine (however difficult it may be) God, with no time frame, at the inception of creation. If creation is to have a beginning, he argues, the universe must begin to exist, and so 'God must timelessly do the equivalent of saying "Let there be light". There is, however, no moment at which this can be said—even timelessly'.[29] Vardy argues that with an image of a timeless God it is very difficult to envisage a 'moment' at which the universe began. Either it must have 'always' existed, in which case God did not 'create' it; or it can never exist. Given a timeless God, creation cannot come to exist when it did not exist before. The suggestion that creation exists in the mind of God as an imaginary construct will not solve the problem, as it raises the further problem as to how an eternal idea could account for a finite realm of changes and chances (a problem with which Plato wrestled). As Vardy says, simply asserting that the initiation of creation is revealed to us by God as a truth will not resolve these difficulties.

The question is this: how, then, can a timeless God give 'daily' bread? In response to these challenges, the notion of God as 'everlasting' rather than eternal has been gaining popularity among philosophers, and recently also among conservative evangelical thinkers.[30] The everlasting God exists in time, or at least with time, and so the future is open for God, although being God he has the ability to guess the future in a way we do not. The future does not 'pre-exist' in the panoramic view of God. God is 'omnipotent' in the sense that he has the power to do what is logically possible for him to do, granted the conditions of creation he has himself established. Similarly, God is 'omniscient' in the limited sense that he knows everything that can be known, given the nature of his own creation. As one modern philosopher puts it:

[God] is omniscient if he knows about everything except those future states and their consequences which are not physically necessitated by anything in the past; and if he knows that he does not know about those future states.[31]

God can be likened to the great chess player who knows *that* he will win and *roughly how* he will win, but not with total foresight of all the details. God knows all the possibilities of the future and all the perils ahead. But if human free will is to be sustained, God cannot 'act' so as to prevent the consequences of evil human activity. Nevertheless God can work around such disasters so as to ensure his purposes do eventually succeed.

God works through the created order more like the course of a river winding to the sea than that of a canal 'blasted through the rock', using John Oman's analogy.[32] This is certainly the pattern of biblical history. The majesty and mystery of God often consist in just this capacity to work through events that are set to contradict his will, and to use them so as to bring about his purposes. Often this happens through weakness and defeat. Moses, the helpless baby left on the river by the persecuted slaves, ends up at the heart of power of the persecuting empire to become the agent of salvation for the oppressed.

'My strength is made perfect in weakness', says God to the apostle Paul, and this seems to be a principle at work in history as interpreted by the biblical tradition. Divine respect for human decisions and actions is accompanied by divine wisdom at work in the weak and despised, which, in due time, and with no little paradox, erodes centres of wrong to build up the good. When we speak of divine action, the biblical tradition speaks often of events being influenced by individuals who are faithful and fearful.

The way of shaping events seems to be through personal agency rather than through the huge processes and forces of history. Perhaps this is better put in terms of the difference between the order of 'knowing' and of 'being'. The biblical tradition commonly focuses upon individuals who act as levers to begin vast movements in time; in terms of what we know, personality counts massively. Supremely the Nazarene who died helplessly and unjustly has projected forces of the spirit for good down through the centuries. God acts in and through human actions and vocations. In this, the process theologians fasten onto an undoubted Christian truth, although they unnecessarily limit *the way* that God acts through human response.

God respects the human free will he has mysteriously created, and limits his action by this free will, at the same time using it as the means of his activity (or at least a major means) in history. God works through persons who obey him to move apparent mountains of opposition. Prayer must be seen in this light, as part of the obedient personal will being open to this God. Somehow the openness of the human spirit creates pathways for divine action, and often saving action according to biblical narratives. The self-offering of humanity to the Father in prayer and worship, the environment in which petition is set, is part of the freedom of the will. This freedom is turned over to divine use in history, and with this genuine offer God works his will. Presumably such is prayer in the name and nature of Jesus; such is prayer 'in the Spirit'.

5. Petitionary prayer and change in God

The choice of the individual, surrendered to God in Christ, opens the way for divine purpose to come about. There is a paradox here; it is as if God needs to be given 'permission' by the free human will as a condition of his activity, which is therefore both his and ours. Such is the depth of respect given to the created being by God. Intercession and petition, 'give us today our daily bread', when prayed sincerely, gives God permission to supply that need, rather than its being provided automatically by the world process as autonomous mechanism. Petition seems to be both acknowledgement and permission. Jesus told the disciples that he must wash their feet, and so he needed their permission to show such love and commitment. Perhaps this is so for God the Father and his care for the world's needs.

But if prayer in any sense gives God 'permission' to act, does it then change God? Can any human event change God? Clearly the process theologians are happy to accept this in a full sense, since God is vulnerable to the world process. But we have seen that this means, in theory, that the 'consequent' pole of deity (immersed into the world) could become degraded, and so degrade in turn the 'necessary' (or absolute) dimension of the divine life. God could become corrupt, dragged down by the world's self-gratification. In contrast, the timeless deity of Thomas Aquinas cannot change. But could such a deity interact with temporal beings at all? 'We do not pray', says Thomas Aquinas, 'in order to change the decree of divine providence; rather we pray in order to acquire by petitionary prayer what God has determined would be obtained by our prayers.'[33] On this view of God, the prayers we pray have been foreseen and also the outcome of the prayers. This indicates a predestinarian relationship of God and the world which rules out free will in any meaningful sense.

The Christian experience of prayer is that God does care and wants to be deliberately invited into situations by his faithful people. Whether or not situations are altered because of petition, it does mean that such prayer has an impact on *God*, that God is 'moved' by prayer, he is not impassive and uninterested. He has and takes an interest in all events, desiring to co-operate with human free will and prayer.[34] Prayer does affect God, and offers to God human wills open to do his Christlike will in the world. When the church prays 'in Christ', she takes part in the communion between Christ and the Father, and so God relates to the church as he related to the human Jesus. As Peter Vardy points out,[35] the conclusion can hardly be resisted that the worship and prayer of believers touches the heart of God as Jesus did in his messianic ministry, and that God regards people of faith as sharing in the project of the kingdom of his Son.

This chimes in with the 'naive' attitude of the ordinary Christian towards worship and prayer. God does have an openness to such worship in which he is glad, and an openness to petitionary prayer which he can use as a means of acting in the world through the freedom of people. God does relate to human time in a way going beyond the logical and formal; he accommodates himself to relate to humanity and wishes this to happen. He freely wills that prayer, of all kinds, be a factor in the sustaining of the universe. God must therefore be said to be 'open' to the freedom of creation, albeit not as vulnerable in his being as the process view implies. We should say that the identity and character of God are stable and exist in themselves without reference to the created order. But the way God relates to creation in its developments is open to the interactive processes of human history. The personal category gains priority over impersonal process, and this is expressed by affirming that God is 'everlasting' rather than timelessly 'eternal'. God, as Temple suggested, continually adjusts and refashions his actions towards and in history.

The transcendent God is open to the world, and seeks the prayerful communion of the creation, reaching into the created order to evoke response and make covenant. In the early centuries of the church, the controversy with Arius established this axiom for the Christian faith: the transcendent Father, not some lesser unrelated God, saves and attracts praise and petition. The group of theologians, led by Athanasius, who triumphed

over Arius affirmed that God the Father was in the most intimate relationship with the divine Son who became incarnate in the world; unfortu-
nately, they also assumed that the Father was timeless in relation to
creation. Whether such a Father could be actually affected, in all senses
of the word, by the prayers of the world seems doubtful, as for Thomas
Aquinas later on. Given the real humanity of Jesus and his deepest interaction with the Father, the patristic doctrine of the impassibility and total
changelessness of God seems to need revision. God's very heart is glad-
dened and saddened by events and attitudes of humanity, and of his
church in particular.

Christian prayer seems to demand that God be not timeless and
unchangeable in the sense that Aquinas and patristic theology envisaged.
God is indeed immutable in the sense that a person is unchangeable; that
is, his identity remains, and his moral character endures. God is not vulnerable to degradation from his interaction with creation, so that the relationship is 'asymmetrical', as is that, for example, of a father to his small
child. This is, of course, precisely the analogy that Jesus himself draws
upon. The relation involves God in limiting his interventions in order to
sustain human free will, thus respecting his good creation. This human
free will at the same time serves as a pathway for divine grace to enhance
and support the messianic kingdom. God's sceptre of rule[36] is that of the
crucified and risen Jesus, the rule of love and strength made perfect in
weakness.

This respecting of freedom begins to explain why, to the human worshipper, the 'answer' to prayer will usually appear ambiguous. Although
occasionally it may be crystal clear existentially and personally, it can
never be provable in the eyes of others. As we saw in considering the
prayer 'your will be done', the overarching plan of God for final good and
fulfilled communion with humanity has been revealed by the resurrection
of Jesus. But the milliard sub-plots and their fine adjustments in the light
of human free will are not readable here and now, although many testify
that the retrospective view does often make sense of things. From this perspective the paradox of grace can be traced even through tragedy. George
Matheson, in his blindness, wrote a now well-known hymn:

> O Joy that seekest me through pain,
> I cannot close my heart to Thee;
> I trace the rainbow through the rain,
> And feel the promise is not vain
> That morn shall tearless be.[37]

Matheson holds on by faith alone, trusting that the purposes of God are caring, despite the appalling affliction he is undergoing. The resurrection of the broken and betrayed Jesus stands surety for the deepest care and victory of the kingdom of God, where other events remain ambiguous witnesses. 'That God did not intervene in answer to my prayer to save the life of some friend during the Great War by deflection of a bullet may perhaps be indirectly a manifestation of His love both for my friend and for me', says William Temple, 'but if He raised Jesus of Nazareth from death, that is a much more direct manifestation of His relationship to the Life and Death of Jesus'.[38]

6. Praying in time: the journey and the place

Christian experience of prayer may reflect different doctrines of the relation between God and time favoured by different families of churches. The evangelical tradition, with its view of personal conversion and discipleship by faith and close attention to the biblical narratives, naturally assumes God to be the one who travels through life with us; he is the constant companion on the journey, the bearer of our sins and the sympathizer with our struggles. God is really affected by our situations and our prayers, however little we can make sense of things at times.

This is not a timeless God. This God sent his only and beloved Son, and so somehow invested himself into the suffering of the world and all its sin, to redeem and reconcile us. God is 'the creative sufferer', to use Paul Fiddes' phrase,[39] complementing the words of William Temple, 'the creative charity of God'. Humanity relates to the Father in a real way, God relates to the temporal order in its struggle into the future. Evangelical spirituality assumes the presence of the Spirit in people of faith, mediating the person of Jesus, in whom praise and petition is addressed to the Father. The position outlined here is the one assumed in evangelical spirituality and increasingly argued for in its formal theology,[40] against the predestinarian theology associated with high Calvinism which continued the medieval doctrines of divine predestination.

Roman Catholic spirituality, however, focuses on the presence of the Spirit in sacramental *objects,* especially the eucharistic host in ritual re-enactment of the sacrifice of Jesus. Time is overcome by this ritual, as the eternal God is offered the eucharistic sacrifice in a timeless manner of symbol and mystery. God himself is utterly transcendent and timeless, and it is the blessed virgin Mary who assumes the role of the

approachable one, the one who will speak for the faithful to the Father
and even to the Son, now exalted to the distant position of the All-ruler
(*Pantocrator*). The telling of the rosary, set after set, brings the worshipper into a timeless mode of circular repetitions of prayer. Candles are lit
as prayers in the stillness of the sanctuary, signals of transcendence overcoming the continuum of this fleeting world. Such a spiritual pattern,
concentrating on the holy place where eternity breaks in, suggests a quite
different understanding of prayer to that of the more historically minded
evangelical on the 'journey' of life.

The way that the Holy Spirit is conceived to work and be present in
the church highlights the difference. For evangelical piety the Spirit is
constantly present to the believer, continually enabling and guiding in the
unique choices each must make in life, constantly promoting personal
sanctification. The Spirit can even be 'grieved' by disobedience. The
Spirit is *primarily* present through the sacramental system in the Roman
Catholic and Orthodox traditions, and also specially present in shrines,
places and holy things; the timeless mysteriously becomes present in
places which have a quality of timelessness. The Reformation might
arguably best be described as a pneumatological shift of emphasis, stress-
ing Christ 'personally' present in the Spirit rather than received through
the sacramental system.

The 'dialogue' structure of the word and response to it typifies evangelical frameworks of prayer. For the evangelical, God communicates
through his word, the living Word of Christ and the written words coming
alive as they rekindle faith. Roman Catholic piety focuses on the visual,
the static, the mysterious. Union with the transcendent occurs through the
tangible and visual by way of *anamnesis*, a remembrance that overcomes
time as the worshipper becomes one with 'the eternal now'. One spirituality assumes that God is leading the believer along on the journey of discipleship, walking in the Spirit; the other is a pilgrimage from place to
place, at each of which the timeless touches this changing flow of time,
providing moments of poise, stillness.

The merits of the evangelical emphasis lie in the closeness of communion assumed, the biblical injunction to regard God as the caring
Father who knows and feels the pain of the tiniest realm of the universe,
the fall of the sparrow. This view, we might say, wishes to have all the
advantages of process theology, while mitigating the vulnerability of God
to certain kinds of change, especially in character, that this theology
seems to entail. The evangelical view is that God is not struggling to

attain his purposes, while he does constantly respect human freedom and works,[41] moving like a river rather than a canal through historical and natural circumstances to achieve the final triumph of love. The weakness of this approach, of course, is that God can be envisioned as too similar to a human person, with just the faults ironed out. God can appear to be a super-parent, with insufficient 'otherness'.

Both the evangelical and the Roman Catholic emphases have their strengths and weaknesses. As Peter Vardy points out,[42] each approach in fact believes in a perfect and immutable God: while the Catholic-philosophical theology conceives this as metaphysical perfection, the evangelical-biblical theology thinks of a moral changelessness. It seems that Christian spirituality, of whatever kind, requires a God who hears and cares genuinely, not just formally; and a God who is 'other' than us, yet not so transcendent that he is beyond our 'appreciation' as worthy of adoration. Karl Barth speaks of the real involvement of God with us as the 'humanity of God',[43] so closely does he regard the being of God as united with the human life of Jesus Christ. This leads him to express the relation of God towards time in a way centred upon Christ; Jesus is 'God's time for us', a 'time in God' that is the basis for revelation in human history.[44]

Any version of the 'everlasting God' who 'journeys with us' must allow for some real relationship of God to time, and Barth's concept of 'time *in* God' deflects the criticism that such a God is simply world history or its mind. There must be some *sequence* in the mind of God, if God is more analogous to a person than a substance. Time of some sort, therefore, exists in God, who has always existed. But this does not mean that time is another object over against God, in a kind of eternal dualism. God has 'time for us' within his own mode of time. Time is not therefore simply endless, a meaningless succession, but has a beginning in God and a goal. Barth tells us that 'the myth of infinite or endless time is shattered by revelation. In revelation, time has discovered its origin and goal'.[45] God, says Barth, bestows time and leaves us time, an aspect of divine long-suffering with the world, a waiting for repentance and faith.

The notion of 'time in God' cuts away any suggestion of a frozen stillness in God, which would be the *inverse* of temporality; Hellenistic philosophy developed such concepts of perfect Being by reversal from this imperfect world of change and emotion. Only non-temporal being, they thought, could be the ground for temporality. In contrast, Barth thinks of 'time in God' by carrying the life, death, and resurrection of Jesus into the divine trinitarian life.

We can also arrive at the same vision of God from another angle. The leading Orthodox theologian John Zizioulas has advanced the thesis that true being is 'communion', and that the human quest for meaning centred upon itself leads to death as the final meaning.[46] God is life and communion in himself, Father, Son, and Spirit. The pattern of such life is ecstatic, reaching out to 'the other' and affirming the other, conferring identity on the other. The basis of 'being' itself for Zizioulas is thus personal; he claims that in contrast to the Western tradition the East stresses 'with regard to God and also with regard to man that the basis of ontology is the person; just as God "is" what he is in his nature, "perfect God", only as person, so too man in Christ is "perfect man" only as hypostasis, as person, that is as freedom and love'.[47] Such trinitarian being cannot be frozen substance or introverted pure mind, but is life, communion, freedom, and love.

Now, if God exists in a communion of love, he cannot be the inverse or negation of time. This God shares his life in pure generosity with creation, seeking communion with the world. God made the world for communion with himself, and in this way is its origin and ground. God is likewise the final end and meaning of the world, its goal and purpose. The communion of God within himself is 'everlasting', but this is no mere mental stability; by analogy with human persons, he imports a vitality and joy that embraces experience as a whole. Hence the divine communion is inclusive of temporal experience rather than seeking to get beyond it to a superior vantage point. The eternity of God as living communion must be a temporally-charged eternity. God is love in his very being as communion, and creation in the Word or the Son is creation in and through this love and life, creation intended to respond to this love.

Prayer for our daily bread is prayer to the one who desires communion with us. Such trustful prayer, out of the context of the world's perverse refusal to love God and fellow man, the first two and great commandments, enacts what God desires. This petition looks to God for the material aspect of life, and this is highly significant for our understanding of the communion that the living and loving God desires. Other parts of the Lord's Prayer look to God for orientation in other ways that we usually label 'moral' and the 'spiritual'. But the material creation—daily bread—is good, equally originating from the love of the Father, equally sustained by the creative Word, equally pregnant with the goodness of the creator. To ask for our daily bread is to ask for the right working of the good creation, to co-operate in the day-to-day restoration of the world to

God's purpose. Furthermore, to ask in this way for daily bread is always to ask for 'our' needful resources, not simply for 'mine', and so fits in with the pattern of prayer in the name of Jesus.

This prayer, centred on God the Father and prayed in Christ, is a matter of communion. God is being asked to oversee not only our souls but our bodies. God cannot be used as a means of gaining bread; such asking for bread, like those Corinthians taking the loaf of the holy communion 'without discerning the body', is asking in bad faith (1 Cor 11:29). Such a manipulative and consumerist approach inevitably attracts divine displeasure and judgement, since God is jealous for our love and trust, not to be treated as a dumb idol. Another way of putting this is to say, with Zizioulas and Barth, that God is personal and that to treat him as impersonal substance or disinterested mind is to offend God.

7. Prayer as the renewal of time

Love transcends time, and the lover transcends time in loving:

> Love's not Time's fool, though rosy lips and cheeks
> Within his bending sickle's compass come,
> Love alters not with his brief hours and weeks,
> But bears it out even to the edge of doom.[48]

John Macquarrie has pointed out that in the act of thinking a human person is lifted above time, or mere succession of events, because he can gain a kind of overview as he considers being in time.[49] But love may provide an even more helpful category than thinking to apply to God and time, since it describes a relationship of a deeper kind than that of knowing about the succession of events surrounding us.

Prayer to a timeless God who has already seen and arranged the events of history would have a quality of pure submission. The prayers themselves would be predestined, pre-arranged events which would be a means of achieving the events preordained. The Christian experience of prayer resists this interpretation. God is really concerned with our lives, God does seek to accompany us on life's journey, according to the biblical narrative of a God dwelling with his people who learn as they go in faith. The divine love leads to life and overcomes final isolation in death. The resurrection of Jesus establishes this. Time as succession of events ends for us with death. But love as relationship transcends mere succession, and the process theologians have realized this in teaching that each event is 'open' to the next in an organic type of relativity.[50] But personal love and sacrifice for another goes beyond a mere principle of 'die to live'; it stems from a core act of a human will, an 'I am' that cannot be linked to other units of reality as some kind of natural process.

God is surely best understood as open to our experiences and to our prayers, sharing our trials and tribulations rather than setting a kind of spiritual assault course in advance. In the created order the future therefore is real, real for us and for God. The majesty of God is his power of bringing good out of evil, life out death, leading his people through gaining their co-operation. The love of God draws out the latent spirit of the created order by the relationship of saving commitment, bringing creation into conformity with the creative Word who patterned it in the beginning.

Prayer is therefore divine time, or renewal of time, an eschatological enhancing of that time which is constituted by our sinful action; for without action there would be no life, no time. In prayer the spirit of God and our spirits unite in a mutual 'Amen' to the kingdom of God, and this affirmation of divine rule includes the blessings of creation, for which creatures cry out. The heart hardened with sin registers the passage of events with a cool and calculating detachment, since even people are reckoned as objects to be used and thrown away. So time is bound to be felt as a mere successiveness. Love seeks to preserve and fulfil life not its own, to overcome death; God's love builds a kingdom of mutual caring and respect, to evoke from all life its created potential. Sin rejects God, the source of all life and relationship, choosing foreclosure of time and control of time, rather than life within the heart of divine relationship which is the basis of all time.

Prayer in the Spirit seeks the fulfilment of creation, the kingdom of God, from the standpoint of Jesus. Such prayer seeks the healing of what has been withered, and the support of the vulnerable in this world of threat. Daily bread, requested for 'us' and not simply for 'me', is a good thing of the good creation which we know God wishes to bestow. Praying for this daily bread coincides with the will of the heavenly Father who wishes to supply it, who will eschatologically abolish all pain and end all separation. The misery of loss and death, the ending of relationship and love, will be overcome by God who is loving relationship in his own being. Death means the triumph of time over mere nature or sinful nature that is turned in on itself and away from God; resurrection is the fulfilment of nature and its transformation. Death cuts off mere succession, but endless time as an everlasting chain of events would not itself constitute life.

Life for humanity images divine life, whose meaning is love; life is not mere continuity and reconfiguration of similar patterns but personal decision, expression, and response. Prayer is a crucial part of this life which transcends mere succession and biological nature. True prayer is deeply personal, a relation with the God who gives the time continuum meaning by relatedness of a personal kind. Petitionary prayer assumes that time has a meaning, that it is not merely equivalent to a print-out of a computer programme already established, no determinism of either a materialist or a theological kind.

God is the God who cares and takes final responsibility for the world as good, as against the view that the world is finally absurd and meaningless. Continuing to pray includes the affirmation of trust that this is so, that God guarantees the rightness of things. Praying for the necessities of life assumes such an order to be right. God, the God of the living and not of the dead, has shown his mastery of time and his power to bring it to fulfilment while engaging with it, by the resurrection of Jesus. By that personal act both space and time are transformed, not abolished, and taken to fulfilment in the purposes of the Father.

In Christ, the church prays to the Father, the Spirit bringing out the potential of creation now redeemed and restored through the resurrected Christ. This is a painful process, new wine requiring new wine skins to contain it. Transformation of lives and of history is the expectation of the Gospel. Prayer, communion with God and his purposes, is part of this transformational activity of God and of ourselves. God acted in the risen Jesus by overcoming the final alienation of death, the final isolation of inward collapse to nothingness. The human life and spirit of Jesus was one of love, one of integration with the Father, a life full of the Holy Spirit, realising the full potential of the Spirit in creation. The truth of creation rose from death in Jesus. This is the guarantee of the kingdom of God the Father, the warrant that love does survive violence and the absence of daily bread, lack of civil behaviour, want of respect and justice.

The Father remains the caring one, despite appearances, despite apparent hopelessness. God knows that the faithful ones of creation will not fall into nothingness, but will be transformed from within time, not escaping from it but transfiguring it. Prayer in the will of God, in Christ, through the Spirit, is prayer from this resurrection perspective of renewal and hope. The faithful pray in the power and love of the new age of the risen Lord, while existing in this fallen world history. This means that those who pray find themselves constantly in need of self-criticism: am I praying aright? Am I praying truly in the way of Jesus, who revealed the kingdom amidst the darkness of historical powers? But this need not be an anxious questioning, for those who pray find that their prayer is 'adjusted' in dialogue with the Father, whose Son refines our sensitivities of communion.

God has acted in raising Jesus in a way which coincides with raising creation to its true self. This act echoes the creation of the universe, with its gift of freedom and its costly underwriting by the cross, 'in the heart of God before there was one planted on the green hill outside Jerusalem'.[51] God created the universe, while existing in his own life of actual love and choosing freely to bring into being a partner with whom to relate. This was the great act of God, intending to create a body of people relating in love and rejoicing in God. God's creative act in creating a self-creative universe is thus one way in which God can be said to act in the world. The fact that this God desires the prayer of humanity indicates his ongoing care of the world within the world. It also shows that communion with God is another vital way of divine action in history, mirroring the being of God as communion. Petitionary prayer in Christ, in the Spirit, to the Father by human beings amounts to an asymmetrical venture in influencing events for the good through communion. The creative act confers human freedom, a prime means of creativity which finds its fulfilment when yielded to the divine purpose. Divine self-limitation in creation, limitation to provide a space[52] for freedom and the development of holiness within creation, unites God with humanity in a covenant of self-giving.

The created creativity, the free will given 'space' to be and to do, was always intended to want and do the good. Prayer in the name of Jesus to the creator Father is prayer in the creative Word, immanent in the created order. The space we are given is filled with this Word of creativity, in communion with the Father's will. Intercession with Jesus, to the Father, in the Spirit, such is the church's stance when she prays for her daily bread.

8. Daily bread: the need and the gift

Asking God expresses our need to God, and this attitude must remain. Our asking is not so that we will one day stock our individual cupboard so full as to gain independence from the giver. Our asking comes in the context of worshipping God the heavenly Father, in a prior relationship and participation. The asking for our daily needs comes in the context of our desire for God and God's for us, so that our desire that our needs be met is part of our discipleship. The desire for God and for blessing by God will never end, nor should we wish for that. It is, according to Rowan Williams, 'impure desire' that desires to stop *having* to desire, to stop needing; it asks for a state where, finally, the ego can relax into self-sufficiency and 'does not have to go on stuffing bits and pieces of the world into itself in order to survive.'[53]

Intercessory prayer is a privilege and no matter of regret. It is part of worship, of a glad dependence which leads to maturity. C. S. Lewis regards our 'need-love' for God as vital, and the reverse as dangerous:

> Man approaches God most nearly when he is in one sense least like God. For what can be more unlike than fullness and need, sovereignty and humility, righteousness and penitence, limitless power and a cry for help?[54]

Asking as part of our approach to God expresses our 'need-love', but when characterized by Christlikeness it also displays a 'gift-love'. The royal kingdom and the priestly sacrifice unite in such prayer, which is the church's only power and her delight in making a self-offering to God and to neighbour. It is important to stress that praying for our daily bread includes the aspect of responsive love, the offering of love as a gift to God, so as to avoid the notion of the oppressive deity who wishes for a cringing and subdued creation beneath his heel. Such a view of God is deservedly criticized, and in their different ways Nietzsche and Bonhoeffer revealed its danger. The Christian petition 'Give us today our daily bread' is made in the security of divine love, and shares in its creativity.

Notes to Chapter 6

[1]Tertullian, *On Prayer*, ch.V, in *The Ante-Nicene Fathers*, Vol. 3, trans. and ed. A. Roberts, J. Donaldson, A. Coxe (repr. T & T Clark/Eerdmans, Edinburgh/ Grand Rapids, 1993), p. 683.

[2]*Jerome Biblical Commentary*, ed. R. Brown, J. Fitzmyer, R. Murphy (Prentice-Hall, Englewood Cliffs NJ, 1968), p. 73.

[3]Cullmann, *Prayer in the New Testament*, p. 51.

[4]John 5:17, 'My Father is working still and I am working', the precise context of this being Jesus' healing on a Sabbath, a restoration of creation.

[5]Hopkins, 'The Wreck of the Deutschland', stanza 5, *The Poems of Gerard Manley Hopkins*, 4th ed., ed. W. H. Gardner and N. H. MacKenzie (Oxford University Press, London, 1967), p. 53.

[6]The phrase was coined by Matthew Fox in his book *Original Blessings* (Bear & Co., Santa Fe NM, 1983). While Fox seems seriously to underestimate the problem of the fall and the need for redemption, his phrase does capture the original goodness of the created order.

[7]Temple, *Nature, Man, and God* (London, Macmillan, 1935), p. 295.

[8]Ibid.

[9]'So the Personal Deity universally immanent—the Logos—may for centuries act in ways that very imperfectly disclose His Character; yet when time is appropriate may submit Himself to conditions which reveal that Character as it had always been.' Temple, *Nature, Man and God*, p. 296.

[10]Ibid., p. 296.

[11]Temple's interpretation of the activity of God in the world comes close to the 'process' view, but with a more personalist and flexible aspect to the divine 'lure'. Temple, in fact, was very familiar with and appreciative of the writings of Whitehead prior to 1939, well in advance of their theological vogue. The principle of individuality, with roots in the lower levels of organic reality, is vital to Temple's interpretation of reality and God, and individuality cannot be subject to a naturalistic grid of predictability. This is so in our consideration of the world generally with its hierarchy of being, and especially when we consider God. The 'lure' of God, characteristic of the process theology, gains a more particularist turn in Temple's interpretation.

[12]Temple, *Nature, Man, and God*, p. 297.

[13]Wolfhart Pannenberg, *Basic Questions in Theology*, Vol. 3, trans. R. Wilson (SCM Press, London, 1971), pp. 94-97, 99-115.

[14]Temple, *Nature, Man, and God*, p. 297.

[15]Herbert Waddams, *Life and Fire of Love: Prayer and Its Presuppositions* (SPCK, London, 1964) collects texts from spiritual writers illustrating this claim. Temple thinks that the phenomenon could be monitored and testimonies of religious people surveyed as evidence.

[16]The phrase can be found in a sermon delivered by F. D. Maurice on this petition of the Lord's Prayer, March 12th, 1848. See F. D. Maurice, *The Prayer Book and Lord's Prayer* (Macmillan, London 1893), p. 335.

[17]Coined by Alan Galloway in his book on Pannenberg's theology, *Wolfhart Pannenberg* (Allen and Unwin, London, 1973), p. 19.

[18]1 Corinthians 2:10; cf. Romans 8:27.

[19]Temple, *Nature, Man, and God*, p. 302.

[20]Ephesians 5:22-24; Hosea 1:1-3; 3:14-20.

[21]See above, pp. 99-100.

[22]Stuart Hall, 'Sub-Christian Prayer: Pelagian Didacticism in the Alternative Service Book 1980', in *King's College Review*, Vol. IV, no. 1, Spring 1981.

[23]Ibid., p. 2.

[24]See above, pp. 101-103.

[25]Aquinas, *Summa Theologiae*, 1a.12-13, esp. 1a.13:3.

[26]Aquinas, *Summa Theologiae*, 1a.10:2-3

[27]That assumption is powerfully argued by Nelson Pike in his *God and Timelessness* (Routledge and Kegan Paul, London, 1970).

[28]Augustine, *Confessions*, XI.30.

[29]Peter Vardy, *The Puzzle of God* (Collins Fount, London, 1990), p. 140.

[30]See, e.g., Clark Pinnock et. al., *The Openness of God*, (IVP USA/ Paternoster Press UK, Carlisle, 1994.). This set of essays argues for the God who does not know the future in detail, who is morally unchanging but interactive with history.

[31]Richard Swinburne *The Coherence of Theism* (Clarendon Press, Oxford, 1986), p. 175.

[32]John Oman, *Grace and Personality* (1917, repr. Collins Fontana, London, 1960), p. 25: 'God does not conduct his rivers like arrows to the sea', unlike the canal blasted through the rock. 'The ruler and compass are only for finite mortals, who labour by taking thought, to overcome their limitations, and are not for the infinite mind. . . . the question is whether God ever does override the human spirit in that direct way, and whether we ought to conceive either of His spirit or of ours after a fashion that could make it possible. Would such irresistible might as would save us from all error and compel us into right action be in accord either with God's personality or with ours?'

[33]Aquinas, *Summa Theologiae* 2a2ae. 83

[34]Keith Ward says, 'As God may justly leave many outcomes to free human choice, and not determine them himself, so he may permit some outcomes that he would otherwise determine himself to be modified and directed by human choices, in the form of requests made to him in the context of worship. Prayer is then seen as an extension of human freedom'; Ward, *Divine Action* (Harper Collins, London, 1990), p. 160.

[35]Peter Vardy, *The Puzzle of Evil* (Collins, London, 1992) p. 138.

[36]The intended reference is to Psalm 2 and its re-use in the New Testament for the rule of Christ; see G. B. Caird, *The Language and Imagery of the Bible* (Duckworth, London, 1980), pp. 180-82, and cf. Oliver O'Donovan, *The Desire of the Nations* (Cambridge University Press, Cambridge, 1996), pp. 144-46.

[37]George Matheson (1842–1906), hymn 'O Love that will not let me go', verse 3.

[38]Temple, *Nature, Man, and God*, p. 303.

[39]Fiddes, *The Creative Suffering of God*, esp. ch. 6.

[40]See reference in note 30 above.

[41]'The Gospel of free forgiveness—in technical language, justification by faith—excludes a despotic God', H. M. Gwatkin, *Church and State in England to the Death of Queen Anne* (Longmans, London, 1917), p. 231. The logic of the evangelical gospel has long been pressing towards a revision of the medieval and Calvinist doctrine of God.

[42]Vardy, *The Puzzle of God*, p. 45. He points out that the philosophically influenced interpretation of God held in Roman Catholic theology does 'not necessarily mean that believers in a timeless God cannot maintain that they have a relationship with this God. However, the relationship is difficult to define or envisage, since their God can never change, react, respond or love in the way that these words normally imply'.

[43]Karl Barth, *The Humanity of God*, trans. C. Deans (Collins, London, 1960), pp. 35-65; cf. *Church Dogmatics*, II/1, pp. 7-10.

[44]Barth, *Church Dogmatics*, I/1, pp. 426-27; I/2, p. 45ff; II/1, p. 611f.

[45]Barth, *Church Dogmatics*, I/2, p. 69.

[46]Zizioulas, *Being as Communion*, pp. 44-47.

[47]Ibid., p. 53. Interestingly, Barth gives the categories of freedom and love pride of place in his doctrine of God, and also regards Jesus Christ as true man. Zizioulas, however, would regard Barth as having an insufficiently 'social' doctrine of the Trinity and being too modalist, a criticism he applies to Western-Augustinian trinitarianism.

[48]William Shakespeare, Sonnet 116, 'Let me not to the marriage of true minds. . . .'

[49]Macquarrie, *Principles of Christian Theology*, p. 208.

[50]E.g., Hartshorne, *Creative Synthesis and Philosophic Method*, pp. 188-90; Cobb, *A Christian Natural Theology*, pp. 40-46.

[51]Charles A. Dinsmore, quoted in Baillie, *God Was in Christ*, p. 194.

[52]Here Jürgen Moltmann appeals to the Jewish kabbalistic concept of *zimsum,* that God withdraws into himself in order to make a space of nothingness for 'creation from nothing'; *God in Creation*, trans. M. Kohl (SCM Press, London, 1985), pp. 86-87.

[53]Rowan Williams, *The Truce of God* (Collins Fount, London, 1983), p. 85.

[54]C. S. Lewis, *The Four Loves*, p. 12.

7

'Forgive us our sins, as we forgive those who sin against us. Save us from the time of trial and deliver us from evil'

1. Seeking forgiveness 'face to face'

The story of Isaiah praying in the Temple, as told in Isaiah chapter 6, has provided a classical instance of prayer for forgiveness. Isaiah perceives the greatness of God, before whom the seraphim cover their faces while proclaiming his holiness. Divine glory dominates. Isaiah senses his own unworthiness in contrast to the pure worth of God. He regards himself as a corrupt person in a corrupt society, 'a man of unclean lips, and I dwell in the midst of a people of unclean lips' (Isa 6:5).

Here we have a classic pattern for Christian confession and repentance. It is a God-centred prayer, not one rooted in self-contemplation and self-loathing but focused on divine goodness, truth, and beauty. The sheer wonder of this divine perfection bursting all bounds, filling the whole earth with glory (Isa 6:3), forms the background to self-examination. As with the structure of the Lord's Prayer itself, the glory of the creator dazzles. He is the great horizon against which the creation stands, and only then does sin intrude.

The sheer positive quality and *worth* of God manifests itself. The negativity of sin falls into perspective against the massive unfathomable holiness of God. Yet sin is no light matter; it is a matter of life and death, and Isaiah senses the awful gap between his own moral state and the goodness of the Lord, and crisis, judgement, falls on him in the realization of his condition. The burning coal from the altar carried by a seraph purges Isaiah's lips, and *atonement is made by God.*

The state of sin discerned by Isaiah in himself and networked into society is felt as no mere blemish but as 'sickness unto death', and Isaiah considers that his existence is wholly compromised, that he has no self-justification whatsoever, and must perish. But the holiness of God is revealed as a transforming and forgiving, *communicative* holiness, coming forth from the altar symbolically with fiery, purifying coals. Holiness in relationship is the purest form of love, the truth unfolded fully in the trinitarian gospel. The sending of the divine, cleansing Word into the world leads to the further sending of the disciples into mission, as the Lord sends Isaiah: 'Who will go for us? Here am I, send me'.

Isaiah, who worshipped and acknowledged his sin, acts in classical Hebraic fashion, a pattern found regularly through the spirituality of the

Bible. Sin needs to be honestly confessed to God, who hears and responds creatively to this utterly real self-disclosure. Judgement by God coincides with self-judgement before and with God. Divine judgement becomes human self-consciousness of sin, a crisis that for Christian theology comes to fullest expression at Calvary.

This is a heartfelt exchange between the individual and the God of judgement and grace, something utterly genuine. Mechanical or purely ritual actions, without genuine personal repentance, are often condemned in Old Testament literature:

> For you have no delight in sacrifice;
> were I to give a burnt offering, you would not be pleased.
> The sacrifice acceptable to God is a broken spirit;
> a broken and contrite heart, O God, you will not despise. (Ps 51:16-17)

Without the heartfelt reality of faith, external religion counts for nothing, and if anything attracts divine judgement. This theme appears in Paul's teaching about the eucharist: 'Whoever, therefore, eats the bread or drinks the cup of the Lord in an unworthy manner will be answerable for the body and blood of the Lord' (1 Cor 11:27), and will attract divine judgement (vv. 31-32). Selfishness and contempt for others at the Lord's Supper mocks the body of Christ as a unity of love. Isaiah is renewed within the cultic context. As Karl Barth teaches, the church again and again becomes the church as God mercifully and lovingly renews it:[1] the finger of the Spirit touches the edge of the old wineglass and makes it sing.

Forgiveness comes to the one who genuinely and honestly repents. The parable of the Pharisee and the tax collector (Luke 18:9) powerfully exemplifies the call for wholehearted and honest repentance in the eyes of God. This persistent fact of biblical spirituality reinforces the claim that Christian prayer resembles and shares something of the quality of human personal relationship. Honesty and genuineness of heart, being 'real' with God, seems to be a prerequisite in the faith found in the New Testament, and also in the Old. God's holiness is dazzling and yet communicated to the one who repents, given authentic turning to God in honesty. Forgiveness becomes restoration of relationship, or covenant, with the God who cares with a passion amounting to jealousy about this relationship.

Forgiveness, therefore, is a phenomenon which opens up the nature of personhood in perhaps the most radical way, in terms of both divine and human relationships, and the Lord's Prayer links the two together very plainly with its clause 'as we forgive those who sin against us'. Right relationships lie at the heart of forgiveness. The sin has wronged our neighbour and God. Offence in the created order offends the creator, a corollary of the 'first and great commandment' to love God and to love one's neighbour. The perception of Emmanuel Levinas, that the presence of the human 'face' confronting us confers an ethical responsibility upon us,[2] finds its final root in just such an encounter with the Lord of Hosts by Isaiah; it is an encounter with absolute worth calling for total response.

This point becomes obvious when we consider the phrase 'as we forgive those who sin against us'; seeking forgiveness from the face of the Lord cannot possibly be seen as gaining a spiritual 'commodity' for ourselves to hoard. Rather we seek renewal that opens us out to others, acting in the mode of generous forgiving love that we have ourselves received.

2. Forgiveness and personhood

Matthew's version of the Lord's Prayer has 'debts' in this phrase about forgiveness, while Luke has 'sins', but no significant difference in meaning is perceived by the commentators.[3] The truth of our condition is faced by either version. Love without truth is shallow and illusory, and the God of Jesus insists on passionate honesty. Someone has been treated without the care due to a person by another person. The wronged person has been treated more as an object than a human being, more as an 'it' than a 'thou'. Wrong can be also committed against beings which are less than human; the philosopher Nietzsche, to take a famous example, became severely ill when he rushed out to prevent a horse from being cruelly whipped. An animal, however, cannot forgive the one who wrongs it, although a person can try to 'make it up to' the creature, to 'atone' for the cruelty done to it, in that way acknowledging the wrong and seeking to make some sort of reparation.

Human reparation to a maltreated animal attempts a moral act of righting a wrong, just as replanting a decimated forest may seek to put right a greedy act of ecological vandalism. Such an act of reparation, born of moral imperative to make good damage done to the world, might be said to reveal an acknowledgement that there is an objective moral order which makes claims on us. In this sense, our 'sins' are indeed our 'debts'. In dealing with the animal kingdom we know that there is a right way of treating the 'beasts of the field', who have their place in the scheme of things. However, to abuse an animal and then to try to atone for the wrong done does not attract the *forgiveness* of the animal, although it may restore its trust, perhaps gradually, so that the human may again deal with it without arousing fear and panic. The link between the animal's behaviour following the reparation or atonement and that atonement itself does not really resemble a relationship restored through repentance and forgiveness; it may in fact look more like manipulation.

The reparation offered to non-human life, for example, feeding a guard dog properly after deliberately starving it, is certainly appropriate morally and does restore good relations between the human and the dog. But it only resembles externally the pattern of apology and forgiveness between humans; the resumption of calmer relations and the easing of the owner's conscience do not entail forgiveness. Repentance may have been made by the offender, both towards the creature and to God the creator, but the animal itself will not be able to grant forgiveness as could a human person. A moral asymmetry thus characterizes the relationship between animals and humans. If a pit-bull terrier maims a child, the dog is not morally to blame; it is simply a ferocious dog, perhaps bred by irresponsible humans to be that way, in the wrong place with the wrong company. Tigers which kill humans in the forests of North India are not culpable; they are merely being tigers (all the less do we apply moral judgements to tigers killing deer, or seals killing salmon).

The moral relation between humans and animals is thus 'asymmetrical'. Human beings can commit moral wrongs against animals, but not the other way around, and humans can and should repent of their wrongs. Forgiveness, a quintessentially moral-personal act, cannot be given from the animal side, although the animal's behaviour and emotional responses may be altered towards a more positive and less fearful mode when some reparative move is made. Likewise, an animal, trained to behave in a certain way, which fails to act as instructed may react submissively before or after being admonished, but this is not repentance so much as a trained dutiful reaction and conditioned fear of retribution. The relationship cannot be sufficiently reciprocal, sufficiently equal, for genuine forgiveness and repentance, although the same might be said for the relationship between an infant and parent. Interestingly, domestic animals can be reared so that they pick up traits of human-like behaviour and moral-like characteristics such as reliability and loyalty. Still, however, the 'beast of the field' cannot be responsible morally as can a human.

Now, in considering the petition, 'Give us today our daily bread', we saw that the character of Christian prayer was also asymmetrical, entailing as it does a communication between different orders of being, the divine and the human. Some understandings of prayer for forgiveness have implicitly assumed that the asymmetry has an exact parallel with animal-human asymmetry. For example, the idea that God can really affect human life but that humankind cannot in a genuine sense affect God seems to be a similar kind of asymmetry as between humans and animals, a one-way causation with God eternally causing human responses and prayers, including prayers for forgiveness. That kind of theology entails the conclusion that praying for forgiveness has been preordained and does not affect the divine heart; similarly, a pet dog's reaction to being treated in a certain way may have been predicted, even conditioned, by its owner.

The dog, after disobeying a command it has learned, may express some plea to avoid punishment that may verge into some kind sense of sorrow for letting down the owner. Some forms of penitence likewise may be performed to avoid punishment, as well as with a sense of shame in offending the holy God. A set pattern of penance and declaration of remission of sins may be part of such a spirituality. This may even stretch beyond the grave and lead to penances and good works being performed in exchange for remission of purgatorial suffering. Such a view of forgiveness certainly takes very seriously the judgement of God as formal judge. But it hardly does justice to the personal sense of forgiveness felt by the one who asks, and indeed not only the *sense* of forgiveness but its reality.

Praying for forgiveness goes beyond entering into a system set up to purge and manage human sins. It means restoration of *personal relationship* with God that has been clouded by sin against our neighbour and therefore against the creator. Thus the analogy of an asymmetrical human-animal relationship can apply in a loose and limited way, illustrating that there are different levels of being involved, but it hardly throws light on the moral-personal dimension. A purely formal recitation or ritual performance without this personally moral reconciliation falls below the experience and theology implied in the Lord's Prayer, and in the teaching of Jesus more generally. Before offering one's ritual sacrifice, one should make up with one's neighbour (Matt 5:23-24). This relationality characterizes the kingdom of God, and is called love.

Repentance is personal; it is not externalist, managerial, or magical, and these aspects must be differentiated from true prayer and worship. 'Magic', according to Buber, 'desires to obtain its effects without entering into relation, and practises its tricks in the void. But sacrifice and prayer are set "before the Face", in the consummation of the holy primary word that means mutual action: they speak the Thou, and then they hear.'⁴ True worship is relational and somehow mutual, because it is a sharing in the task of the kingdom in history. There is a face-to-face quality about worship and prayer, as classical theology has always held.

D. M. Baillie rejects a secular analysis which regards a sense of sin as rooted in a pathological repression of some incident of earlier life, which will disappear once brought to light and recognized for the illusion it is.⁵ Rather, we need to confess our sin to God, and not repress the truth about it or interpret it as a psychological effect of something else. What is needed is forgiveness by God, and forgiveness entails honest repentance of wrong. Baillie interestingly regards the view that the sense of guilt is a product of repression as itself repressing the spiritual reality of sin, which has to be faced up to personally before God.

The Lord's Prayer presses the analogy with human relationships and human forgiveness in the clearest possible way: we ask God to forgive us *as we forgive* those who sin against us. There could be no more powerful way of emphasizing the relevance of the analogy of human forgiveness. Practical human forgiveness really does *share* in the quality of divine forgiveness. Eberhard Jüngel, speaking of the analogous nature of our speech concerning God, says, 'To grasp God as love certainly means to grasp God as self-communication. That however explodes the thesis of the unspeakability of God.'⁶

At this point we seem to run into a difficulty in interpretation. Matthew introduces this subordinate clause with 'as', Luke with 'for'; so Matthew has 'as we also *have forgiven* . . .', while Luke uses the present tense 'for we ourselves *forgive* . . .' Cullmann, however, explains that the tense in Aramaic which lies behind the language used in Matthew indicates a continuing effect flowing from the moment of action, a present perfect. In Cullmann's opinion, 'As we hereby forgive . . .' may then be a good translation.⁷ He argues that the implication of the petition is that we stand in the sphere of divine forgiveness *as we pray* for it:

> 'As we forgive . . .' does not relate to the divine fulfilment of our petition but to our human petition itself, i.e. to our inner attitude when uttering the prayer. We can ask for God's forgiveness only if while praying we are ourselves in the realm of the forgiveness that he wills. We must know that God's forgiveness is not some property, but belongs to his

inmost being, his infinite love. Faith in God is faith in the forgiving God. So we must know that when we ask for forgiveness, in the light of this forgiveness we must forgive those who do harm to us, just as in general, in the light of God's love we must practise love.[8]

God is not denoted here as a royal potentate administering an empire for his own benefit, at a distance from his subjects, but as a heavenly Father who is holy and transcendent but at the same time present and approachable. Vermes says that 'what lies at the heart of Jesus' intuition and gives individuality and freshness to his vision is the conviction that the eternal, distant, dominating and tremendous Creator is also and primarily a near and approachable God.'[9] The power of God is revealed as love, but an effective and transforming love, far beyond the sentimental, colluding, and transient phenomenon often bearing that name.

Vincent Brummer describes prayer for forgiveness as embodying fellowship characterized by *agape*-love, rather than by rights and duties:

> If we were to interpret the relation between God and human persons in terms of rights and duties, this would either make prayers for divine forgiveness inappropriate, or turn them into acts which somehow merit the restoration of one's rights before God, or into requests for divine condonation or remission of penalty.[10]

'Agapeistic fellowship' is restored to its full state by way of repentance and forgiveness. While the divine character is reflected in the moral law of the cosmos, God does not relate to us merely as a lawgiver who seeks to maintain a system by means of credits and debits earned and forfeited.

The involvement of others in forgiveness raises the question of traditions which regard the mediation of a priest, who may set down certain penances, as being necessary to forgiveness.[11] Peter Vardy stresses that this is the 'sacrament of reconciliation' with the holy church with which the sinner has broken by sinning. The notion of breaking fellowship with the church, the community, by sinning and needing to be reconciled back to it through the secret mediation of the priest may seem strange to Christians who are not Roman Catholics, since the community of believers know nothing of the sins being confessed in strict privacy, and hence to be regarded as out of communion with the church seems artificial.[12]

The Pentecostalist practice of mutual confession of sins openly in the congregation may take the community aspect of sin more seriously in terms of the actual community. The Anglican *Book of Common Prayer* makes provision for confession of sin to a priest in its service of Visitation of the Sick. A rubric reads, 'Here shall the sick person be moved to make a special confession of his sins, if he feel his conscience troubled with any weighty matter'; the minister prays to Jesus Christ that the sins be forgiven, and then declares 'by his authority committed to me, I absolve thee from all thy sins, in the name of the Father, and of the Son and of the Holy Ghost. Amen.' The rationale of this is the easing of the troubled conscience at a time of special unease and a need of special assurance of forgiveness. It is not the regular mode of confession to God, which is the general confession made during public worship.[13]

Richard Foster suggests a form of 'sacramental' confessing of sin by writing it down and burning the paper.[14] Sometimes people may need such opportunities of confession for particularly troubling moral failings; sometimes they need to tell another church member or their minister. Foster points to the sense of release and help in the path of discipleship such moments can bring. They do not, however, elicit or guarantee forgiveness any more powerfully from God. The Holy Spirit mediates divine renewal and forgiveness to the Christian heart, but at times the assurance of this can be assisted pastorally by some kind of symbolic act. Holy communion may be the most obvious with its character of pure gift.

3. Praying for forgiveness in the movement of divine love

Praying for forgiveness, while committing oneself to forgive others, may be the quintessentially personal act of a human being, soldering together honesty and responsive love in the heart. Here is utter reality. The prayer of the Christian cannot be seen as simply individualistic but arising from the community of faith, the people of the Spirit, the body of Christ. This context remains as true for private prayer as for corporate acts of liturgy.

Members of the body of Christ know that they depend on Christ and his saving action for us and in us. The Spirit knits together the members into Christ, the one whose sacrificial death and victorious rising to life broke the bonds and barriers of sin. Forgiveness has been achieved by this great act, and yet forgiveness needs to continue among the people of God since we continue to sin. 'If you sever Jesus of Nazareth from the Church and His work through His Spirit in the Church, you make the claim that He is divine a fabulous myth and the doctrine of atonement both immoral and grotesque', according to William Temple.[15] This is because, he suggests, we find in the world 'a power which can be identified as the Spirit of Jesus which is steadily bringing the world into obedience to that Love which he revealed as the inmost nature of God'.[16] The church in the power of the Spirit thus continues the reconciling work of Jesus.

Christians pray for forgiveness out of a sense of fundamental security; they do not believe that they are in and out of divine acceptance from one moment of confession of sin to the next, moving in and out of a 'state of grace'. Rather they are in the family of God, accepted and reconciled, having trusted in Christ and his victory. Praying for forgiveness happens *within* this overarching context of security, acknowledging the painful slippage from the way of the kingdom. Christ has been let down, the Spirit has been 'grieved'. This picture presumes the constant presence of God, our turning away, and repenting for our lack of love and constancy.

The cross of Christ was a real historical act and event, but did not remain trapped in the past; since Christ rose, so did the power of his redeeming act, and hence Paul can say, 'He died for our sins and rose for our justification'. The living Christ is the basis of being for the church, the once-for-all judgement and the sanctifying enemy of false motivation in the heart. Turning our face again to the Father is responding to the promptings of the divine love poured out in Christ: 'God has sent the Spirit of his Son into our hearts, so we cry Abba, Father' (Gal 4:6). We pray in Christ and not outside of him, baptized into his death and part of his life, seeking to 'become what we are'. As a recently agreed statement between the Roman Catholic and Anglican Churches puts it, the church, the body of Christ, is 'the reconciled and reconciling community'[17] in which the unholy find forgiveness and reorientation.

In terms of the historical Jesus teaching his disciples to pray, we pray beside him who forgives and heals us. Jesus reveals and implements the divine character in time and human will. The Spirit, says Paul, searches the deep things of God, that is the wisdom of the cross, and searches our spirits with this wisdom,[18] nurturing the baptismal pattern of dying to sin and living to righteousness. Repenting of our sins is part of this relationship with the relational, self-giving God. We own our responsibility for our actions and attitudes, find them badly wanting, and open them honestly up to the purity of God. We break out of our insularity and again seek to reaffirm our relationship with the Father and humanity.

Jesus Christ effected the reconciliation of sinful mankind with God and created the environment of forgiveness, peace with God, in which disciples live and move and have their being. This is the clear message of Colossians,[19] which envisages Christ, the 'image of the invisible God' and first born of all creation as holding all things together, having 'made peace by the blood of his cross'. This is indeed the Logos, the principle of the universe, sustaining and supporting creation, but also the head of the church, and the one who died on the cross. The reconciliation is of all things to himself, by this sacrificial death undertaken in favour of those who were 'estranged and hostile in mind' so that they may be presented as holy and blameless to God. The death of Jesus transforms the situation, enabling all things to participate in the life of Jesus. 'See, see Christ's blood streams in the firmament', says Marlowe's Faustus: the life of Christ holds all things together, not so much as merely a principle of rationality but as personal presence revealed in the man who was crucified.

Martin Buber points to the paradox that persons are limited by the existence of other persons and things, and that this cannot be true of God. God is however 'absolute person', a paradoxical definition, and as absolute person God enters into direct relation with us,[20] and not only with human beings: 'God's speech to men penetrates what happens in the life of each one of us, and all that happens in the world around us, biographical and historical, and makes it for you and me into instruction, message, demand.'[21] We must add to Buber's insight that the cross was made into the supreme undertaking and enacting of the 'instruction, message and demand' with morally transforming effect, reaching across the limits of time.

Praying 'in' the trinitarian life of God means becoming more human, sharing in the image of God shining through in Jesus. It means a relational mode of prayer, in God to God, and outwards to the human network of relationships. Praying for forgiveness in a positive sense is realigning our life with the generous outreaching movement of God into the darkness of the world. God is so worshipped and valued as true and holy that offending this love galls us, indeed injures us as it hurts God the Father and God the Holy Spirit within. It might even be the case that the death of Jesus brought together in one crisis of history both the pain to God and injury to humanity arising from sin. Our prayer for forgiveness therefore is a penumbra of that crisis; we pray, as it were, out of the dark shadow cast by that eclipse.

Contempt for God and for our fellows defines sin as relational and also organic. We are sharing in the life of the Holy Spirit, and we are fellow human beings one with another. Our sin tears and wounds these bonds of communion; they are knitted together by the grace of Christ. The bonds of fellowship flowing out from the coming of the divine Word extend like concentric circles. We owe our love and care to our immediate family, local community, nation. But the gospel of Christ pushes our concern wider into care for other peoples, nations, and tongues, even to loving our 'enemy'. This principle finds voice in the phrase 'as we forgive those who sin against us'.

Our prayer for forgiveness is no isolated prayer but integrated into the fellowship of believers and always sustained by the presence of the Spirit. Our sins do not banish the supporting faithfulness of God: rather we sin against God while sustained by God, and we pray for forgiveness in his presence. The break in fellowship does not mean the absence of God, but rather the presence of a forbearing God whose judgement and grace come afresh in upon us as summons and challenge. 'God is the Being', says Buber, 'that is directly, most nearly, and lastingly, over against us, that may properly only be addressed, not expressed',[22] God is the Thou who underlies all relationship, even when relationship is spoiled.

The organic nature of our bonds with the Father and with fellow believers never ceases to be 'personal' in kind, and only such a relationship can be sufficiently 'adjusting'[23] and pastorally sensitive to our individual state. We can 'grieve' the Spirit just because the Spirit searches our hearts, and so we are constantly called to repent afresh and rejoice again. Process theology calls this the divine 'lure', and correctly understands God as pulling us to new openness, but it may have insufficiently appreciated the fact that only personhood has the finesse and the moral judgement to understand the subtle state of each individual heart. The whole spiritual complex of sin, guilt, repentance, and forgiveness coheres with the personal reality of God as Trinity.

The fact of sin shows that we are free and that God gives us 'space' in which we may grow; we are created beings. On the other hand, we are not isolated or autonomous, but are sustained and upheld as both created and as adopted into the family. God's loving movement into our situation insistently upholds, surrounds, and summons us to become the partners intended at creation, through our own act of freedom. Creation is creation, not divine being; but it is filled with the glory of the Lord whose presence is both 'externally' sustaining and 'inwardly' or personally relating.

William Temple offers here the picture of a father who runs his household at some levels 'automatically' (paying bills, buying food) and at others in total 'existential' individual love and passion (loving his wife, comforting his children).[24] The presence of God in the world is a complex presence, not to be interpreted on a single monochrome model. In particular, the deeply personal and utterly basic spiritual reality of sin and forgiveness cannot be interpreted as any kind of mechanical or impersonal system. Christian believers know that they are treated and loved as moral individuals.

This tells us about God and about our own identity, which is rooted in our origin, destiny, and salvation. Sin substitutes this divine and generous context for one we prefer to construct, centred on our autonomous will. Failure to repent, to reorientate to the divine ambience, is self-justification, a form of idolatry, which takes an ever tighter grip. The release from this grip, according to the Christian vision, is *Christus Victor*, Christ the Conqueror. In praying with trust to the heavenly Father for forgiveness, the disciple shares an identity with Christ. The very act of prayer, being utterly honest, in itself constitutes a putting aside of false identities and personal constructs. It reclaims the proper identity of the self as a joyful worshipper of the creator: on earth as in heaven. The goal of the process and the means of achieving it are 'personal'.

Some modern astrophysicists speak of an 'anthropic principle' at the heart of the cosmos, a sense that the whole universe is finely tuned to support the emergence and growth of human life.[25] Theologians are rightly suspicious of this phrase, because God and not humanity is at the centre of reality. Nevertheless, a kind of 'top down' way of interpreting the world around us, starting with the moral and spiritual experience of humanity and unfolding lower strata of life in accord with these insights, is a wise method of procedure. It is more in tune with God's creative project than reducing the 'personal' and moral to impersonal phenomena. The same anti-reductionism holds good for our praying: we ask forgiveness of one who is at least 'personal', although obviously transcending the merely human and individual. When we speak of the personal character of God we mean something social and personal, relational and triune. We mean a personal character in God which is infinitely caring and tender, creative and strong.

4. Real relations in forgiveness

Forgiveness is real for the one who genuinely repents and turns to God, whether regarded in terms of subjective feeling or of an objective state. God is not 'pretending' to forgive, either because he is cruel or because our behaviour does not actually matter, as if we have simply been led to believe it matters in order to have a well-regulated world. Something just and loving *does* happen which affects the disciple as convertedness to God is renewed.

The nature of the 'something real' which happens takes us to heart of what is meant by personhood and relationality. Active hatred, or careless negligence, damages people, both the hater and the victim; violence is done to both. Married people who divorce report the real sense of loss, the wrench and sense of tragic failure of potential, the pity of missed opportunities, of arrested development. The genuine, objective damage done to people by sin shares this nature of tragic waste, of failure to develop vast potential, of deep woundedness which never fully heals.

Forgiveness creates afresh. The 'creative charity of God' (William Temple) and 'the creative suffering of God' (Paul Fiddes) together aptly describe the nature of the benefit of forgiveness. Love reaches out at cost and restores relationship, transforming what has become a technical, manipulative 'I-it' relationship into the mutual respect of 'I-Thou'. Personhood has been retrieved and reaffirmed. The hater has been, in a sense which is more than merely metaphorical, 'made alive in Christ' as he receives forgiveness afresh from God. A dying to the hardness of heart, a rising to a new way of life destined by God, occurs through the whole act.

Perhaps we might even regard this 'turning' to the face of God in genuine sadness as itself part of the gift of the Spirit, who evokes and rekindles the Christ-life in us. The consciousness of being forgiven in response to a definite act of repentance, on further reflection, forms part of the larger whole and is a moment in a personal journey whose beginning and end is in Christ. Being Christian is being in Christ, living in an identity from which we can tend to depart but in which we are most fully our real selves. Falling back into less personal and depersonalising modes of relating to God and to others does happen, and yet the love and grace of God forbears and endures to melt the heart that reverts to a coldly autonomous life.

The ongoing need to be forgiven our sins and the continual pastoral activity of the Spirit who evokes repentance fall within the ambit of the crucified and risen Christ. Communion with Christ means communion with the basis of that communion, the judgement of Calvary. Baptism into Christ crucified secures and challenges, justifies and sanctifies, accepts and breaks. Being in the body of Christ is living in the influence of the Spirit of Christ crucified and risen, a truly personal and person-making influence. Seen in this way, the once-for-all moment of cosmic judgement in the obedience of Jesus at Calvary and the ongoing forgiveness of God cohere in the act and presence of the triune God.

In this way the disciple relates within the body of Christ to God, in a transformatory way which is nevertheless wholly real, dealing with the person as having vast potential but also with deep-seated moral problems to be struggled with through life. The question then arises, however, as to how such a path of human discipleship might affect God. If God does relate to his faithful people in the agapeistic mode of the I-thou relation, as well as by the creative sustaining grounding of all being, then God interacts with the repentant person in a particularly deep way, more searching and profound perhaps than in the case of petitionary prayer in general.

God transcends time while occupying it, according to Macquarrie.[26] That is to say God is not a victim to time, although he feels the impact of events in time and interacts with them as the lord, judge, and saviour of time. The moral act of sacrifice actualized by Jesus in his life and death was in time, hence part of the being of human history and human response; but this act was also divine and so, if a matter of true moral commitment and love rather than a revelation of a regulative idea, it was real for God. Conviction that the sacrifice of Jesus was real for God, that 'God was in Christ reconciling the world to himself, not counting their trespasses against them' (2 Cor 5:19) means that God suffered for this reconciliation. Therefore there must be some distinction of relationships within God to allow both for this suffering and for its being embraced securely by God.

God is the God who goes out to bring back, who rejoices at the lost sinner repenting, at the finding of the one lost sheep. The parables of Jesus on this subject are clear indications of divine care and ceaseless pastoral activity. God is 'always more ready to hear than we to pray', never foreclosing on humanity or creation. This is the God of hope, and of a longsuffering of an active and positive kind, provoking and forcing the issue with in-turned humanity. We remind ourselves yet again that while such a description is analogous, the analogy runs along the line of personal relations, and not along the line of a mechanical system.

The biblical witness to Jesus has him speak of a joy in God at repentance (Luke 15:7), a joy matching resurrection from death to new life and peace with God. It matters to God when human beings harden their hearts against him; it matters when they fail to give what the medieval theologian Anselm called the 'honour' due to the generous creator of all things and benefits of life, preferring loyalty to created things. The New Testament speaks of the Spirit being 'grieved' at such behaviour, desiring repentance and repair. This is part of the creative suffering of God, inseparable from the creative charity of God, its more active counterpart. God is negated by our sin, God is honoured again when we repent and are set right: there would be no 'creative suffering' *in* God (William Temple's preposition), nor *of* God (Paul Fiddes' preposition) if the suffering were not felt somehow by God. While 'suffering' is analogous, the phenomenon to which the analogy refers must be akin to hurt. If God is love, if God is a 'jealous God', if God grieves for his wayward people, then God does absorb the impact of sin in a way going beyond the administrative.

Likewise, the biblical description of divine anger, or wrath at wickedness, cannot be easily discounted. The person who colludes in wrong shares in the resulting evil, and this may be immense damage and destruction. The objective evil in history is vast and raises the question not only of the *existence* of God, as 'protest atheism' makes clear, but of what *sort* of God there might be and with what sort of reaction to wrong. God cannot be a God who is happy with murder and oppression or indifferent to them. Rather, God must detest such evil and wish to destroy it, that is to uproot it from the will of human beings who brought it about. God's anger burns against evil, but in a way superior to our purely negative and destructive anger. We view it through the cross and resurrection.

Divine freedom does allow itself to be limited by human freedom, by human centres of action, and so by the sin which Calvary reveals. As we have already seen, the very act of creating the universe logically entails some limitation on divine freedom, which defines itself therefore as being more than a static, frozen absolute quality. The freedom given to creation to oppose the divine will and character does not, however, mean that divine holiness is limited. The Christian doctrine of Christ reveals this distinction, in holding that God chose to limit his power in the life of Jesus, but that this if anything magnifies the revelation of his holiness; in this sense, as P. T. Forsyth put it, *kenosis* is *plerosis*—self-emptying is fullness.[27] The holiness of God enacted in time and space is Jesus Christ, and this holiness is no less holy by coming forth into the created order.

Divine freedom is holy, and therefore inextinguishable while being vulnerable. True holiness cannot be conquered, as the resurrection of Jesus both symbolized and enacted. Freedom and holiness cohere in an ultimate fashion in the life of Jesus, giving freedom a new quality not normally associated with it in human experience, although it may well be the case that holy people do exhibit a strange freedom over the networks of influence pressing in on the human spirit. We do see traces of Christlike freedom in the lives of Godly people, a freedom far from other-worldly detachment.

Divine self-communication reaches deepest into human hearts in forgiveness. Analogy fails to suffice as a description of how language functions at this point in the theological explication of the gospel. Forgiveness by God *is* forgiveness, and not merely *like* forgiveness, and this forgiveness is both enacted and revealed in Jesus Christ. God's holiness transforms and heals human sinfulness, in a way which can only be described as 'real' and 'relational'. This fact lies at the very heart of the Christian faith and worship: the holy one stoops low into our condition, magnifying his holiness by this act of love. God really forgives, an act far exceeding the mere regulation of the unruly human race by way of external control. 'Good faith' on the divine as well as the human side of this act is utterly fundamental: without it, the Christian gospel collapses. That is, divine forgiveness entails 'cost' which is as genuine for God as for us.

Divine forgiveness must be rooted in the holy character of God, and this must be changeless, yet the changelessness cannot be of a Platonic type, no mere idea or mind disconnected from the realm of change. Here we reach the paradox that God's holiness is secure and yet in such a way as to include 'real relations'. This must be so as regards the death of Jesus, if that death did mean the judgement of humanity and the justification of God, rather than being a terrible absurdity. Our prayer for forgiveness rests within this divine judgement and justification, reaching the very heart of God in and with 'our great high priest' and brother, Jesus. The notion of 'real relations' must be set theologically inside this trinitarian reality: the real relations are enjoyed and volunteered by *this* God, who thus cannot be a philosophical principle of the absolute, which by definition could not relate to the finite and contingent world.

The process theologians stress this real or 'internal' relationship of God with the world,[28] luring the sinner back to the divine will. God can indeed feel the pain of rejection. Yet, according to the process vision, God also has a primordial pole of being which is invulnerable, so that he is in no danger of being rendered impotent and paralysed. While this kind of 'dipolarity' in God has been rightly criticized,[29] any Christian theology must have some way of upholding the unchanging character of God, the fact that God is not going to become evil or degraded. The holy character of God cannot be lost, can never change. A deity who is not holy could not forgive, and indeed would not be worthy of worship at all. That God is crucified does not mean that God changes in identity or attitude; rather it means the reverse, that God cannot collude with untruth and falsity, that he is the foundation of all truth and reality. The unholy reveals itself in violence against God who reveals himself as changeless in holiness, judgement, and love.

The death of Jesus unmasks the falsity of human self-justification while simultaneously disclosing the divine character as unchangeably holy. The death of Jesus reveals what sins means to God, and what forgiveness costs God. This demonstrates in history that God really does relate to human history in a reciprocal kind of way, albeit an asymmetrical one. The doctrine of the atonement most clearly underlines this point, but the reality of prayer for forgiveness likewise brings this home to the hearts of believers.

5. Forgiveness and time

God does have something to forgive. The sin of the world affects God, who cannot collude with it, and forgiveness costs God the pain lived out at Calvary. Such basic gospel facts entail the reality of temporal events and acts for God. The Christian experience of walking with God through life in trust and faith, frailty and doubt, reinforces this interpretation. Praying for forgiveness makes little sense if God does not or cannot relate to time. Our experience of repentance especially calls for the Christian God who knows and understands our framework of time.

Our moral actions do not die at their birth. While nothing could be more obvious, we need to be reminded of the truth that the past stays with us in the sense that the impact of our actions do not simply fall away. The past is not an abyss of nothingness. Not only do we remember it, it becomes causally and morally influential on what follows. The past, in fact, is our past; 'it' is personal to us, part of us; what we have done and thought transcribes itself into our very brain cells, and into our hearts. To try to destroy the memory and the responsibility for our deeds is itself an act of self-hardening, of sterilising the conscience. Our past also includes the reality of the past history of the human race, and of the whole cosmos. The effects of moral actions of years back remain, subjectively and objectively, in history and the fabric of the universe.

Praying for forgiveness recognizes the enduring character of responsibility for what we have done, and recognizes the fact of God's presence to events then and now. In a sense, bringing a matter before God completes it, owns it, marks it, and brackets it. It is finished, and judged by ourselves as we view it and interpret it with God. Praying in Christ, and in him crucified and risen, we judge ourselves and are judged—and justified or 'put in the right'. What Forsyth called the 'supreme moral act' of self-giving by God happened in time, with its roots in the character of God, and endures throughout time.[30]

There can be little doubt that time is real to God, but more significantly that moral acts are what God called upon time to produce, in particular loving, holy relationships. A time-line of mere events, including the vast tracts of time barren of any relationships, are of less significance to God than an act of caring love: the kingdom of heaven indwells neutral time and fulfils it at such moments. Space and time were brought into being for the responsive love of creation, headed up by the human race, and consummated in Jesus. Time for us leads to death, the wrenching out from life of what God made for relationships and love. We fall away. Before we do, our actions in time fall away into the past, in terms of a time-line. But in terms of a narrative of who we are they remain part of us, and we take them with us, good and bad. They will determine our character, and by them we judge ourselves. Our sins are small deaths, small wrenchings of relationships, tearings of the fabric of care and love —in thought, word, and deed. They mortify us and hurt others, they affect the race, even the cosmos. They repress the kingdom of God, the reign of God on earth, as in heaven.

God knows and feels this. He is 'the great companion' on the way (as Whitehead put it)[31] who suffers and redeems as we each travel on our own time narrative. Some people usher in the kingdom; some negate it. The heritage of some acts will promote the good. No historian can write the vast web of life narratives of humanity; only the one who is present throughout knows, cares, and saves. The Spirit of the Lord cannot be escaped spatially or temporally; as ever present, he is immanent to all and everything, alone the interpretative historian of all life stories, and constantly mediating the things of Christ to human life.

Lives are real to God, and therefore time is real to God. God thus gives space for time, or provides time for time; this is, to use Barth's phrase, 'God's time for us'. Christian faith believes that there is no Spirit-free patch of time and that God is constantly, intimately, subtly working with us as we use the time given to us. God 'remembers' (with a 'memory' coloured by the sacrifice of Jesus) and 'thinks ahead' (according to the purposive plan of the kingdom), as we can. God's act of creation is one, yet full of actions in which we are a part, intended to share in the kingdom in ways totally fitted to our characters. Forging people who wish to choose as the heavenly Father chooses is the work of the kingdom, the work of love; time is needed for this to happen.

The link between fulfilled time and our time cannot be Platonic, with ours as merely a shadow of the reality, since our time goes to make up the fulfilled reality, and since in Jesus the fulfilment of the kingdom has been enacted and we share in that, here and now. We relate to the heavenly Father and his Spirit who knows our hearts throughout our lives, fostering relationships pleasing to God and Christlike in pattern. The link of the Spirit to the future, the heavenly presence and guarantee here and now, means that relationships will actually endure in the kingdom, that we will not pass out of our time into the night of nothingness. Our prayer for forgiveness bandages the tears and cuts in our relationships with God and with others, knitting up what seemed to have unravelled in temporal actions, healing and restoring, bringing back hope that we travel to the light.

God has committed himself to the ongoing forgiveness of those who turn to him, having initiated the process of turning recalcitrant human will back in Christ. Tracing this forgiving intention and will back to God's electing will was done in the New Testament writings such as Revelation and Ephesians where we read of 'the Lamb in the midst of the throne' (Rev 7:17) and the 'plan of the mystery hidden for ages in God' (Eph 3:9). Divine forgiveness reflects the divine character that can never be subject to change: 'Love is not love/ Which alters when it alteration finds'.[32] The holy love of God persists through all resistance and rebellion, even to the bitterest of ends.

Just as we are not simply the product of time, nor fully explicable by it, all the more so is it with God, whose sheer imaginative love brought our time into being. God works by the Spirit in myriad ways upon the hearts of all people. Divine forbearance, according to the New Testament, is real and is linked with the critical act of righteousness carried out by God in Christ (Rom 3:25). God seems therefore to travel both *in* human history, in time and space, and also *with it* as its Lord. Praying for forgiveness, common to all believers, marks out with utter clarity the reality of our moral lives, of ourselves as perduring agents, and of the Lord of time who has a purpose for us as we use it. Time is no illusion, nor are our moral decisions, nor our relationship with the God who is love.

Ultimately we are related to the Lord who has entered our fallen time and death, whose moral companionship and energy will achieve his victory over it.

6. Deliverance in trial and deliverance from evil

Our prayer for forgiveness means we feel that we do wrong, and that evil thus is no illusion nor a psychological phenomenon to be smoothed away. As Austin Farrer puts it:

> Men have never, in the mass, felt the Maker in his works, without at the same time finding their wills engaged with the action of a Saviour . . . Religious naturalism may conceal, but cannot eliminate the saving function of the godhead . . . A theology which stops short at creation and disinterests itself in the conflict of evil with the divine goodness, handles a one-sided abstraction, which is not even a diagram of an actual belief.'[33]

Farrer is right to point to the sense of evil felt by humanity, and the pressure exerted by it. So we move on from the prayer for forgiveness to the prayer to be delivered from evil.

Defining the word translated 'temptation' in older English versions of the Lord's Prayer has proved a difficult task. It brings prayer from the past of failures forgiven into the present struggle of the kingdom of God in the world. Whatever the precise sense of the word, the general meaning is plainly that of some kind of pressure and situation in which the will of God becomes hard to do. A 'time of trial' or 'testing' is what the one praying seems to be seeking to avoid, or perhaps testing beyond the capacity of the worshipper to endure.[34]

Testing forms a mysterious motif in the gospel story; according to the Synoptic Gospels, Jesus is driven into the desert to be tested, or tempted, by the devil, under the impetus of the Holy Spirit (Mark 1:12). Discipleship and struggle go together, and the struggle is against those things which draw us away from the purposes of God. Jesus agonizes in Gethsemane before his death, and prays that the cup may be taken from him, a version of the prayer to be spared testing (Matt 26:39). In this scene Jesus urges his disciples to pray that they 'may not come into the time of trial' (v. 41). The prayer is honest and realistic, acknowledging the hardness of the path of faith and the frailty of our will in the face of challenge. This petition assumes the difficulty of the challenge, and also the fact of divine permission allowing it to happen: so we pray 'save us from the time of trial'. At the same time there is a deep intimacy between the Father and the disciple in the battle, as the Gethsemane prayer models in practice. The moral position implicit in the petition is that difficult situations will happen, that divine empathy knows the pressures and suffering involved, and somehow the divine will is worked out most powerfully through human endurance and moral conquest. The petition recognizes all this, and very humanly prays the Gethsemane prayer.

The petition for deliverance from evil likewise assumes opposition, the relative dualism found in the Gospels between the kingdom of God and the 'powers and principalities'. Barth's description of these dark powers as the *nihil*, sheer negativity preying on the good creation and distorting it, will serve as a useful way of putting the dualism.[35] It is asymmetrical, for God is not to be compared with the negative of God. But the experience of being dragged from the purposes of God is very real, and the petition addresses it.

We find ourselves exposed to evil influences by the very fact of living in a sinful society with structures and value systems sometimes deeply opposed to the way of Jesus. We can be caught up in such structures subjectively and objectively. They can pull us toward the easy, comfortable but wrong option as firmly as the tide in the sea. We can resist or collude, go with the tide or swim against it. We are not isolated from society and its influences, and in fact we ourselves help to strengthen or weaken them by our activity. Networks of good can be built up or weakened, and we have a part in that; these networks in turn pull us, and we respond again. We therefore freely contribute to the building up of networks of what is less than holy, and then find ourselves victim of such networks. The biblical category of idolatry describes precisely this pattern. Even to fail to use our vote morally in an election will be, however minimally, a contribution towards implementing a value system more or less good. Buying a less than edifying newspaper likewise strengthens or weakens the cause of honesty and respect. This in turn affects others, now in future years. In such a way we are part of the ambience, the influence, of society on ourselves and others.[36]

Deliverance from evil means rescue from collusion with influences which seduce us, and we need to make no decision as to whether a 'personal' or purposive devil lies behind such forces acting upon our will. It is as coherent to argue for an individual 'Satan' as against one, and the weird irrationality of human connivance with evil might confirm a level of hostility to the good that belies explanation or any fitting into any reasonable pattern. Evil has to be defined as sufficiently evil so as to exclude itself from any smooth reconciliation with normality in the created order; this was the problem with the over-rational interpretation of evil offered by the philosophical system of Hegel and his followers, in which evil became necessary to promote the good.

The evil of the Nazi holocaust, for example, cannot possibly be patched into any tapestry of overall good; it has to be seen as a shriek of sheer wrong, of pure devilment, wilful perversion of the good, absolute crime. We may do well to acknowledge such a threat to ourselves, objectively the evil that damages us, and subjectively the evil with which we connive and collude, making our own what is of the kingdom of darkness.

Deliverance from evil can also be seen as a strengthening in holiness and love, and this should be a perspective in the petition to avoid any sense of the worshipper being somehow isolated and adrift, alone and pulled hither and thither between God and evil. Rather, prayer arises from the security of being in God, but in the real experience of life's trials and seductions as a free disciple living out the paradox of grace. To pray is to orientate oneself towards God and to alert oneself to the perils of idolatry in the world and indeed in the religious worlds we inhabit. To pray this prayer is therefore part of the openness to God's grace which prevents evil taking root in our heart. This petition plays an important part in the deconstruction of sin's attraction, laying bare what is going on with regard to our relationships in society.

To say this about prayer is not to reduce it to anthropocentric therapy, to a kind of socio-psychological interpretation of my place in the world, as if God were not a reality. But to *pray* against evil is in a sense to pit oneself against it, to engage in the struggle and so to open oneself to God. This God, it hardly needs saying, has to be enduringly good to be worshipped in such fashion. A God who might conceivably also be seduced by pleasures deriving from evil, on whatever scale, would not be one to whom such a prayer could be offered. The Christian God is indeed holy in an absolute sense, who has in fact already proved victorious over evil.

Human resistance to evil and divine protection from it relate together to holiness. Evil is conquered not by merely external power but through love and holiness of relationship, and that persistent holiness is the drive and energy behind *kenosis* and incarnation. The evil heart is not overcome by force; only the power of love can conquer by gaining a free response. Identification with God's holy love in Christ by the disciple means that evil will break on the cross and resurrection. In the person of the human

Jesus the created order, as intended by God, broke the power of the potential destructiveness inherent in the freedom granted to creation. This victory was human, and divine as human; it was not the operation of an artificial divine intrusion into the human condition.

The subjective aspect of the cross of Jesus, however, involved genuine pain and anguish of spirit. Gethsemane demonstrates this. Baptism into the death of Christ surely involves not only the objective gain but also the subjective readiness to face up to the evil involved in Christ's passion. Prayer for deliverance from evil is therefore quite natural and normal for the disciple of Jesus. Jesus' genuine humanity involved him in faith and prayer, and in prayer for strength against all the threats arising from the power of alienation and evil.

The petition for deliverance from evil arises from disciples who live 'between the times' of the overcoming of evil by the victorious second Adam and the final abolition of the very possibility of evil. Evil has been overcome in the human life of Jesus, and we as disciples share in that victory, but we remain in the world of history with its ambiguities and confusions, its struggle and frustration over the persistence of what is finally to fall away, the power of evil. Praying to be delivered from evil equates with the prayers of the saints beneath the altar in the book of Revelation, the cry of the persecuted, 'How long O Lord?' (Rev. 6:10). The righteous suffer, and indeed are told in the Gospels that they must take the way of the cross and find themselves treated no better than was their master. The prayer faces the reality of the life of faith, its difficulties, injustices, and even oppression.

7. Deliverance within time and history

The final deliverance from evil comes with the *eschaton*, the reign of God, the judgement and vindication, the putting right of what has been so wrong because of human disobedience and misuse of freedom. But until then, does God intervene to prevent evil happening, and in particular does prayer have any relevance to such divine activity? What are we expecting to happen when we pray, 'Deliver us from evil?' The biblical motif for such divine activity seems to be that of restraint. The theology of history found in the book of Revelation, for example, symbolically indicates that the forces of conquest, war, famine, and death will wreak havoc but will not wholly destroy. Hence the strange fractions used such as 'power over a quarter of the earth (Rev 6:8), or 'a third of the earth was burnt up and a third of the trees' (Rev 8: 7-8). The idea is that evil is great but relative, God is sovereign and ultimately victorious.

This apocalyptic pattern of history, putting evil in its place and looking to a final triumph of good over evil, joy over pain, gives the context for the prayer for deliverance. God restrains evil from absolute abuse of created freedom; indeed, perhaps it is because evil is merely parasitic on the good and has no real being of its own, that it can never achieve finality. There can be no absolute dualism between good and evil. The Gospels tell us that evil undercuts itself through itself, murdering that which it feeds off. Divine holiness, as lived out in history, suffered but did not cease being holy and so destroying evil patterns of life.

The holy one lived in human time, but his holiness cut through the waves of pride, hypocrisy, and hardness of heart that washed against him. The nature of time becomes complex when it is related to holiness and the God of Jesus. God's very identity is intimate with 'the holy', that is pure goodness and worth, which will never alter. What will not change in the face of time is love; God's changelessness is not some principle located in a detached cosmic mind. 'Love is not love that alters when it alteration finds', and love will not cease relating itself even to those who have alienated themselves from divine love. Evil, however, exists in created beings only as an orientation away from the creator; so although at heart it seems to be a Promethean urge to 'be as God', it is confined to the temporal order and cannot transcend it. Unlike God, it is trapped in time. Evil can only remain until the redemption of the world is complete and creation is restored to harmony with God. Until then, during the period of time which exists for the sake of the redemptive purposes of God, the negative will play upon the richness of the positive.

Love, or the subject who loves, relates to others in space and time, while it has the overarching project of building up and helping those others. Self-giving is the projecting of life outwards, a 'gift love'. Evil cares nothing for the other, who is an object merely to be used, an it. Evil deals in the quantitative only, asset-stripping what can be plundered from persons and from created being, for the sake of self. 'You can't eat the orange and then throw the peel away—a man is not a piece of fruit!',[37] says Willy Loman in Arthur Miller's play, *Death of a Salesman*. Loman is the tragic figure who discovers that his unquestioning faith in commerce as the way to fulfilment and reward has been totally misplaced, and that his life has been sucked away by an uncaring company.

Such a process dehumanizes persons, even as they can dehumanize themselves and become increasingly merely objects. Loving others reverses this and restores to us the quality of persons transcending the iron law of temporal flow. We can identify ourselves with the quantitative passage of nature, becoming complex beings and yet motivated by idolatrous modes of life; we thereby become items in the cosmos. Or we can identify ourselves with the divine love of self-giving and outgoing generosity, so gaining a qualitative distinction that transcends mere existence. It is interesting to note that Nietzsche, the greatest modern critic of Christianity, became convinced of the reality of the eternal recurrence, the reliving of precisely the same experiences over again. The self therefore becomes the process of time as experienced, and is not in fact free over against that process.[38] There is no 'God of the open future' for Nietzsche who might break into our life cycle and transform it by remaking our moral will.

The bleak doctrine of Nietzsche effectively confirms the axiom 'become what you are', in this case without God. You are, not what you eat, but what you do, and what you do comes back to haunt you, a kind of judgement akin to that of Sisyphus in the ancient Greek myth, who was condemned to roll the same stone uphill eternally. This eschatology, or anti-eschatology, renders us mere *quanta* of experience. From such a fate we may well pray to be delivered. Our deliverance from such an identification with mere temporality is by the qualitative difference of love given through the infinite moment of the cross and resurrection of Jesus. Here Kierkegaard, with his confidence that the eternal moment has paradoxically broken into time,[39] surely corrects Nietzsche.

Prayer for such deliverance recognizes the dialectic of sin and grace, but not as divorced from creation and history, for there is 'time in God' and 'God has time for us.'[40] The process of God's kingdom, of the Spirit enabling the disciple to live Christianly in the face of the world's confusions and evil, is not an escape from the world but its transformation by love and goodness. We pray for deliverance from evil, not from history and the created order, however depressing that may seem. God is the God of creation and of redemption, and is active within them in many ways.

The sustaining activity of God in the created order is represented, for example, by the sheer power of nature to renew itself and recover from the most terrible blows of pollution. 'For all this, nature is never spent', says Gerard Manley Hopkins[41]; despite despoiling by humanity, the capacity of nature to absorb destruction and still push up the small green shoots through the wastelands and slagheaps stands as a symbol for divine resilience.

The sustaining power of God in the historical process works through sacrifice and renewal, the way of the Kierkegaardian 'moment' which, however, opens out into new relationships of care and transformation. The good suffer drastic reverses and tragedies, but somehow through such moral sacrifice the kingdom of God makes gains. 'The historical process' is not an impersonal process, but fashioned by human will, sometimes by an individual's supreme act of conquest or genius, sometimes by the aggregate of behaviour patterns responding to conditions.

God has acted decisively to break up the sinful patterns of human behaviour, to redeem the will and build the kingdom. This decisive act initiates the struggle against evil, and praying is close to the heart of engaging in the struggle. The baptismal pattern of dying and rising, dying to sin with Christ and finding new life and new potentialities, continues to harrow and plough the stony ground of history for God. At the same time evil seems continually to oppose and re-harden what the disciples have cultivated in their hearts, and thereafter in institutions and structures of life.[42]

Entering into prayer against evil is a subjective participation with God on behalf of his kingdom, against the cultural tendencies working against it. Such prayer reinforces the conviction that God is involved in the bringing to birth of his reign *in* creation, and not just *over* it. He seeks the conquest of the heart through freedom and love; such is the difficulty of the re-creation. The very action of praying this prayer is a taking part in the will of God for the world, as the disciple in Christ pits his will and desire with that of the creative charity of God against the hatred of the world.

Baptism in water symbolically puts off sin and evil; prayer continues to engage in that putting off both individually and for the creation. Christ's lordship remains ambiguous in the confusion of history, but it is real and final; it is purposive and creative. The church exercises her only power as she prays. She has no calculus of divine action, merely trust in the sovereign lord who has certainly entered the world fray, settled the battle and secured the victory. The petition for deliverance from evil requires much faith, given that so much destruction has been wreaked on countless people of faith who have sought divine deliverance from violence and death. The theological position after Auschwitz needs only to be mentioned to underline this point. Evil not only seems to have run riot uncontrollably, but the aftermath of the carnage has led to God being placed firmly in the dock, and found guilty, thus giving a double victory to the powers and principalities. Does God not care to defend his reputation in history?

Apparently not, or not to the cynical enquirer who cares nothing either way. The death of Jesus was a kind of Auschwitz experience as far as the disciples were concerned: so much innocence destroyed, in the face of promise and trust and hope. The testimony to the victory over this pure injustice was given only to those with some seeds, at least, of care about Jesus and the kingdom; it was not granted to the detached and merely interested. Nor was the victory an event of impersonal force and terrifying power, reducing the recipients to frozen fear. It was shot through with love and holiness.

Even such ghastly and massive events as Nazi extermination camps are only part of the process and picture, whereas the whole is revealed in the resurrection: judgement and vindication. The resurrection of Jesus discloses the final product of the divine redemption; the breaking up of the sin of history yields its final harvest. But the disciple has to trust that this is so, for he has no historical proof from the face of the historical record; he has only 'the sign of Jonah' (Luke 11:29). The church prays, as it were, from within the belly of the whale, for the deliverance from evil. Disciples recognize the risen Lord with joy, at the breaking of the bread.

Sin and evil appear at the close of the Lord's Prayer, put into their proper place as subordinate parasites to the merciful, gracious God and the creation which is filled with his glory. While so much wrong may crowd into the foreground of our view of life, objectively and subjectively, our prayer puts the picture into genuine perspective. Sin and evil are transient flares against the vast ocean of divine holiness and love. Evil and confusion in the world, so overwhelming and depressing a reality, is temporary. The steadfast love and holiness of the Lord stands forever, inviolable and eternal. This grounds the confidence of the church, whatever the appearances of the chaos of the world. The notion of 'the fall' presupposes the good creation and the holy creator, whose love never fails, and overcomes 'the world.' Our orientation to prayer for forgiveness is fundamentally positive; we honestly acknowledge our deep failure, but we wish to become what we are.

Notes to Chapter 7

[1]Barth, *Epistle to the Romans*, p. 157.

[2]See above, p. 73.

[3]According to Oscar Cullmann, 'There is no difference in meaning here, and the two Greek terms go back to the same Aramaic word. Matthew's more concrete translation here is probably to be seen as the more original, especially as Jesus was fond of using the situation of financial indebtedness as an illustration'. Cullmann, *Prayer in the New Testament*, p. 55.

[4]Martin Buber, *I and Thou,* trans. R. Gregor Smith (T & T Clark, Edinburgh, repr. 1959), p. 83.

[5]Baillie, *God Was in Christ*, p. 163f.

[6]Eberhard Jüngel, *God as the Mystery of the World*, trans. D. Guder (T & T Clark, Edinburgh,1983), p. 260.

[7]Cullmann, *Prayer in the New Testament*, p. 56.

[8]Ibid.

[9]Vermes, *The Religion of Jesus the Jew*, p. 180.

[10]Vincent Brummer, *What Are We Doing When We Pray?* (SCM Press, London, 1984), p. 82.

[11]Peter Vardy explains the system in *The Puzzle of God* (Harper Collins, London, 1990), ch. 16.

[12]The last chapter of the Epistle of James exhorts its readers to confess their sins to each other, a rather different concept to confession to a mediating priest, and one that takes the community of faith as a genuine pastoral community which cares one for the other; the exhortation is given in the context of sharing troubles and prayer for healing.

[13]Richard Hooker, the greatest of the Anglican Elizabethan theologians, expresses the classical temper of the Anglican position as follows: 'And in regard thereof, the Church of England hitherto hath thought it the safer way to refer men's hidden crimes unto God and themselves only: howbeit, not without special caution for the admonition of such as come to the Holy Sacrament, and for the comfort of such as are ready to depart the world.' Hooker, *Ecclesiastical Polity*, Book VI. iv. 15.

[14]Richard Foster, *Celebration of Discipline* (Hodder & Stoughton, London, 1980), p. 131.

[15]William Temple, *Fellowship with God* (Macmillan, London, 1920), p. 134.

[16]Ibid., p. 137.

[17]*Salvation and the Church*, Agreed Statement of the Second Anglican-Roman Catholic International Dialogue (Church House Publishing, London, 1987), p. 24.

[18]1 Corinthians 2:10-12, cf. Romans 8:27. On this theme, see Gordon Fee, *Paul, The Spirit, and the People of God* (Hodder, London, 1997), p. 46.

[19]Colossians 1:13-20; 2:13-15; 4:1-3

[20]Buber, *I and Thou*, p. 136.

[21]Ibid.

[22]Ibid., p. 81.

[23]On the idea of 'adjustment', see above pp. 139-44.

[24]Temple, *Nature, Man, and God*, pp. 284-89. Cf. also A. E. Taylor, *The Faith of a Moralist*, Vol. 2 (Macmillan, London, 1932), pp. 162-69.

[25]See John D. Weaver, *In the Beginning God. Modern Science and the Christian Doctrine of Creation*, Regent's Study Guides 3 (Regent's Park College/ Smyth & Helwys, Oxford/Macon GA, 1994), pp. 10-11, 68-71.

[26]Macquarrie, *Principles of Christian Theology*, pp. 195-210.

[27]P. T. Forsyth developed his Christology on this premise. See *The Person and Place of Christ* (Independent Press, London, 1955 [1908]), lectures 11 and 12.

[28]See, for example, Charles Hartshorne, *A Natural Theology for Our Time*, pp. 26-28.

[29]See above, pp. 10-11, 102-103, 110.

[30]Forsyth, *Person and Place of Christ*, p. 356.

[31]Whitehead, *Process and Reality*, p. 532.

[32]William Shakespeare, *Sonnets* 116.

[33]Austin Farrer, *Love Almighty and Ills Unlimited* (Collins, London, 1962), p. 13.

[34]Cullmann, *Prayer in the New Testament*, pp. 58-66, discusses the range of options possible for the exegete.

[35]Barth, *Church Dogmatics*, III/3, pp. 302-303.

[36]P. T. Forsyth, in his *Justification of God*, pp. 28-29, interpreted the failure of politicians to implement values of the kingdom of God in the pre-1914 arms race as a gradual building up of spiritual and moral evil, a kind of pustule in history, which came to a head with the catastrophe of the terrible war.

[37]Arthur Miller, *Death of a Salesman*, Act Two ([1941] repr. Penguin Books, Harmondsworth, 1961), p. 64.

[38]Further on this, see above pp. 118-19.

[39]Søren Kierkegaard, *Philosophical Fragments* [1845], trans. D. Swenson (Princeton University Press, Princeton, 1962), pp. 79-86.

[40]This insight qualifies the 'eternal moment' of Kierkegaard. See note 39 above, and p. 113.

[41]Gerard Manley Hopkins, poem, 'God's Grandeur', *Poems of Gerard Manley Hopkins*, ed. Gardner & MacKenzie, p. 66.

[42]Hendrikus Berkhof speaks of 'an ambiguous and internally contradictory world, a society which is busy cutting down the gospel tree from which it is picking the fruits.' Berkhof, *The Christian Faith* (Eerdmans, Grand Rapids, 1979), p. 515.

8

Conclusion
'For the kingdom, the power, and the glory are yours now and for ever.'

The phrase that usually brings the Lord's Prayer to an end catches the mood of the whole prayer. It expresses trust and joy in God, following the offering of a petition for deliverance from evil, very much in the pattern of many Old Testament psalms. This phrase is not found in the New Testament texts, but occurs in the *Didache*, a very early manual of Christian practice datable possibly in the first century. The *Didache* version ends with: 'For yours is the power and the glory forever'.[1]

1. The character of prayer: God-centred

This mood is the final thing to catch about Christian prayer, a resolute trust in the goodness of God, going beyond knowing how 'it works'. The intellectual issue of the mechanics of how prayer affects God falls away, as the child takes the hand of the parent in times of trouble. 'The power and the glory *are* yours for ever.'

The epistemological questions about prayer (for example, 'how can we know the will of God?') can receive some answers, but soon give way to ontological statements about divine care, statements with which the Lord's Prayer begin. Ontologically, as a matter of sheer *being*, the church is in God and not calling across a chasm in the hope of being heard. This relationship is being enacted again and again in prayer. As our study has shown, the sacramental structure of faith, the baptismal dying and rising in Christ, undergirds prayer and is reflected in it. The eucharistic feeding 'in the heart by faith with thanksgiving', prompting a responsive self-offering which shares in that of Christ, mirrors the shape of prayer.

The disciple prays in the Spirit, with the Jesus of Gethsemane, to the Father: never alone nor detached from the one to whom he prays. Thereby the struggle in prayer is a joint one, since God is already in the world and its conditions, and the church is hid with Christ in God. The relationship of prayer has to be deeply co-operative, a shared vision of the world and the kingdom; so the Spirit, we recall, prays for us when we are unable.

In this way prayer may be compared with the celebrated 'ontological argument' for the existence of God, developed by Anselm (Archbishop of Canterbury 1093–1109). Like prayer, Anselm's theological argument focuses on the highest, purest being, and the thinker is drawn into the desire of God for the world, including his purpose for ourselves as individuals.

The argument goes that God must exist, since a greater than God cannot be conceived; if God lacked existence, then a greater *could* be conceived. This sounds like a highly abstract concept (and philosophers find all kinds of problems with it), but the real thrust of the claim is clear: God is absolute worth, worthy beyond all else, and so is to be acknowledged. We are drawn into this worship as we attend to the being of God.

In fact, Anselm sets his so-called 'argument' in the context of prayer and worship rather than dry philosophy. He prays as he paints the picture of surpassing greatness and worth:

> And so, O Lord, thou art not simply that than which a greater cannot be thought; rather, thou art something greater than can be thought. For since something like this can be thought, if thou are not this very being, something greater than thou can be thought—but this cannot be.[2]

Anselm is addressing God as he contemplates God in praise, in a doxology: 'yours is the glory. . . .' He is far from suppressing his mind in mystical union of being, but rather his thought seems heightened along with his heart, fired by the divine reality. This is praying as believing.

Anselm's prayerful meditation arises in the midst of his Christian community, in the monastery of Bec where he was Prior at the time, and it addresses the God of Jesus and the Spirit, the revealed God, not a philosophical principle. It is this God of love who is 'a greater than which cannot be conceived'. Merely by philosophy one might conceive, instead, of an existent 'first principle' which was indifferent, the 'unmoved mover' of Aristotle's thought, for example. But Christian worship is magnetically drawn to the God who reaches out in Christ, and it knows that the Spirit is drawing us to our worship.

Prayer is offering, a setting of the will and person into the flow of divine life. The will, feeling, self-understanding, and identity of the disciple gains its clearest focus in prayer. We are most ourselves at that point, fully honest with God, prompted by the Spirit into reality. We reach a point of trust in God, and in ourselves as known by God; we know that we are objects of his deep care—with all our failings. A certain perspective comes from prayer, illustrated by Isaiah's crisis before God, his acknowledgement of wrong, being forgiven and being set on his way (Isa 6:1-8).

To have possession of some 'calculus' of the action of God in relation to prayer would mean that one was not dealing with Christian prayer at all, more a kind of manipulative mechanism whereby God becomes a factor in human will being done. We do not stand over against God as we pray, working a system. In the previous chapter we saw that this was true of repentance: we are assured of forgiveness by God if we trust in Christ and frankly acknowledge our sins, but our security is not in the working of some sub-personal system of payments. There can be no 'naturalization of grace' (Barth's phrase), either in terms of 'indulgences' or of 'prosperity' gospels.

This God-centred character of prayer, which acknowledges God as the free and sovereign one, never to be manipulated, does not lead to the equal and opposite attitude of fatalism. God is not to be manipulated, but that is not to say that prayer is purely a ritual, a form of words good for us, but never impinging on the divine life. God is love, the outreaching God. He is always more ready to hear than we to pray. Prayer is sharing his kingdom in a special way. Karl Barth puts the point with great power:

> In [Christ] God came to our side and entered into our humility. And in Him we are set at God's side and lifted up to Him and therefore to the place where decisions are made in the affairs of His government. . . . It is not the Christian in himself, but the Christian in Christ, who is the servant and child and also friend of God, and as such he is free lord with him over everything.[3]

Prayer is a sharing in the body of Christ, as we share in the bread we break and the cup we drink, a sharing in the kingly office as well as the prophetic and priestly. Prayer is indeed centred in God, but in *this* God, the God of Jesus. God has made space in Christ for the membership of Christ to pray freely and gladly, in a real way. Discipleship builds up to a large degree in this fashion. Prayer is active, as well as passive, demanding the energy and discipline of the person and the group as well as the quiet and the contemplative phases. The Spirit who searches the deep things of God, searches also our spirit, bonding together and identifying God and his people.

2. Answers to prayer: the agenda of the kingdom

Just as time is most deeply defined by divine activity and purpose, so are 'answers to prayer', because our time is not God's time. The greater includes the less. God 'has time for us', and so divine oversight of the cosmos somehow associates itself with humble prayer, but the way this is so defies our comprehension. Yet we can say, 'I greet him the days I meet him, and bless when I understand'.[4] Answers to prayer go beyond the agenda we use in praying, and the dialogue often takes us beyond the assumptions we brought in the first place.

Our prayers pass through Christ and will increasingly reflect the priorities and wisdom of Christ, the more we pray in and with his presence, drawing on the Gospel portraits given to us. Indeed, many Christians today are re-appropriating the method of praying developed by Ignatius of Loyola, using the biblical narratives of Jesus in imaginary fashion. Modern disciples are encouraged to place themselves into the Gospel narrative, and to allow the Spirit to speak from it into our current life experience. The mystically present 'Christ within us' gains definition and shape from the biblical narrative of Jesus, making a new version of the union and distinction between the 'Christ of faith' and the 'Jesus of history'. The presence of the narrative element provides an important corrective to any drift towards an amorphous spirituality of an 'inner light', and its contemporary equivalents of subjective psycho-dynamic phenomena as the matrix for spirituality, apparently now popular among some evangelicals.[5]

Providing the narrative element remains strong, such a procedure may be of real help to all Christians as an element of prayer, not simply to 'go back' to the 'then' and seek to *understand* better through a mystical route, but as part of the project of God's kingdom here and now. We pray in the movement of the divine outreach—into our context of life. Jan Luis Segundo sees in the Ignatian Exercises 'a groping attempt to link Christian perfection to a project, a project for which God needs human beings: human beings in the world and endowed with traits that can be translated into historical force.'[6] Segundo, known especially as a liberation theologian, wishes to see the Ignatian tradition move into this direction towards which he detects initial 'gropings', with a greater integration into the concerns of the kingdom than Ignatius himself proposed.[7]

Answers to prayer will always be aligned with the interests of the kingdom: 'for the kingdom, the power and the glory are yours.' But the real difficulty in any theology of answered prayer relates to that of suffering, in the light of claims of 'answers' to prayers for what seem far less vital concerns. If God is interested in *this*, why not *that*? That is a major issue in discussion of the value of prayer. It is the question of theodicy in different guise, and points inevitably to Calvary. Why could God do nothing about *that*? 'Save yourself', mocked the soldiers (Luke 23:37). We are asked to trust in the God of Jesus that the whole creation and history of the universe will be seen to be vindicated and glorious, that evil will fall away, that goodness will bring joy. We are asked to trust in the risen Jesus as the supreme testimony to the ultimate vindication of God's good creation and salvation of sinful history. We are asked to trust in the character of God as holy and caring.

The Christian experience of prayer links up directly with our doctrine of God. God is this God and not another God. He has, according to the life and death of Jesus, sought to overcome the negativity of the world by choosing to conquer by love. That means he has chosen to sustain creation, rather than terminate it. His mode of action in bringing the kingdom is this. Love needs careful definition; it is not merely bland, nor selfish, nor costless, nor uncommitted, nor amoral. It is tough, demanding, and transforming. It is not, however, 'raw power' in bringing his many sons and daughters to their fulfilment in Christ: that level of creation involves perfecting through freedom, the power of sacrificial love. God recreates us by love that reaches victoriously into our hearts.

3. The God of prayer: present in the world in many ways

With this power of insistent sacrificial love God seeks our response. The poet Gerard Manley Hopkins speaks of Augustine's final response being won after a prolonged, soft wooing ('stealing as spring') of his heart, while others are sharply struck by the grace of God, as by a hammer on an anvil.[8]

> With an anvil-ding
> And with fire in him forge thy will
> Or rather, rather then, stealing as Spring
> Through him, melt him, but master him still:
> Whether at once, as once at a crash Paul,
> Or as Austin, a lingering-out sweet skill.
> Make mercy in all of us, out of us all
> Mastery, but be adored, but be adored King.

Hopkins, consciously echoing many psalms, also felt his discipleship tested to the utmost by the fierceness of divine love that 'batters' the hearts of his followers, allowing apparent cruelty, abandoning them to a dark night of the soul.[9] Francis Thompson writes in his poem 'The Hound of Heaven' of the one who pursues relentlessly:

Rise, clasp my hand, and come!
Halts by me that footfall:
Is my gloom, after all,
Shade of His hand, outstretched caressingly?

The redemptive calling of God to individuals is part of the whole creative work of love, but it reveals a different aspect of divine presence in the world from that of the constantly supportive Being. The divine Word follows and addresses; the Spirit challenges us to respond in the present situation that is as unique as our fingerprint, and unrepeatable. These two aspects of divine presence and activity are not to be interpreted as some kind of dualism in God, but point to a richness and complexity not to be subsumed under a single 'model' of action.

The 'heavens declare the glory of God', and 'the word of the Lord came' to the prophets; the Hebrews understood the creative word to be the saving and revealing word, with no dichotomy between them. They made no distinction, as Kant later made it, between the principle beneath the *material* order and that underpinning the *moral* order. The existential theological tradition has helped theology with its stress on the summons of the divine Word to the disciple now. Process thought has rectified other errors by insisting on the divine in the processes of nature and history, which strict existentialism treats either agnostically or non-theistically, setting up a dualism between the mind and the world.

Process thought, as we have seen, unnecessarily restricts the mode of divine activity to that of a lure immanent in the vitalities of history for the promotion of universal pleasure. But there is little doubt that its criticism of 'classical theism', not undertaken at the Reformation when the medieval doctrine of God was retained unexamined, has been deserved and has been fruitful. The biblical God cares passionately for the world, and is not 'apathetic' about it in any sense of that term. Anselm knows about doctrine as a form of prayer, but he falls prey to the medieval assumption of divine impassibility when he says to God in his *Proslogion*: 'When thou lookest upon us, wretched as we are, we feel the effect of thy compassion, but thou dost not feel emotion . . . thou are not affected by any share in our wretchedness.'[10] The medieval deity could have no emotions, indicating changeability. The biblical analogies point in the opposite direction, indicating passion, joy, and response in God. The trinitarian relationship indicates at the very least some such reality in the divine life.

God is present to the world and present in it, and this indicates more than one kind of immanence. God *is* not the world; divine being is not 'as' the world. The world is not a form of deity at a lower level of being or historically stretched out as time. Nor can it be said that the world is 'God's body', a parallel form of modalism in which God the Son is confused with the created order. The divine sustaining of the universe is a divine activity, not the divine life itself existing as another form, an emanation of divine being. God has made and maintains the world, but it is invested with power and life, with the stamp of the maker so that its being often sings of its maker. The heavens declare the glory of God, rather than being God.

How God created and sustains the universe is not known to us, and here the theologian must have sympathy with those scientists who tell religious thinkers not to complete the cosmic mechanism (or organism?) by splicing high cosmology into doctrines of creation; to do this would be neither good science nor good theology. That there is a connection is sure to the believer, but how the connection 'works' is not open to observation or mathematical projection. The poet Coleridge was right to point to the imagination as a key category for understanding creation[11]; the imagination of the merciful and gracious Lord, not merely rationality and morality, does justice to the joy and wonderment of our experience of the world and our perception of it.

God acts in the cosmos, knows it intimately, loves it, has a purpose for it. Therefore, God is in it as well as present to it. The term 'panentheism' may be useful in suggesting the picture of the cosmos resting in God, simultaneously suggesting the 'space' or room accorded to creation by God. The analogy suggests the principle of 'displacement'; we recall how the ancient Greek philosopher Archimedes discovered this principle when he observed how his body displaced the water from his bath, prompting him to a famous piece of exultation! God, we might say, gives the body of creation space to be creation, while surrounding it, supporting it, and also being present to it, 'face to face'. We need then to develop a multi-dimensional understanding of divine creative activity; using a more personal analogy, we may say that it should be *at least* as multi-dimensional as that of the mother who surrounds, gives birth to, and brings up her child.

Such a use of the 'panentheist' picture of 'everything in God' leads to a fairly orthodox vision of God and the world, one of sustaining *and* relating as 'I and Thou'. Anselm praises God with the words 'For nothing contains thee, but thou containest all things'.[12] The picture need not entail the notion that the cosmos is so suffused by the being of God that divine being actually constitutes the fibre of creation (technically speaking, 'emanationist monism'). The language of God as Being that inevitably expresses itself in beings, as derived from Heidegger by Paul Tillich and John Macquarrie, does take the 'panentheist' model a bit further in this direction, and needs to ensure that sufficient distinction is left between the divine and the creation.

Creation is an act of God, rather than an emanation of God, but an act cannot exist apart from the being *who* acts; it cannot be understood as free-floating, a sliver of existential decision rooted in nothing. The act of God reflects the goodness, purpose, and generosity of the one who is present to act. That act conveys the well-being of creation, and only such an act could bring about a free creation to be a partner to God. By contrast, if the creation were an emanation of God, it would simply be God in another mode, and could have no freedom over against God. Freedom in creation must be recognized as real for the Christian view of sin and evil to have any ground.

Now, the experience of praying reflects precisely such an understanding of God and the world. The disciple offers prayer to God, one who cares, one who is present and close, who understands. The Psalms, central to the church's whole tradition of prayer and worship, sing and cry out to the Lord, the one who has a name and a purpose, however veiled and hard. The Lord's Prayer takes up this tradition, sharpening the focus on God as the caring heavenly Father. Prayer assumes that God is good and wants the best for his created children, that it is therefore right to ask; seeking to stand in the will of this good God while asking ('your will be done') purifies the intercession. God's close involvement in the world of nature and of history is presupposed in the prayer for daily bread; the creator is the redeemer, and so bread and forgiveness come one after the other. God is present both as the ground of being, and the infinitely particular God who knows in detail the lives of all.

4. Prayer as human partnership with God

Prayer for forgiveness presupposes our freedom to sin, our accountability, and the changeless character of God's holiness. The absolute, though not static, quality of this holiness poses interesting questions about the openness of God to the world. Can human deeds surprise God? Can God envisage or imagine the evil that is committed in his creation?

Forgiveness might be compatible with a divine foresight of ill deeds, as a parent might foresee a wrong to be done by a child known very well, and still forgive. The biblical image of a 'lamb slain before the foundation of the world' (Rev 13:8) likewise indicates some kind of foresight of sin and judgement on the part of God. Nevertheless, the biblical motif of God's deep disappointment at idolatry and betrayal on the part of his people indicates that although the possibilities for wrong are given along with freedom, the actualisation of these possibilities for evil are surprising and distressing to God. With all due deference to the character of language about God as being analogy, we must take seriously the statement that God's Spirit can be 'grieved'. This means that God must be capable of having fresh experiences, and the figure of Calvary again becomes vital in the Christian understanding of this insight. The cross signals divine love, judgement, and also divine sadness at human wickedness; this is not a mournful sadness that enervates, but pain that acts purposively to get beyond and to repair the moral disaster of generic Adam. The passion of God pours itself into the passion of Christ: here one can indeed speak of an 'emanation', although it flows from free, personal self-giving rather than from any necessity laid upon God.

The deepest challenge of prayer may be that, just as God chose to act kenotically ('emptying himself') in Jesus to work out his kingdom in the world, he may also have chosen similarly to work through the human medium of faithful prayer, to use this as the sceptre of his divine freedom in the creation. This might be better expressed in terms of a prayerful mode of being. God's human agency now is the body of Christ, the body of people open to divine grace, prepared to struggle faithfully, 'to fight and not to heed the wounds, to toil and not to seek for rest, to labour and not to seek reward save that of knowing that we do thy will'.[13] The worldly weakness and folly of the Christian people may be the fuel of God, the means of conquering the hardness of the hearts of the indifferent and ungodly. Prayer is the power of this 'foolish' group (1 Cor 1:26-7).

God has chosen the foolish and weak of this world, has restricted divine power, and has translated his strength into the moral heart, supremely in Jesus but derivatively in the church, whose prayer is 'may we who drink his cup, share his risen life'.[14] There was one incarnation, and the church is not its continuation, as some modern theologians wish to say.[15] But the *work* of the incarnate one continues through his people by the Spirit, and prayer is perhaps the point where the risen Christ and his disciples most nearly are identified with each other in their interpretation of the world and their engagement to transform it.

The place of worship in the midst of the confusion of the world, of praise despite conditions, of getting beyond human perspective and potential, should be the focus for the church as it approaches a third millennium. Yes, we need intellectual defences of the faith and critical wrestling with it. But the people of God need above all to settle their heart and minds on this heavenly Father, to orientate themselves to the movement of infinite grace whereby 'God has sent the Spirit of his Son into our hearts, so we cry Abba, Father.'

5. Prayer and the meaning of power

The worshipper prays amid the confusion of history, but the map must be that of heaven rather than earth: if there were no jarring between the kingdom of heaven and the realities of earth, we should need to examine the presuppositions beneath our praying. Praying in the Spirit, Christian prayer, means praying in the heart of God where the cross is found, or 'the Lamb in the midst of the throne', as the Seer of Patmos puts it (Rev 7:17). The jarring of Calvary should therefore be accepted as deeply woven into the praying experience of Christian prayer. This includes the desolation ('my God my God, why have you forsaken me?') and sense of alienation from our own culture and 'our times' in all sorts of ways. It excludes worldly counter-hatred, bitterness, and despair ('Father forgive them, for they know not what they do').

Can we take this point further and suggest that the path of Jesus should be reflected in our praying experience? Does the fact that the Spirit mediates the Christ life to the church mean far more than we usually realize in this respect, in that our life of prayer will incorporate judgement and grace, abandonment and glory, sharing the sufferings of Christ and the risenness of Christ? Knowing that our worship and prayer are linked by the Spirit to the death and resurrection of Jesus, and so to the heart of God, can help to explain the irrational difficulties we experience in worship and our commitment to it.

One useful typology here may be that of the disciples sleeping during the 'agony in the garden' of Gethsemane. We are torn in the collusions and compromises of the world and fail. Our priorities can exclude the kingdom of God, for many reasons. We can even crowd out true prayer by well-meaning efforts to work a system of spirituality which attempts to abolish our 'earth' and function on what is taken to be the life of 'heaven'. The injunction to 'pray without ceasing', taken in a woodenly literalist fashion, can lead to difficulty. The point here is that prayer is part of the project of the kingdom of God, and as such it can be no smooth experience but one bound to be charged with challenges of many kinds.

The divine 'kingdom, power, and glory' appear through the 'humanity of God', and this is made manifest in the very earthy life and ministry of Jesus. Theologians working with the concept of 'kenosis' or the 'self-emptying' of God, and trying to find a way of explaining how the divine Word could become human, have often tried to work with a supposed distinction between the 'metaphysical' and the 'moral' attributes of God. It is suggested that while the former attributes, such as power, could be emptied out in taking the form of the servant, the latter attributes, such as love, were magnified in this movement . Kenosis of the one meant 'plerosis' (filling) with the other.[16] The putting aside of divine power was one thing, while divine goodness and love could remain and flourish in the person of Jesus.

But would this then mean that we worship a completely helpless God, who has allowed his hands to be tied behind his back as the increasingly cynical children behave with more and more violent destructiveness? Is the 'crucified God' in fact rather irresponsible, since he has apparently laid aside the power to maintain order in the cosmos, therefore handing control to chaos and pride? The biblical testimony does include an element of sensing the 'holding back' of God, despite the breaking out of the kind of violence among his children that is well described in William Golding's fable of children on an island, *The Lord of the Flies*. But on the other hand this prophetic and apostolic witness regards the divine victory as having been accomplished and its total manifestation as merely delayed, chaos and destruction as temporary. The Lord's Prayer ends in the confidence that 'the power . . . is yours'.

In fact, when we consider the nature of love, the distinction between 'metaphysical' and 'moral' attributes in God is rather artificial. 'Kenosis' finds its root in God's moral character, as does the act of creation itself: a self-limitation was involved in bringing about free beings. Creation and incarnation therefore share the one dynamic of gift and cost. All the metaphysical attributes of God are coloured by the character of holy love; divine power is not to be split off as an independent phenomenon—at the very least it works towards one and the same purpose and kingdom as do

Calvary and prayer. So the *whole* of God's being is involved in self-emptying, and thereby exercises true power.

God sustains the galaxies and the atomic structures at the same time as bringing sons and daughters to fulness of life through trust and faith. Molecules and love are related, but one is not reducible to the other and both can be spoken of as forms of agency or power. William Temple's reminder that persons 'act' at many levels of intensity is important. The mode of power most expressive of the divine character is manifest at Good Friday and Easter. God is not a helpless victim, but chooses to work through the avenues of freedom to create space for others and potential for relationship in its deepest sense. This choice of God, stemming from the character of God, lies behind the power of God as seen by us.

The 'helpless' God, in fact, is not a true description of the 'crucified God', even taking that phrase in a strong sense and ignoring the trinitarian distinction between the Father and the Son, according to which the Father's will is the primary agency through the redemptive self-giving of Jesus. To ask the question whether the divine choice to rule through self-giving means the loss of 'external' forceful power, has already fed in an assumption deriving from our own kingdoms of this world, which is that force always triumphs over the good, and that *realpolitik* has the last word.

Prayer 'in' Christ may be part of the way out of this imprisonment of our spiritual imaginations. We pray not to a frozen or dead God, but to one who has taken on the experience of human abuse and death as part of the true conquest of malevolence. Mere application of threat and violence could not conquer it—in fact, such an application would be capitulation to it. Baptismal life means dying to the ways of the violent, and living to the mode of the kingdom. The truest power in all the universe, the deepest effect exercised on the highest order of being, is love. That is revealed truth, and it is the most challenging and transformatory summons.

Our perspective on nature and history is an individual one. We cannot have the perspective of the universal good of the human race, let alone that of the cosmos. But this perspective is revealed to us as 'the blood of the cross', which is the key to the cosmos (Col 1:19-20), alone with the power to break down the truly implacable barriers of hatred and fear. A new and living way is introduced by the gospel. Only entry into the church of Christ, according to the Orthodox theologian Schmemann, can bring us to true freedom and free us from false ideas of freedom defined over against worldly authority or power.[17]

Schmemann claims that the Holy Spirit brings true freedom from the externality of things:

> The proper role of the Spirit is to connect and to unite, not by a form of 'objective' link, but, by revealing and manifesting the interiority of all that exists, by restoring and transforming the 'object' into the 'subject' (the it into the thou, in the terms of Martin Buber).[18]

Schmemann takes forward the point that *external* power and authority are worldly and fallen modes of being. He argues that the tragedy of the Western Church lies in an acceptance of worldly power and authority, which inevitably led to a reaction in the name of freedom at the Reformation. Externalist authority structures and counter-claims to 'freedom from' such power have controlled the histories of Roman and Protestant Churches. While his diagnosis is a historical one, modern instances such as that of Northern Ireland match it with a terrible accuracy.

But true authority and freedom are found in the Spirit, and we must add to Schmemann's account[19] that they flow from the cross, which alone has the power to end the terror of power and reactive fear. The deepest power is indeed that of love, and when this collides with hatred, it seems to be crushed but in fact conquers. This is the truth of the gospel, and should be the pulse running through the churches, Eastern as well as Western.[20]

God is the God whose deepest power is love and not coercive power, which we so commonly regard as the only effective power. God is not to be regarded as a helpless victim, a hand-wringing deity, powerless and pathetic, unable to hear and answer prayer. Prayer, sharing in the project of the kingdom, is 'heard and answered' for the ends of the kingdom and according to its own power and glory. The infinite adjustments to this purpose[21] continually maintain and develop it, for individual, generic, and cosmic good. The last judgement when we shall at last understand what is now hidden will be the vindication of this way of love that enables free response.

6. Contemplating God

We are not only caught up in the purposes of the kingdom in our baptismal life, with prayer as an essential aspect of that summons. We are also to contemplate the goodness of God simply for the sake of praising the holy and loving heavenly Father, confessing that 'the kingdom, the power, and the glory are yours, now and for ever'. Our 'attending' to God like this resembles attending to a great work of art which expresses truth and love in pure form. But we do not *relate* to a work of art, however much we are filled with inspiration from its author through its form.

The philosopher and novelist Iris Murdoch has spoken of giving attention to a work of art as being something like prayer, and regards art as a visible manifestation of the invisible supreme Good behind the virtues. Yet she has also asked:

> If one is going to speak of great art as 'evidence', is not ordinary human love an even more striking evidence of a transcendent principle of good? . . . One cannot but agree that in some sense this is the most important thing of all; and yet human love is normally too profoundly possessive . . . to be a place of vision.[22]

She regards the Christian God as an incredible and a degenerate idea, something merely to console us, but she identifies what may be the key paradox of God, that the Good is transcendent and not 'visible', while love is its 'most striking evidence'.

The Lord's Prayer leads us to address God as our Father in heaven. He is the caring 'good' behind all things, revealed in the unpossessive love of the human being Jesus, who teaches us so to pray and contemplate the goodness of God. The life of Jesus takes us to the Father's 'face'. We notice that even the philosopher cannot rest content with merely conceptual goodness or love, or even expression of such qualities in artistic form. The heart of reality lives in holiness, goodness, and love and relates these outwards.

'Our Father in heaven', reaching out in creation and redemption, needs no philosophical defences, and yet our prayer describes what is craved by the whole human personality. This God we praise now and for ever.

Notes to Chapter 8

[1]*The Apostolic Fathers,* trans J. B. Lightfoot and J. Harmer, ed. M. Holmes (Apollos, Leicester, 1990), p. 153.

[2]Anselm, *Proslogion* ch, xv, in *A Scholastic Miscellany, Anselm to Ockham,* ed. and trans. Eugene R. Fairweather (SCM, London 1956), p. 84.

[3]*Church Dogmatics* IV/3 (T & T Clark, Edinburgh 1960), p. 287. Barth continues to stress that the disciple is a member of the community in prayer.

[4]G. M. Hopkins, *The Wreck of the Deutschland,* stanza 5, *The Poems of Gerard Manley Hopkins,* ed. Gardner & MacKenzie, p. 53.

[5]Richard Lints has some disturbing words to say on this phenomenon of what he calls the evangelical fascination with self-help and the self, with 'the trend toward pop psychology and analyzing the "inner self" in evangelical radio programming'. He concludes that 'Simply put, evangelical subjectivism reflects the trend in modernity at large.' Lints, *The Fabric of Theology: A Prologomenon to Evangelical Theology* (Eerdmans, Grand Rapids 1993), p. 326.

[6]J. L. Segundo, *The Christ of the Ignatian Exercises*, trans. John Drury (Sheed & Ward, London, 1988), p.111.

[7]Segundo makes the judgement that Ignatius's period was 'not yet the hour, of course, for a christology from below—one which would permit the kingdom of God as proclaimed by the historical Jesus or even the humanisation and maturity of humanity espoused by Paul's christology—to take shape in a spirituality.' Ibid., p. 111.

[8]Hopkins, 'The Wreck of the Deutschland', stanza 10, *The Poems of Gerard Manley Hopkins*, ed. Gardner & MacKenzie, p. 54. Text copyright © The Society of Jesus.

[9]See his so-called 'dark-night sonnets': e.g., 'Carrion Comfort', 'No worst, there is None', 'I Wake and Feel the Fell of Dark'.

[10]Anselm, *Proslogion*, ch. viii, in *A Scholastic Miscellany*, p. 78.

[11]E.g., S. T. Coleridge, *Biographia Literaria*, Vol. I [1817], ed. J. Shawcross (Oxford University Press, London, 1907), ch. xiii.

[12]Anselm, *Proslogion*, in *A Scholastic Miscellany*, p. 87.

[13]Prayer of Ignatius Loyola. For the whole prayer, see George Appleton (ed.), *The Oxford Book of Prayer* (Oxford University Press, Oxford, 1985), p. 86.

[14]*Alternative Service Book of the Church of England.*

[15]See, for instance, John Robinson, *The Body. A Study in Pauline Theology.* Studies in Biblical Theology 5 (SCM Press, London, 1952), pp. 49-55

[16]There is a good critical discussion of this kind of kenosis theology in Baillie, *God Was in Christ*, pp. 94-98.

[17]Alexander Schmemann *Church,World, Mission* (St Vladimir's Seminary Press, New York, 1979), p. 187.

[18]Ibid.

[19]Schmeman's failure to mention the cross in his analysis means that 'ecclesial' life tends to become unhistorical and unreal.

[20]Unfortunately, post-Soviet Russia exemplifies one counter example to Schmemann's ecclesial vision of the Eastern Church, given the efforts to deploy state power against minority churches.

[21]For this idea of William Temple's, see above pp. 139-44.

[22]Iris Murdoch, *The Sovereignty of the Good* (Routledge & Kegan Paul, London, 1970), p. 75. Murdoch however exalts the place of art by going on to remark: 'That the highest love is in some sense impersonal is something which we can indeed see in art, but which I think we cannot see clearly, except in a very piecemeal manner, in the relationships of human beings.'

Index